Where Soldiers Fear to Tread

John Burnett is a former investigative reporter and speechwriter for Congressmen in Washington. Getting out of politics, he worked for the US Department of Interior, before spending years as writer/adventurer and considerable time as a professional seaman. He is the author of one previous book; *Dangerous Waters: Modern Piracy and Terror on the High Seas.*

Praise for *Where Soldiers Fear to Tread*:

'Burnett's energy is riveting and his robust style is suited to the narrative, resulting in a propulsive story which never flags. This is a gripping, often sad account of a devastated land.'
Telegraph

'Part journalism, part fictionalised narrative, *Where Soldiers Fear to Tread* makes compelling reading.'
TLS

'The book speaks well to the complicated web of motivations involved with relief work in high-risk zones. Be it altruism or ego, a desire for adventure or isolation, the compulsion for relief workers to leave lives of relative comfort for dangerous war zone makes for a compelling take on human motivation.'
Financial Times

WHERE SOLDIERS FEAR TO TREAD

At Work in the Fields of Anarchy

John S. Burnett

arrow books

Published by Arrow Books, 2007

7 9 10 8 6

First published in Great Britain in 2005 by
William Heinemann
Random House, 20 Vauxhall Bridge Road,
London SW1V 2SA

www.rbooks.co.uk

Addresses for companies within The Random House Group Limited
can be found at:
www.randomhouse.co.uk/offices.htm

The Random House Group Limited Reg. No. 954009

A CIP catalogue record for this book
is available from the British Library

ISBN 9780099464990

The Random House Group Limited supports The Forest Stewardship Council (FSC), the leading international forest certification organisation. All our titles that are printed on Greenpeace approved FSC certified paper carry the FSC logo. Our paper procurement policy can be found at:
www.rbooks.co.uk/environment

Printed and bound in Great Britain by
Cox & Wyman Ltd, Reading, Berkshire

Contents

To the men and women who have fallen in the service of helping others—quiet heroes of humanity

and
for Jacqueline

Men are not made for safe havens.
The fullness of life is in the hazards of life.
—Aeschylus

Author's Note

SOME of the names have been changed; while all knew I was taking notes with the purpose of possibly converting them into a book, it would be unfair to hold my colleagues responsible for what was done or said during times of such ineffable duress.

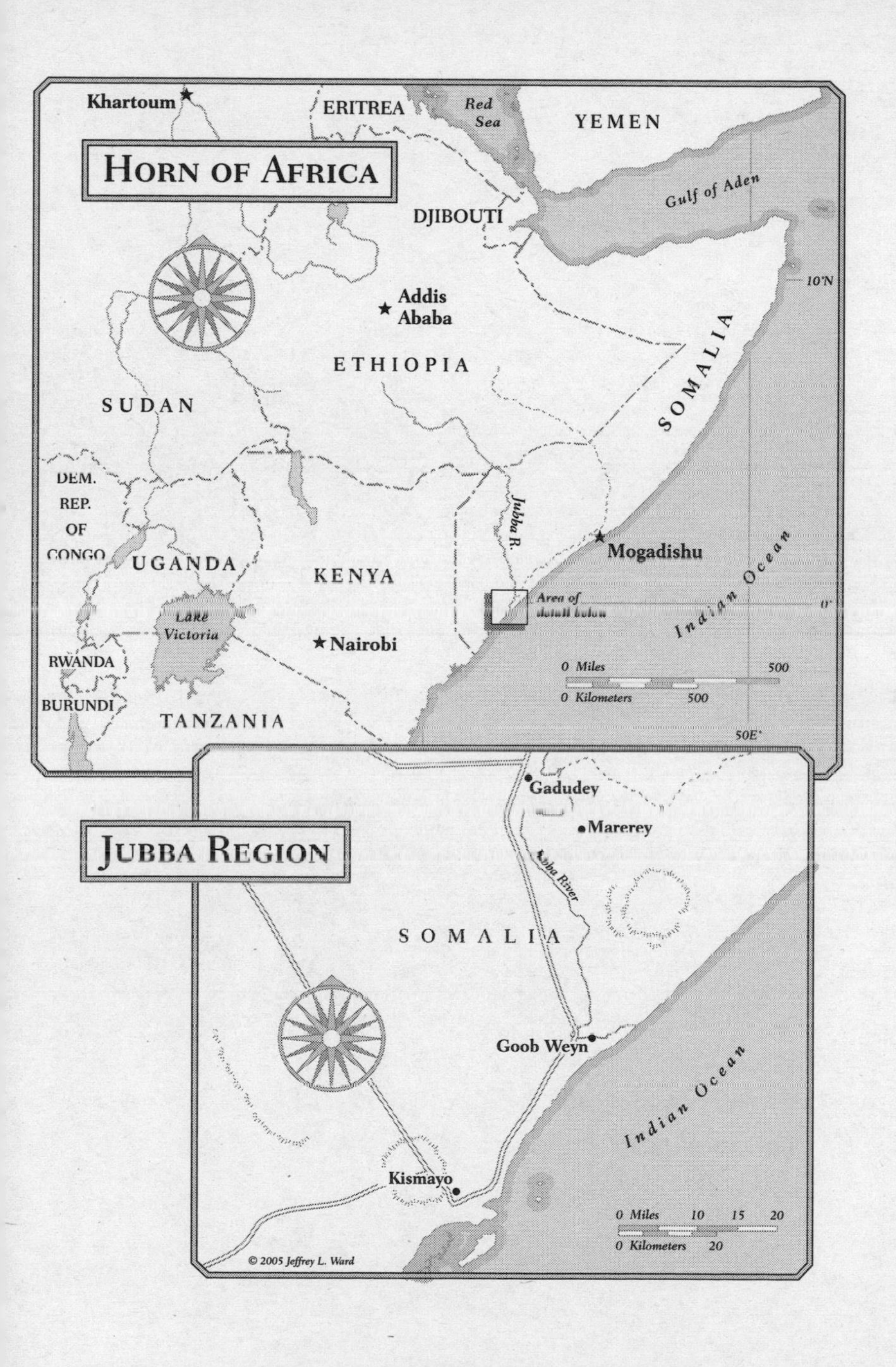

Horn of Africa
Khartoum
ERITREA
Red Sea
YEMEN
Gulf of Aden
DJIBOUTI
10°N
Addis Ababa
ETHIOPIA
SOMALIA
SUDAN
DEM. REP. OF CONGO
UGANDA
Jubba R.
Mogadishu
KENYA
Lake Victoria
Area of detail below
Indian Ocean
Nairobi
RWANDA
BURUNDI
TANZANIA
0 Miles 500
0 Kilometers 500
50E°
Jubba Region
Gadudey
Marerey
Jubba River
SOMALIA
Goob Weyn
Indian Ocean
Kismayo
0 Miles 10 15 20
0 Kilometers 20
© 2005 Jeffrey L. Ward

Where Soldiers Fear to Tread

Prologue

THERE is going to be a shooting here, and it is a toss-up who is going to get the boy's first round. The soldier, about ten years old, is jamming the barrel of his gun hard against my driver's face, and unless the kid decides to go for me, the relief worker, my driver is going to get his head blown off.

There is something in the back of the boy's eyes. Not an expression of anger or fear or hatred that might cause someone to want to kill, but the icy indifference of a child's ignorance. He has a gun. He pulls the trigger. So what? There is no dealing here.

In the few weeks of serving as a relief worker in Somalia, a nation rent by a decade of anarchy, I have come to fear children with guns. It is one thing to face an adult with a full load. But children, unlike grown-ups, do not have a personal history to balance, to offset the matter-of-fact, to work out anything rational; few adults, no matter how experienced, know how to persuade a child not to shoot. If killing is what he knows—and ten years of war is a long time to a ten-year-old carrying a gun—then there is little chance for reasoning, any one-on-one communication. Cock it. Shoot it. Next.

* * *

SOMALIA is in the throes of what is known in the jargon of humanitarian work as a "complex emergency," a rather oblique way of acknowledging that we have been sent into a hostile, unstable region. Unusually heavy monsoon rains spawned by El Niño have triggered floods that have submerged most of the country's agricultural heartland; thousands have drowned, nearly a million are homeless and starving. The United Nations, desperate and in a hurry, recruited civilians with maritime experience off the streets to drive riverboats. We were to deliver and distribute tons of medical supplies, food, clothing, and emergency shelter in a land still classified as a war zone.

When we joined this relief mission, we were told it should be safe, that we would be among a friendly people who welcomed our help, that there were no troubles in Somalia anymore. Somalis, we were informed, knew that we were sent on a mission of mercy, an attempt to keep people alive, clothed, and sheltered, and that we represented the goodwill of the developed world. Somali resentment was a thing of the past, a conflict long ago between Western peacekeepers and warlords. Yet we are discovering that in the eyes of Somalis, any international assistance, no matter how well-intentioned, is still foreign intervention—whether the international community is represented by a peacekeeper with a gun who rides herd on a relief convoy or by an unarmed aid worker delivering life-saving medicine through the malarial and crocodile-infested floodwaters. We also were assured that we would be pulled out if the bullets ever started to fly. We took their word for it. Yet from what we have already seen, from all the missed and unanswered communications to UN headquarters, I am beginning to wonder if they remember that they sent us out here in the first place.

This past week, feuding warlords have kept our little compound under siege and held us hostage, ambushed one of our food convoys, and taken potshots at us. We try to convince ourselves that they do not want to kill us, that we are far more valuable to them alive than dead. Not as distributors of Western largesse but as hostages who would fetch enough ransom to keep a warlord in guns and bullets for months. These terrifying games are played with calculation by adults, men who know how vulnerable we are without the protection of peacekeepers, who know what a bullet can do. Our fear, however, is getting shot not by the bullet aimed at us but by the stray that had been aimed at someone else.

Then there is the child with the loaded gun.

We get accustomed to seeing proud little boys strut through the hot and dusty streets with their militia buddies toting assault rifles and grenade launchers. Here in the port city of Kismayo, there are plenty of kids and plenty of guns. Anarchy, it seems, does not soften the Somalis' ability to make children.

* * *

GRITTY and exhausted, I duck into the UN Land Rover for the trip back to the compound after another futile day sorting out the pieces of what is left of the bombed-out port facilities. As acting port manager, an exalted reward for being the only one available with any merchant-marine experience, it is my job to help prepare for the arrival of chartered ships bringing emergency supplies that will be delivered to the refugees Up Country. It is also my task to set up a logistics base for the small riverboats from which to mount these relief operations.

I slump between my militia guards in the back and stare out at the harbor as our old mufflerless Land Rover, hired from some local warlord—no doubt booty from the last conflict—chugs past rusting shipping containers on the pier. The muzzles of the guards' assault rifles stick out of the car windows like deadly quills of a porcupine.

Harun, my cheerful young Somali driver, who wears an old sweat-stained New York Yankees baseball cap backward, is very suave, and he loves to chew his leaves of *qat*. His tough, uneven face, charred with several days' growth, is belied by remarkably sympathetic eyes. His youthful swagger seems unaffected, enviably natural. He could be at home on any dark city street. He has the moves.

Harun hums along to a scratchy Arabic tune on the radio; his Kalashnikov rests against the front seat, its barrel just visible above the dashboard. His electric incense burner plugged into the cigarette lighter emits a resinous smoke.

The harbor is little more than a large open bight carved out of the coral reef. It is surrounded by white sand beaches littered with the shells of burned-out vehicles, rusting razor wire, and garbage. A causeway into the city leads from an abandoned packing plant, the shell-cratered port office headquarters, and the wharf. A helicopter landing area once used by the escaping UN military forces is painted as a faded white cross within a faded white circle on the pier.

The tide is out. On a nearby mudflat under an unstained blue sky, broad-shouldered black-and-white marabou storks on stilted legs rip apart something human-size—heavy and meaty. In one smooth, easy motion, they strip the flesh with their long and powerful yellow bills, swing their long necks skyward, and, with a couple of impatient gulps, swallow whole the chunk of meat.

The armed militia manning the barricade at the port gate has a good idea of my schedule. Rifles on their shoulders and bandoliers of bullets strapped across their chests, they stoop to window level to inspect those within the white vehicle with the stenciled blue UN lettering on the hood; with *qat*-stained grins, they return my thumbs-up and shout *"Diep maleh!"*—No problem!—and wave us through.

Beyond, on the other side of the gate, the children playing in front of their rounded stick-built homes covered with animal hide also know when to expect my rig. Despite the barrels of the guns poking out the windows, these naked urchins, with grand smiles and excited voices, chase alongside the vehicle through the puddles of water and scattered rubbish, waving and laughing hello to the lone white figure inside. I lean across the guards and wave back. I am a sucker for kids.

"You have children, Captain?" Harun asks over his shoulder.

"Yes, Harun."

"In Somalia, you are rich man when you have a cow, a gun, some wives, and many children."

"You have children, Harun?"

"No, Captain. One wife. A cow. A gun. But one day—children."

The last barricade before entering town is formidable; razor wire, steel girders, and a scattering of heavy artillery casings block the laterite road. It is in a beautiful location, on the flat with the Indian Ocean on one side and the bay on the other.

The roadblock appears unmanned. Strange. I am edgy today—more so than usual. There was an artillery exchange near our quarters—the sound of distant incoming, although not unusual, is hardly conducive to a night's rest. I suppose the clan that currently owns the city and the other clan near the airport, which wants it back, occasionally need to lob shells back and forth to keep their boys alert and the machines working. Still, anything out of the usual fires the adrenaline, and this unmanned roadblock is unusual.

Harun honks impatiently. I sense my guards tighten.

There is some movement in the shadows of the portal of the cement blockhouse. A little boy not more than ten years old emerges from out of the darkness and marches toward the car, cradling an AK-47; one of the attractions of the rifle is that it's so light, even a child can carry one. He wears a full-length yellow smock, torn at the shoulder; the rip exposes his brown baby skin. His clean round face and his soft eyes display that precious naïveté of youth—he looks like a nice kid.

With a charming attempt to snarl and with a manful squeak he orders us out of the car. My guards and Harun look at one another and laugh. A sudden black cloud of anger twists his little-boy face; his small soft eyes narrow with the petulance of a child who isn't getting his way. He is not going to be humiliated.

He steps up closer. He jabs his rifle into Harun's face; the barrel presses the flesh of his cheek. Harun secretly reaches for the door handle. The boy realizes he is vulnerable and backs away. His gun is leveled at the driver's head. He has been trained. The boy says something in Somali, and Harun shuts off the car's engine. Sweat begins to form on my unshaven face.

Noticing for the first time the foreign relief worker, he swings his gun toward me.

Introduction

FEW fears, except perhaps those experienced during the process of dying, are more acute, more commanding than when facing a child whose finger is on the trigger of a loaded gun. It is at that instant the adamantine faith in our own ability to influence and control our fate becomes a delusional conceit. No one should ever experience that terror, and yet it is not uncommon for humanitarian workers, serving in countries torn by internal conflict, to find themselves suddenly facing their death—at the whim of a child soldier, or a militia seeking to make a political point, or belligerents in a local war who are convinced the relief worker is not neutral but is working for the other side.

Humanitarian workers serving in strange, politically violent lands expect to offer themselves tirelessly to feed, immunize, heal, rescue, teach, house, and relocate; they never expect to have to give up their lives. Today, relief workers are as likely to be killed in the line of their civilian duties as are well-trained and well-armed soldiers. Indeed, more UN aid workers during the past five years have been killed than peacekeepers. Between 1999 and 2004, more than four hundred fifty men and women working for UN agencies and nongovernmental relief organizations on nearly every continent have been assaulted, kidnapped, raped, or murdered. Eighty UN staff members are still missing.

The dangers of the work could be no more tragically demonstrated than the killing of twenty-two humanitarian workers in the bombing of the UN compound in Baghdad in the summer of 2003, and the bombing ten weeks later of the Iraqi headquarters of the International Committee of the Red Cross that killed two staffers. In Afghanistan, five members of a Médecins sans Frontières team were ambushed and murdered by returning Taliban. In Darfur, Sudan, nine aid workers of the U.S. Agency for International Development were attacked and killed. These are only a few of the deaths recorded during 2003 and 2004.

Relief work has always been dangerous, but it has become more so during the past ten years. Tragically, the security of those humanitarians has been less a concern than getting the job done. This was dramatically illustrated during the hastily conceived flood-relief operations to Somalia in 1997–1998, about which this book is written.

Somalia was then and continues today to be a shambles, torn apart by more than a decade of lawlessness and near-classic anarchy. It is perhaps the only nation without some form of central government, and it is considered still to be one of the most dangerous places on earth. Its demise as a member of nations occurred in 1991 when dictator Mohamed Siad Barre was overthrown and feuding warlords began to battle over the spoils. In 1992, Somalia suffered a famine of catastrophic proportions—three hundred children a day died in the capital city—caused in part by natural events and to a greater degree by warlords who used starvation as a weapon. The United Nations created an emergency relief mission and sent peacekeepers to protect the humanitarian operations. Mogadishu, the capital, turned into a battleground among warlord militia, armed civilians, and peacekeepers; eighteen American soldiers were killed during a two-day firefight in the streets and alleys. The soldiers withdrew, never to return.

Somalia was no less a hell five years later during another humanitarian crisis. In November 1997, torrential rains on the Horn of Africa spawned destructive floods that poured through the Somali heartland, sweeping away whole villages and displacing nearly a million people. Despite the bloody history, the United Nations considered the crisis severe enough to return to this pariah land. It threw together emergency relief and rescue operations and sought those with some maritime experience to deliver desperately needed emergency supplies up the swollen rivers. I was one of those volunteers. This memoir of waking nightmares is not just my story, but is representative of the horrific experiences of relief workers elsewhere, whether facing down child soldiers in Liberia or being held hostage in the Caucasus, not knowing whether tomorrow you will be shot or released. This is one account of our fears, our challenges, our confrontations, our frustrations, our pleasures, our successes—and our deaths. Writing this story is finally a purgation of my own ghosts.

Many of us joked that we were mercenaries, missionaries, or maniacs. Which begs the question, why would relatively normal people knowingly risk their lives to help others in areas too dangerous to send soldiers? Personality deficiency? Or merely a different personality? It is a question that I sought to answer, not just about the others in the field but about myself.

I had not exactly lived a life of the mainstream, and perhaps my own background is not representative of the others. Yet I feel I have to lay some of it out, for what follows in these pages is often so outrageous, so frightening, and so typical of the lives of aid workers that it is necessary to look into the reason why one person, at least, might willingly enter such work.

After graduating from boarding school, I rebelled from the highly disciplined cloistered life that prepared its youth for careers in medicine, law, business, politics, and diplomacy, and signed on as a "workaway" aboard merchant ships—pay the captain a hundred bucks and work your butt off for the passage to Europe. Signing off a ship in Baltimore, I found a job as copyboy on a local newspaper, sharpening pencils for reporters, and after years of local journalism wound up with United Press International as one of their correspondents covering the State Department and the White House. I left the newsrooms to write speeches for congressmen on Capitol Hill, then tired of the claptrap of politics, took my family to northern Michigan, where I worked on oil rigs and built a log house. I went north to Alaska, ran a political campaign, did a short season on a crab boat, then skippered a commercial boat fishing for halibut in the Gulf of Alaska. I wrote a steamy dime novel about the Last Frontier that was published, then briefly wrote for the daytime television show *Search for Tomorrow.* I had been writing the soap aboard my little thirty-two-foot sloop in San Francisco Bay and, suffering intellectual burnout, I sailed across the Pacific to Tahiti and beyond. I met my Dutch wife, Jacqueline, in Malaysia, and together we sailed across the Indian Ocean to East Africa. It is upon our arrival on the coast of Kenya that this story begins. While my own past may not be one that many can relate to, it is a history that led up to the day that I joined the World Food Program to save lives in Somalia.

Yet this background does not explain why. Was the money enough to risk my life? Was my marriage so rocky that I had to get away? Did I sign up because I really wanted to help people? Had my own past required that I merely find another adventure? Each of us had reasons to disappear into relief work, reasons that reflected an individual's personality and personal history. One humanitarian worker, a former schoolteacher, admitted as the bullets were flying overhead in Baghdad that she remained in the aid trade because of the adrenaline rush. Another, who had been kidnapped and held for twenty-two days in a moldy root cellar in Chechnya, said he was in it for altruistic reasons, that he really felt good about himself when he was helping those who suffer. One with whom I worked in Somalia was in it only for the money that the job paid. Myself, I really did not know at the time what I was getting myself into and I signed up without much thought, eager for adventure that was well paid. I had no idea what relief work was, what it would require physically and emotionally. I had never considered myself an altruist or a missionary much interested in helping anyone, simply a restless sailor. I was to discover, however, that at the end of the day, the reasons for getting into relief work for many of us were not the reasons to stay in it. After saving a life, I was hooked. There is something selfishly satisfying about saving lives.

Saving others, saving yourself is not without its price. Some of us were emotionally scarred by our experiences. It was unavoidable. I was as much of a stranger to violence as anyone else, the last to throw a punch. There was nothing in my own past to prepare me for the horrors that my colleagues and I were to face in Somalia. Despite a much-practiced ability as a journalist to disassociate, I found myself unable to avoid emotional intervention. I tried to disconnect, to see the horror, the deaths through the cold eyes of a professional observer. I was sometimes successful when the bullets came my way, but not when the bloodshed occurred to others within a few feet of where I stood or, indeed, in my arms. Out in the field, we saved the lives of dozens or more, many more, and that was gratifying; nothing, however, can expiate the unremitting guilt, the memory of that child for whose death I was responsible.

* * *

FIELD workers go where they are sent, rarely working again with those they have known in other areas of crisis. The time shared is frequently in a foxhole, under stress and immediate. And then it is over. Word comes over high-frequency radio to pack up and move to someplace else where you are needed. And then it is simply good-bye, hope to see you again somewhere. Relief work during a humanitarian emergency does not often permit intimacy or promote long-term friendships.

Relief workers charge weaponless and without protection on missions that are frequently away from the eyes of the international community, their quiet bravery considered only when their deaths make the news on the back page. What they endure in other parts of the world is frequently more horrifying than what is recounted here. For some, working for the UN or for nongovernmental relief organizations in the field during a humanitarian crisis is the last job they will ever have.

Part I

Will the Last One to Leave Please Turn Off the Lights?

1.
The Crisis

ONE villager reported the building simply collapsed without warning. The woman and her three children and the two old people on the tin roof vanished under the fast-moving brown floodwaters and were swept away.

Marerey was one of the villages on the banks of the southern stretch of the Webbi Jubba. It was disappearing fast, ripped apart by the rising river that had broken its banks and was sweeping away everything in its path.

Its people were a strong lot, used to hardship. They had weathered searing droughts and previous floods, the pestilence of locusts and mysterious diseases. They were more fortunate than others.

Once time not so long ago, there had been a sugar factory on the other side of the airstrip, where many worked, and so the villagers could afford tin roofs instead of thatch, could afford to build their homes of mud bricks instead of wattle. There had even been a school. But the fighting had come and families fought families and the area had been divvied up by the warlords and their clans. The sugar factory had been destroyed in one of the many seesaw battles for turf and was now no more than a skeletal ruin. There had been things to salvage, however, and the youths who remained in the village, who had not left to join the fighting, had scavenged wood and cement blocks, slabs of Styrofoam, wire and rope, furniture and vessels, poles and plastic.

Marerey was in the breadbasket of Somalia, a land of cultivated fields and grazing plains, veined with a complex network of irrigation canals and roads; those who had not worked at the factory had raised cattle and goats, sugarcane, bananas, maize, and sorghum. Although they lived on the river, they were not fishermen and they seldom ate fish. They were pastoralists. The Jubba, one of Somalia's only two perennial streams, existed in their eyes mainly to provide the water for the fields and to carry away the effluence. The muddy river originating in Ethiopia to the north was not very polluted; there had been few pesticides in use and little industry and it was still pretty clean by the time it got this far, tainted only by the raw sewage from the communities on the river. The men usually quit their homes around dawn and took their places in a row, lifted their sarongs or dropped their trousers, squatted over the river, and performed their ablutions. The women performed theirs on the bend downriver where the Jubba took a turn.

The rains that were causing the floods had started suddenly. They say that one day, one month, it was normally dry and plans were made for the harvest. Then the next day the black clouds rolled in off the ocean to the east, merging with storms that drifted down from the north, and the skies opened up. And still it rained.

There were not many left in Marerey. Most of the residents had fled earlier to the narrow earthen dike about a half mile downriver, taking what little they could; the dike was bigger then and it had looked solid and safe and indestructible. They were, however, only a little safer there than had they taken refuge on the roofs of their homes, for the fast-moving river was steadily eating away at the dike; sections of earth peeled away, broke off, and tumbled into the flood.

Those who decided to stay in Marerey huddled together for warmth on top of their roofs under the pelting rains that never seemed to end. Some had tucked themselves under plastic sheeting; others had only cotton cloth as cover, and that only deadened the sting from the deluge.

The waters were rising steadily, two to three inches an hour. The night before, the river had climbed over the embankment and crept through the village, slowly, like a serpent searching, covering, consuming everything in its path. By daybreak, the roads, the town center, and finally the floors of the homes had disappeared under the flood. Those who took to their roofs watched the water below reach ever higher and spread out over the plains nearby, through the fields of maize that had been nearly ready to harvest, and vanish in the distance toward the untilled savanna. In this gray and dismal afternoon, this was a landscape without definition. In days—perhaps in hours if the rains didn't let up—the entire region would be just one large lake with only a mound of dry land here and there isolated as islands.

As the floodwater continued to rise, it no longer extended gradually as spillover but picked up the swiftly moving current and became the river itself. It tore at the foundations and sucked away the ground from under the heavier homes. Those on the roofs grasped the sharp edges of the corrugated iron, fearing, sensing, that these were their last moments on something solid before falling into the turgid waters below.

The buildings under them swayed from the pressure of the current; the mud-daub houses with thatched roofs were surprisingly solid, but they could never be expected to withstand the force of the flood. They stood defiantly against the rising waters until finally, one by one, they loosened their hold on the land and began to move slowly with the river. They broke apart and became just so much unidentified flotsam.

There was a grand old mango tree on the submerged embankment on the other side. One witness told of an old man who balanced on a thick bough on the second level. He clasped two small children in one arm and circled the tree with the other. He stared in frozen disbelief, too afraid for panic, at the water pressing against the trunk on its passage down to the sea. The bloated, whitening carcass of something bigger than a cow, a camel perhaps, broke the surface just below as if emerging from some depth; it floated briefly, then vanished, pulled under the swirl of the furious river. He felt the force of the raging stream as tight vibrations. Occasionally there was a shudder as the current changed and a more massive wall of water challenged the tree.

* * *

RUSS Ulrey, the regional logistics officer of the UN's World Food Program, stood beside his desk staring out the window at the steady rain and tried to suppress his frustration. He had just left the meeting of diplomats, agency heads, representatives of nongovernmental organizations, donor groups, and donor nations. He shouldn't have expected anything different for this crisis: The competition, the gentlemanly infighting, the need for public approbation, the breast-beating—these were the negative elements that bothered him the most during these emergencies. There were already signs that the same conflicts were cropping up again. Despite it all, however, the job always did get done: Many of the malnourished and starving were fed, some of the refugees relocated and housed, many of the sick and dying treated and saved. Yet he damn well regretted that there was such competition on the way to saving lives.

The rain outside his office swept across the manicured lawn of the UN compound in Nairobi like a moving wall. The cement walks were almost underwater and he watched two women pause under an overhang, slip off their shoes, and sprint across to the next building. The steady heavy rains were an irritant to the office workers.

The crisis on the Horn of Africa had come suddenly. Last year, the *Deyr,* Somalia's secondary rainy season, had been unseasonably sparse, and the expectations had been that this year the drought would be more severe. This was an El Niño year, however, and it had been anybody's guess what the season would bring. Local farm knowledge didn't help: The mangoes were hanging heavily on the trees as usual and the sugarcane was a little stunted, but that didn't mean much (it was not like looking at woolly-bear caterpillars in Russ' native Michigan and measuring the black stripe to determine how severe the winter would be). Nothing, according to the locals on the Jubba, heralded the disaster that was to come.

Among the papers on his desk were the reports from the U.S. State Department's Agency for International Development Famine Early Warning System:

> Unusually heavy and sustained rains have fallen in the Jubba Valley during October. Many homes in Gedo and Middle Jubba regions have been destroyed by floods and possessions swept away, prompting a new wave of displaced people in need of food, medicine, drinking water, blankets, and shelter. Floodwaters are moving downriver to Lower Jubba. Waterborne diseases are a threat. Hundreds of underground grain storage pits have been flooded.

A low-pressure trough had dropped from northern Europe to the Horn of Africa and had collided with the retreating Inter-Tropical Convergence Zone, the band of permanent low pressure that circles the planet near the equator. The combination of the two systems created a low-pressure belt over the Horn that pulled in moisture off the Indian Ocean. Unusually heavy rains in the north began falling in the Ethiopian highlands on the Great Rift Valley in October. There were some breaks in the weather, but in early November another wave of storms charged in from the ocean and the rain never stopped. Above-average sea temperatures fed the drifting storm clouds, and meteorologists predicted that until those temperatures fell, the rains would only become more frequent and more intense. The swollen streams poured into the Ganale River, and in Ethiopia thousands were left homeless. The Ganale fed the Webbi Jubba and the Webbi Shabeelle, and the normally arid Ogadĕn region had been flooded. While Ethiopia faced a crisis, it paled compared to that which was to strike downriver in the fertile midsection of Somalia.

Russ had flown over the region the day before. Keeping just above gunshot range, the small airplane followed what he guessed was the original course of the Jubba to the ocean port of Kismayo. Many of the dikes already had been breached. He saw, felt the panic of those massed tightly on the small patches of bare land, on their roofs, on the few remaining raised roads, even in the trees as they waited for help.

There were a half million people stranded on the high ground, and most of them had no access to shelter, food, drinking water, medicine. How was he going to deliver hundreds of tons of food out to these remote and isolated communities? Airdrops into the floodwaters were not an option. Trucks could go only so far before running out of land. Helicopters could deliver to distribution bases, but only small boats could get the supplies to those huddled on islands near their flimsy shelters, surrounded by the rising water. That was his priority—boats and people to drive them.

Russ was not unaccustomed to the challenges of putting together a lifesaving mission: delivering emergency supplies, coordinating with other often-competing agencies within the UN and assisting nongovernmental organizations (NGOs) like the Red Cross, Médecins sans Frontières, Oxfam, CARE, and dozens of others. As WFP regional logistics officer, Russ handled humanitarian operations for the entire Horn—parts of Eritrea, Kenya, Somalia, and Sudan—an area as large as the landmass from New York to the Mississippi. Until now his primary task had been Operation Lifeline Sudan, a WFP mission that provided food for more than two and a half million people displaced by the civil war or suffering from massive crop losses. He had been responsible for putting together the largest humanitarian airlift in history in terms of tons per day delivered, he was proud to say.

Then suddenly there was Somalia, a complex emergency in one of the most hostile places on earth. The country had been rent by civil war since the overthrow of the central government in 1991. Somalia was said to have more guns per capita than anywhere else on earth. Stitching together a multiorganizational, multinational emergency operation in a war zone amid competition with other agencies was a challenge beyond imagination. Russ never questioned his ability to put it together. It was a matter of delegating; it also required begging, borrowing, cutting corners, and creative thinking.

Russ had personal, hard-won experience with Somalia. While head of logistics for operations in Sudan, he was assigned to arrange cross-border relief deliveries into Somalia during the famine crisis in 1992. Warlord militia had been looting and hijacking his trucks as soon as they crossed the border. To get the emergency supplies through, he knew that clan and subclan militia first must be disarmed. Indeed, Somali leaders had requested UN assistance in disarming the population and had suggested that Somalis would voluntarily turn in their weapons for a basket of food or other inducement. Russ recommended to the American troops who had been sent to assure delivery of humanitarian assistance that their first priority be to get the guns away from the locals. The demobilization program never got off the ground. "I asked them to disarm the Somalis as soon as they landed and before I authorized any further delivery," he recalled. "They could have done so. But they didn't—it was a formula for going sideways." Because of this dispute with the military, Russ was unceremoniously sent back to Sudan, and the United Nations operation in Somalia (UNOSOM) later ended in disgrace and tragedy. There was little conviction in his mind that the current flood emergency mission would be any more successful.

Russ had started his humanitarian work years back driving a relief barge on the Nile in the Sudan. He had been hijacked and kidnapped by bandits, toward whom he holds no ill will. Before that, he had been a sailor, a licensed mechanic, a boat builder, had swung a hammer on construction sites, had a pilot's license, and had the schooling, a degree in geophysics. Today, in his early fifties, with a peppery beard and dark, concerned eyes, he says he was convinced at the time he could put the Somali operation together, although he recalls wondering if he was not beginning to wear down. WFP missions are 24/7.

Indeed, the WFP fed a hundred four million people in eighty-one countries in 2003, at a cost of $3.3 billion. Despite these Herculean efforts, one person starves to death every four seconds. That is twenty-four thousand people a day worldwide—three quarters of them children and women.

Working alongside the WFP in most of these humanitarian crises is the United Nations Children's Fund, and because of Unicef's more sweeping mandate, which includes funding appeals, child welfare, health, nutrition, hygiene, and development, it was the agency assigned to coordinate the Somali flood-relief mission.

As Russ stared out his window of the UN compound waiting for two of his logistics staff, Dr. Agostino Paganini of Unicef, the interagency coordinator, was describing the situation at a news conference in the conference room on the ground floor:

"Unless we get helicopters and boats now, immediately, we may as well hang our hats on it. Instead of saving lives, we will be helping to bury the dead. Thousands of people will die. The response team's plan of operation is in place; a lot of relief equipment and food rations are ready to go, but what we absolutely lack is the means of getting these things to the affected population. . . . It is deeply frustrating. The world community cannot remain indifferent in the face of a disaster that is slowly and cruelly evolving before our eyes, hour by hour. Nor can bureaucracy ever be an excuse for inaction." A few hundred families had been reached by donkey cart out of Kenya, Paganini added. "The hideous situation is compounded by the presence of deadly crocodiles, snakes, and land mines."

Only a few months before, Paganini had launched a hundred-million-dollar appeal to help Somalia pull itself out of its continual state of lawlessness and reintegrate with the international community. There had been few sympathetic listeners. Following the controversial humanitarian and military intervention in the early nineties, contributors had tired of Somali horror stories and the contributions were drying up, a clear sign of "donor fatigue." Paganini was announcing at the press conference that the current Somali flood crisis would require at least an additional $10 million.

There was only a finite amount of resources that donor organizations and donor nations could contribute: money, food, material, and personnel. The inter- and intraorganizational competition for these resources, often a matter of an organization's solvency, is frequently unpleasant. Russ wondered how intense the competition would get this time—between WFP and Unicef, between the WFP and other UN agencies and the NGOs, which often relied on the WFP for logistical support. A war of egos—the efforts to strengthen their empires and to remain financially secure, as well as to assure their eminence in the eyes of the donors—is often waged on the battlefield of public relations. It occurs during nearly every humanitarian emergency.

The origins of this self-serving puffery began in earnest in 1992. International attention had been focused on Somalia, where more than three hundred thousand people already had died of hunger and hunger-related diseases and at least three thousand people, mostly women, children, and the elderly, were starving to death daily. In a high-profile media blitz, one agency, CARE, not the first on the scene, airlifted and distributed supplies from ships anchored off Mogadishu. Then someone in CARE with a sense of marketing saw an opportunity and distributed agency T-shirts and baseball caps to its workers, which were highly visible to the world media. WFP and Unicef, not to be outdone, quickly did the same. "It was a chance to get recognition and to impress the donors with their efficiency, their high-profile presence," Russ remembered. "A photo opportunity. Everyone kept score—how many people have we saved today?"

Competing press conferences were held, the numbers inflated and presented, and some NGOs that had been little known before were assured that, as a result of their high-profile media efforts, they would be kept funded and operating. (The need for public exposure, however, did a one-eighty following the bombing of the UN compound in Baghdad in August 2003: Many agencies, including the well-respected International Committee of the Red Cross, removed their logos from their cars and offices, fearing they were targets of the forces opposed to Coalition occupation.)

Each humanitarian crisis is different, but the Somalia flood crisis had all the ingredients of the worst that could befall mankind: It was a natural disaster that had occurred without warning; thousands suffered from malnutrition and starvation and required immediate rescue; it was in a part of the world that was poorly mapped; it was within a combat area; there were diseases known and unknown; and so far there was not much money to do the job.

The reports from the towns on the Jubba River had been urgent, desperate. Russ had received one account from the Médecins sans Frontières staff upstream in the Ogadĕn that malaria, dysentery, watery and bloody diarrhea, cholera, and snakebites were already taking their toll, and as usual the first to die were children under five. Hippos and pythons, confused and displaced, were moving into the quieter waters that covered the villages, and there was one confirmed report that a child had been taken by a crocodile. One community of two hundred fifty families was reported stranded on a narrow coastal sand dune north of Kismayo, an island with the Indian Ocean on one side and the swift floodwaters on the other. They had no possessions, had not eaten for five days, and had only rainwater to drink. The need for rescue, food, and medicines was immediate. MSF, World Vision (an international Christian relief NGO), and Somali Community Services (an NGO that liaised with the hard-hit villages) also were asking Russ to help them arrange delivery of staff and equipment and supplies.

Russ cataloged some of the items he had to consider. In addition to meeting the requests and needs of other UN agencies and NGOs, there were a few other pressing matters: He was desperate for helicopters, and Russ thought he could contract an Mi-8 from South Africa and another from Ukraine. He had a line on some cargo planes: two venerable C-130 Hercules—each with a payload of fifty thousand pounds of food, enough to feed a hundred twenty thousand people for a day—standing by at the Lokichoggio base in southern Sudan and one at Jomo Kenyatta International Airport in Nairobi; and there was that Ukrainian Anotov still without charter at JKIA. He had to meet with Kenyan government officials—Customs, Immigrations, Interior—always a headache because of the corruption, the money needed to get things done. There were houses to rent for staff in Nairobi and arrangements to be made for accommodations in some of the villages in Somalia. Locations where Unicef had semipermanent quarters—Kismayo, for example—could house some of his crew. The former military base at Garissa in northeast Kenya would be a good staging area for relief flights into the Somali heartland. He would offer to repair the landing strip, cheaper than paying landing fees every time a WFP plane landed. He would have to contract for smaller cargo planes—the Buffaloes and the Caravans—that could land on the dirt strips. Aviation fuel would have to be trucked through the bush from Nairobi to Garissa and a fuel depot built for the planes and helicopters. Problem: How was he going to prevent *shifta,* wandering Somali thieves, from hijacking the fuel trucks, as they do occasionally in the Sudan operations (aircraft fuel is ideal for their lamps and cooking stoves)? And there were the boats; there could be no effective relief mission without them. All this had to have been done yesterday—the waters were rising and people were being swept away.

He expected this emergency to be stressful, but he had a staff upon which most of the grunt work would fall. Saskia von Meijenfeldt had been loaned to the WFP by the Dutch government as a junior projects officer, an intern. A tall, slender blonde in her late twenties, Saskia was to become indispensable to the relief operation. With boundless nervous energy and remarkable efficiency, Saskia learned quickly the intricacies and politics of the bureaucracy. Russ gave her a permanent posting with the WFP and appointed her Somalia logistics officer.

WFP headquarters in Rome had pulled Matt Wolff from a posting in Iraq and seconded him to the regional logistics office in Nairobi for the Somali emergency. A square-bodied former racing yachtsman from the UK with time on the ground in Rwanda, Matt was to run the river operations.

Saskia and Matt sat across the desk from Russ, waiting for an update.

"The meeting went as I expected," Russ began. "You'll be attending them in the future, Saskia. They will be held every morning at seven-thirty. Unicef, of course, wants the limelight—wants to run the river operations, thinks those are the glamour jobs. Photo opportunities.

"But they are not ready to do the job. They are starting an operation in Kismayo, but they have no boats. I think we should give them a hand. If we send boats and drivers to Kismayo, we can work the flooded areas of the river from both ends. Saskia, you see what we can arrange in Kismayo."

Saskia nodded, took notes on her pad.

In this early stage of the emergency, Russ knew that the boats were vital not only for rescue but for access. He recalled that the agencies couldn't get out to the villages by airplane or truck, and access was also politically difficult: Many of the villages were either on one side of a combat line or the other. The gift of food provided an opening, an entrance, and he could make decisions based on that.

Russ continued: "I told them, 'If you give me a quarter of a million dollars, I will hire twelve boat guys and I'll get those little boats I already have for our Sudan operation and in the next couple of days we'll fly them in on the Buffalo with some food and save those people. We will get them out of the trees.' "

"And?" Saskia asked.

"What could they say? It looks like we will keep the river operations as well as the airlifts. And of course we'll help them any way we can. Unicef is holding a news conference as we speak."

"Where do we get boats?" Saskia asked.

"I'm flying two down from Loki that are on standby for Sudan, but we are going to have to find more. The Norwegians are supposed to be donating ten boats to Unicef but I expect we will be in charge of them; some safari operators probably have some that we can hire. I know there are a few in the Mombasa area—you should check on that. We may have to borrow some bigger dinghies from 'yachties' on the coast. You'll have to figure where to put the boats on the river, figure out where to set up distribution sites, and arrange for the transport of the boat operators."

"Where do we get the drivers?" Matt asked.

"Well, you're the sailor. I guess that is your job."

This was one of the most pressing issues, Russ recalled later in an interview:

"There was an immediate need to go into the bush—in the next couple of days, in fact. We didn't have the people for the jobs; we required people who had skills that were not common to our organization. We don't have bosun's mates. The WFP usually hires contractors, but there weren't any contractors in the area whose job descriptions, whose skills, were such that they rescue people out of trees in the bush in Somalia. It wasn't the case where we could have done an open tender. We needed people who were very unique. So we hired yachties, round-the-world sailors, and anyone who was familiar with boats.

"This was going to be some of the toughest and most heart-breaking work in the world, and some of those guys were perfect for it. If you can sail the Third World and get through the Customs and Immigrations and negotiate in the marketplaces and live for a while with the locals, you probably have the right attitude to negotiate with a tribe in southern Sudan or in Somalia. I was looking for self-sufficient people used to living in rough conditions and willing to make some sacrifices."

"Write a fax," Russ told Wolff, "and send it to anyplace where you think there are boat people. Might try the Dar es Salaam Yacht Club, Mombasa Yacht Club, the Tanga Yacht Club, and the boat-yard in Kilifi. I am sure we can get some yachties to sign on.

"Oh, and, Matt," Russ said, raising his eyes directly to the solidly built figure opposite, "this is going to be one very frustrating job. You are going to have to do some of the things that I haven't got the time or space for. You have a bit of a history—so keep your temper, keep your patience, and go with the flow, eh?"

"Yeah, sure, no problem. Are you going to tell the drivers that it could get a little dangerous?"

"Everyone has heard about Somalia. You could add in the fax that there are some security problems they should be aware of. Also better tell them that it pays more because of those risks."

Security of humanitarian workers sent into the field was an issue. So was the urgency to get the operations under way and save lives. Security balanced against operations was an administrative conflict that dated back to the very first relief mission in a hostile area. While Russ was mindful that already that year nine WFP staff members had been killed in the line of duty, he was just as concerned with getting the boats, food, water, medicine, blankets, tarps, and tons of other material out to the field and to the flood victims as soon as possible. Security measures were based on an assessment of conditions in the field and officially categorized by phases. Somalia was Phase Four, an area unquestionably hazardous, where only the most essential personnel required to carry out the mission would be permitted. As long as people were dying and the UN had committed a relief mission to save them, then the workers in the field could be expected to face some risks; that came with the job, always did. The applicants would be warned of the dangers, would get some security training, and they would get additional pay, of course. This time, however, it was not as it had been in 1992, when the UN Security Council authorized a military force into Somalia to protect the aid and those relief workers distributing it. For this emergency, there would be no troops. Better because, in the eyes of the locals, his people would not be associated with any foreign nation's military or political policies. Worse because his people would have to face the guns alone and fend for themselves. While security of the staff was important, operations—getting the food out to those who so desperately needed it—were more so.

"We should get a security window," Ross told Wolff. "Usually happens in an unexpected natural disaster—the locals put down their guns and help. Who knows? Our window might last the crisis. It is not like they are going to shoot at each other over a worthless patch of water. Run the list of those you want to hire by me first."

2.
The Consultant

MY wife, Jacqueline, and I had arrived in Kenya after a voyage down the East African coast on the *Unicorn,* our thirty-two-foot yacht. Our temporary home was the ancient slave port of Kilifi, where we had stopped for provisions and maintenance. The passage had taken us from the Mediterranean through the Suez Canal, down the Red Sea to Aden. From Yemen, another thirty-three days to reach our landfall, a frustrating nonstop passage of fickle winds, heavy rains, and a contrary north-setting current around the Horn of Africa. The trip was not expedited by the need to add hundreds of miles and tedious days to keep far off the coast of Somalia, a notorious feeding ground for pirates.

The rains seemed to chase us down the coast right into the harbor, and they'd kept us cooped up below nearly continuously since our arrival. God never intended Man and Woman to live together for twenty-four hours a day, week after week, in a small sailboat—a space smaller than many modern prison cells—and while the slow, interminable passage had been made in harmony, it was during the comedown, the soggy period following, that we had reached near boiling point.

It hadn't rained since noon and, hoping a change in scenery would help, we had motored into the large bay up the creek, past the imposing mansions on the cliffs owned by white Kenyans who had sold their Up Country holdings and retired gracefully to the coast. I sat alone out on the deck against the doghouse, gazing across the water at the colonnaded villas, the well-manicured lawns, the deep jungle beyond, and the cumulonimbus that built over the interior. This was the season of the traditional Short Rains, a transition between monsoons, but the locals said it had rained straight through the dry season and there were no signs that it would stop anytime soon. The thunderheads, tops splaying off into the upper reaches of sky, emptied heavy rains on the interior. Lightning, a brief swelling of silent light, throbbed within those powerful storms. Here on the still waters of the bay, the humid air was redolent of the strange smells of tropic jungle and unseen flowers, of the tang of salt from the exposed reef. Carmine bee-eaters, tucking wings missilelike to intercept the insects of the evening, swooped and darted above the boat, twisting and diving in the frantic last hour before dark. Broad-winged fox bats flapped heavily and erratically across the water at mast height. They came as many and they flew scattered and alone. Other than the distant rumble of thunder, it was quiet and peaceful, and mercifully dry. This evening, this anchorage, this peace—any anchorage and peace like it—were the destinations, the reasons. Yet I still stewed a little over our recent sharp exchange about something now forgettable, and I was thankful for the brief solitude.

Jackie came from below and sat next to me without speaking, without touching. I felt her body from a distance. In her middle years, her pretty Dutch features had become more defined, giving her a handsome quality. I was pleased she had joined me; I chose to believe she was feeling at peace and forgiving at this moment. She leaned forward, her chin on her knees, staring outboard, abstracted.

She sighed, whether from aggravation or contentment I could not tell. But it was communication, an opening.

"Peaceful," I said.

"Yes . . . I need space."

"And?"

"I need a break."

"I don't blame you. It was a difficult trip."

"No, I mean a long break. I need to do something with my life."

"I've heard that before."

"So what? I need to get off this damn boat."

It was a night of a late moon, and the darkness this close to the equator comes quickly. The silhouettes of fronds of the palm trees that lined the ridge on the hills before us were growing indistinct. Despite the gentle tropic air, I felt chilled, and cheated of a moment.

"It sounds like something more serious than the boat."

Silence.

This had been gathering since the end of the passage like the turbulent Up Country weather, smaller blows building to the big one. The tension was electric and dangerous. I needed to postpone, to deny. We had had too many good years to say something stupid. I realized, perhaps with some relief, we were too defeated to begin yelling at each other.

Jacqueline had owned a bar and restaurant on a resort island in Malaysia when we met. I was a solo blue-water sailor with a thirst. Some months later, she had sold her interest in the place and was crossing the Indian Ocean with me on a passage to Europe. That was eight years and a few adventures before.

I started the engine, hauled up the anchor, and motored us back down the river. I looked at my watch; if lucky, we would get to the bar at the boatyard before they shut it down for the night.

Deliverance arrived the next morning in the form of a fax, an urgent appeal for anyone with any sailing or maritime experience to contact the UN's World Food Program in Nairobi. The WFP was looking for boat drivers to deliver emergency relief supplies up some river in Somalia and they paid well. For me, it didn't matter whether the UN job was in Mogadishu or in Paris. It appeared that I had found my own modern-day Foreign Legion.

Without hesitation or consultation, I faxed back my interest, determined to sign up. The immediate response instructed me to go to Nairobi for an interview, arrive prepared "to camp in the bush, like going on safari." I had never camped in the African bush, never gone on safari: I did know enough to borrow a tent and raid the boat's galley of our Snickers bars. The fax also warned of "some security problems in Somalia." I could imagine that a few sacks of food disappeared from time to time. Admission of security problems probably represented the caution with which the UN undertook its relief missions.

The day before my departure, Jackie left for her flight from Mombasa to the Netherlands. At our brief good-bye, I jokingly announced—with some self-pitying malice—that I was off to war. I would imagine that those running away into the unknown might enact similar peevish scenes. It is the annunciation of our intentions, the note left behind—you're going to miss me when I'm gone—before jumping off a bridge. We hugged briefly, almost like strangers: "Be careful. . . . I am sorry," she said, and took refuge in the shadows of the taxi. As the car pulled away, I thought I saw her face turn toward the rear window—and a brief uncertain wave.

Back on the *Unicorn*, I stood in the darkened cabin, owning myself completely after so many months, accepting with equal measure the bitter silence, the sense of loss, the emptiness, and the bubbling excitement of liberation. This is what I had needed. Yet the sense of loss prevailed and, like a thief in the night, I sought out the things she had left behind. If any. I rifled her drawers and at the bottom found her cherished photographs of family: her sons and their partners, her elderly parents, us. At her departure, at least, she intended to return. I was relieved.

* * *

AFTER flying into Nairobi the next day, I dickered with the driver of a clapped-out rogue taxi, a cheerful youth with dreadlocks under a red, black, and gold woven Rasta cap, for the fare to the UN headquarters that I was told Kenyans would pay. "Okay, okay, *bwana,* I give you friend price, *Rafiki* price."

The taxi sputtered and clanked past the cargo terminal. A row of airplanes wing-to-wing, a few with UN stenciled blue on their tails, appeared eager to spring over the horizon. Forklifts heavy with pallets of cargo drove onto the gaping ramps and disappeared inside their cavernous bowels. Dark half-naked human figures, balancing boxes and heavy sacks on their heads, marched toward the aircraft—relief supplies, I supposed, destined for faraway places in need: the Sudan, Somalia, Rwanda, the Congo, Burundi. The pace of this industry provided a singularly subjective interpretation: Hurry up, hurry up, people are dying, relief workers need to get out there to save people, to get on with it. I felt a wonderful childlike proprietary pride in those aircraft, a sort of home team rah-rah—they were more important than anything and they were ours. And I had yet to be interviewed.

The four-lane Uhuru Highway passes through an Africa of less than postcard beauty. This was still the era of Daniel arap Moi, one of Africa's longest-reigning autocrats. For twenty-four years, hundreds of millions of dollars of international funding for schools, sanitation, roads, and poverty relief were flushed down the latrine of corruption—convincingly displayed by this trip from the airport to the city. Squatters huddled over small cooking fires alongside their small homes of sticks and rustling plastic, and their naked children scrabbled in the dirt only a few feet away from the gravel-kicking lorries and buses that belched gagging exhaust. In those early-morning hours of washed-out light, with the dew still heavy on the ground, the smoke from the cooking fires snaked across the surface of the road. On the raised center median partially veiled by the haze, an old man, his trousers lowered to his knees, squatted and watched both sides of the rush hour.

The traffic moved fitfully, past the wealthy estates, clusters of residences protected by high cement walls embedded with shards of broken bottle glass.

An hour later and a little closer to the city, steam drifted out from under the taxi hood and from under our feet. The stop-and-go traffic was taking its toll and the car needed a break. That came at the roundabout at Kenyatta Avenue. Away from the industrial section, the air had begun to clear. But at the circle, we ran abruptly into a wall of thick, white semisweet smoke, caustic enough to be tasted. The familiar stench conjured up a distant memory. Tear gas. Not since as a reporter during the heady days of anti–Vietnam

War protests and urban riots following the King assassination in the sixties had I tasted this.

Our taxi was suddenly quite alone and at the head of the line of slow-moving traffic; drivers honked and cursed behind us. Ahead, a phalanx of near-empty *matatus,* minibuses normally packed beyond the limit, charged toward us the wrong way on this one-way avenue. The taxi turned sharply, slithered up the muddy embankment, and, at the top, coughed and shuddered to its apparent death. The minibuses below, plastered with reflective decals warning ***MISTER DOOM, BLACK MAGIC MAN, LOVE FURST***, charged the oncoming commuter traffic that we had left behind, sideswiping some cars and running others off the road. Gangs of youths jumped off the buses and beat on the hoods and windscreens with their fists. Helmeted police armed with shields, truncheons, and assault rifles piled into the rioters. Blaring horns, popping tear-gas canisters, angry exhortations amplified by megaphones, the cacophony of a riot mixed with cheerful bouncy African music that came from somewhere else.

"*Bwana,* you come with me. Quick smart!" The young Rasta man grabbed my sea bag, took my hand, and ran with me down the other side of the embankment into the relative quiet of the city. The noise from the demonstration grew faint, the smell of tear gas now only another memory. But I was shaken.

"Nairobi, *bwana,* Nairobi."

* * *

THE World Food Program/Somalia Office headquarters was not what I had expected, not a scrubbed modern office building but a sagging tin-roof settler's house in Gigiri, the hilly suburbs of the city. During the days of the Empire, this might have been a substantial home that a new colonialist would have been proud to build, when a trip to the center of town was a full day's outing through untamed bush. These days, it served as temporary quarters for the UN during one desultory humanitarian crisis or another. A small foyer had been turned into a reception area that was manned by an indifferent guard. The wooden floors sloped unevenly, and the 1940s-era wallpaper of pastel-colored posies—wallpaper that the imagination allows may have been eagerly awaited on the ship from England—was stained by the years. Flimsy walls painted pea green had been hastily nailed together to create small offices. Staff emerged from out of one closed door and disappeared into another, bumping into each other in the narrow corridor. There seemed to be a sense of urgency. But perhaps it was my own. I presented myself to the Kenyan guard behind the desk and announced that I was there to join the aid mission to Somalia. He shrugged, pointed down the hallway. I peered into another office and announced myself, and no one there seemed to know what to do with me either. I began to wonder if I was the only one being interviewed for the relief team or if in fact there even was an ongoing emergency operation in Somalia. The thrill of adventure, of belonging, of being part of an international effort, of being part of a mission for which I was desperately needed, all this began to evaporate and I saw myself returning on the next flight to the coast.

Sitting back on my haunches against the wall in the hall, I waited for someone who looked like they had some authority. The morning newspaper had a story about the planned demonstration by *matatu* drivers and their touts. Two days before, one of Moi's bodyguards in the presidential motorcade had lost patience with a slow-thinking *matatu* driver caught in the inevitably slow-moving Nairobi traffic. The guard had pistol-whipped the driver, then shot him and his tout. He was to be charged with the double murder, but not before this morning's riot.

Reading the account, I thought that if all went well I soon would be working with the United Nations in Somalia. Not in some nuthouse like Nairobi.

"Here to sign up?" A tall, stern-looking woman in her late twenties had emerged from an office and stood over me.

"I heard you were looking for boat drivers," I said, rising awkwardly to my feet. "I'm from Kilifi—on the coast. I faxed that I was coming."

"Good, excellent—yes, we do need drivers. When can you start?"

"Immediately." I hadn't thought about getting a hotel. I'm not sure what I was thinking—that the UN was a compound that offered barracks? It was apparent there was no room in this place, except perhaps some space on the uneven floors. Maybe they'd send me to Somalia tonight.

Her eyes fixed critically on my sea bag, a large canvas laundry sack with the faded stenciled name of some forgotten merchant ship. She looked up and smiled. She reminded me of the nerdish little girl with oversize glasses whose pigtails I pulled in class. Yet her strong blue eyes, short hair, and reluctant smile briefly kindled some other curiosity.

"I'm Saskia, WFP logistics officer. You have gear?"

"Not much. I wasn't sure what I would need."

"Well, to tell you the truth, neither are we. Your own things should be enough to keep you in the field for a month or two—your own food, of course—anything you think you would need for the bush." She led me down the hallway to meet the manager of the Somalia boat operations.

The tight quarters in the rummy little office pinched the young administrator's heavy features. Here was a harried, overweight, overworked, hard-smoking bureaucrat who appeared to take things very seriously. Possibly it was the nature of the work. Organizing an emergency relief operation to save lives, I imagined, was serious business. Wearing a short-sleeved white shirt with sweat stains under the arms, Matt Wolff sat imposingly behind a battered wood desk of mottled stain and varnish; a four-blade fan overhead provided some relief, occasionally stirring papers on the desk and the edges of maps that were tacked haphazardly to the wall. An ashtray of heavy ebony wood filled with cigarette butts kept some loose forms in place.

He shuffled some papers on his desk, lifted tired eyes, and inspected the figure before him with the enthusiasm of a drill sergeant checking out a raw recruit.

"I'm looking for people who aren't child molesters, don't have prison records, and who aren't sought by the police." It was evident by his scrutiny that he was assessing which of the above might disqualify me.

"Tough requirements. All other vices accepted?"

"Most others. No pissheads. No journalists. And they should have some knowledge of boats."

"I know the difference between port and starboard."

"Good, you'll do fine."

No journalists? There was no danger of being a journalist again. There was no story in Somalia, just another African famine crisis.

"We've got people hanging on to tree limbs out there, dying by the minute, and bloody Customs won't let us get the boats out of their warehouses. What absolute crap!" Responsible also for dealing with Kenya Customs, he was up to his neck battling the notoriously greedy bureaucracy, their efficiency proportionate only to the amount of *kitu kidogo*—bribery money—to grease the skids.

"I'll probably send you to Kismayo. You'll set up a logistics base, prepare the boats, and deliver the supplies upriver from there. Ever been to Somalia?"

"I've seen it from offshore."

"Know anything about it?"

"Not a hell of a lot. Some American soldiers got killed in Mogadishu a few years back."

"That was UNOSOM—United Nations in Somalia. A real fuckup and we're still paying for it. You don't need to know the details—it's in the history books. The success of our mission, whether or not we are able to help these people, save these people, depends, as it did then, on the locals. To be more specific, on a bunch of crazy warlords letting us do our job."

"Warlords?"

"Regional tribal leaders. Somalia has no central government and the country is run by warlords. It is like Europe in the Middle Ages; each warlord has his own fiefdom—a twenty-first-century feudal system. No knights in shining armor, just militiamen with guns. The warlords can make our job easier, or impossible."

A passing shower pelting the tin roof like thrown pebbles drowned out the last of what Matt Wolff had to say.

". . . so nothing much has changed since the UNOSOM days of 1992, except that there are no soldiers to protect us."

The chain-smoking young Brit revealed that he had just arrived from Iraq and had worked in Iran, Rwanda, and Azerbaijan during the past eight years. He was hardly the stereotypical out-of-shape starched paper-pusher with green eyeshade and suspenders that I imagined. I was to learn later that when not involved with relief operations for UN agencies, he was working toward his Ph.D. His subject: management—or mismanagement—of UN relief programs.

The logistics officer knocked on the partially opened door and entered, followed quickly by a dour, preoccupied figure with a black beard and a distant impersonal air.

"You've met Saskia," Wolff said. "And this is Russ Ulrey, the regional logistics officer—he's in charge of the whole WFP operation. He and Saskia—"

"Yeah, hi," Russ interrupted. "Matt, you got those Norwegian boats out yet? I got the donors on my butt. They don't want to hear that they are still in the Customs hangar when they see reports on television about how many people a day are being flushed down the rivers."

"They promised me one out this afternoon, another out tomorrow. At the latest."

"Well, stay on it—maybe you should go over there and shake some cages. You a boat driver?" he said, turning to me. He didn't seem unfriendly, merely stressed.

"Don't know. I'm here for the job."

"Yeah, he's on board," Matt said.

"Good. Let me know when that boat is released." He disappeared, leaving the three of us in silence.

"Russ also runs our Sudan and Kenya operations. Busy guy."

"So, you are ready to go?" Saskia asked me.

"Almost—I have to buy some things."

"Kismayo?" to Wolff.

"I think so." He turned to me. "Kismayo is Somalia's southern port on the Jubba River. For the next day or so, I want you to assemble the boats at the airport here. Then you take one of the fast boats to Kismayo—there is another already there—and set up an operations base. While you're at it, you might help the locals put their port back together. We have some ships ready to deliver supplies from Mombasa, but first the port has to be up and running."

"Also, when you are in Kismayo," Saskia added, "I'd like you to check on the security situation. Unicef has a security man out there, but I haven't got much sense of what to expect. Radio us a report, daily if you can, about what's going on."

"You don't know?"

It was evident by her expression that she took my question as criticism.

"We do know, of course. From others. But you will be representing the World Food Program, the first from our office, and I would like to hear it from you. Okay?"

"We haven't heard of any problems," Wolff interceded, lighting a cigarette. "But the port and airport are prime real estate. Whoever controls those controls most of southern Somalia. Things change by the minute. We can bonk a few threatening crocodiles but we can't do anything about the militia and the AK-47s. Everyone there has a gun, and they don't need an excuse to shoot. And if it gets tense, well," he paused, running his fingers through his short sandy hair. He snorted. "Well, we are all quite sure it won't get that tense."

"And if it does?"

"We will pull you and the others out. We'll all go home. The Somalis bloody well know that. They know that we're the good guys. We rescue them and provide them food. They know this is their last chance for any assistance from the international community. Oh, here," he said, taking a blue baseball cap embroidered with *WFP* from a box on the shelf. "Help keep the sun off."

I left the office feeling like a man who had just won the lottery, but at the same time, I had the misgiving that maybe I should not have bought the ticket. I chose to dwell on the positive. I would have a job and at the same time earn a bundle of money for a new adventure. As an aid worker I hoped I would get the satisfaction of doing something worthwhile for others for the first time in my life, not for lovers, partners, friends, sons, or a daughter. I would help alleviate the misery of a thousand strangers, of those I would not know, normally would not care about. I might even save lives—for that was the purpose of this mission. (Saving lives—such a portentous concept. Saving someone from dying, not something to spend too much time thinking about; if you are there, you save a life. If you are not, a person dies?) At least I would not be standing on the sidelines, reading about some faraway humanitarian disaster that really did not interest me, or scribbling some throwaway words about an event that I would soon discard—I was being sent out there where I might even make a difference.

It was further reassuring that I would be a neutral, working for not one nation but for all the nations. There were to be no guns, no uniforms, no enforcement of a nation's Manifest Destiny. I would not be a representative of any military or political power. Moreover, while there might be some danger to the work, I would be part of a mission for the UN, reason enough to be convinced that it was safe.

3.
The Contract

TWO of the boats donated to the WFP lay in various disassembled parts of polished and painted aluminum at the mouth of a hangar at the airport, looking like pieces of wreckage and suggestive of the initial re-creation of a plane crash.

One was a small eighteen-foot open red runabout to be equipped with an outboard engine, and it appeared ideally suited to the task; put a couple of seats in it, a case of beer, and we could all go bass fishing. The other, donated by the Norwegian government and built in Finland, looked like something out of *Star Trek,* a toy of the space age that bespoke an ineffaceable arrogance. The sleek metallic-blue aluminum craft, low slung with sharp pointed bow, was built to skim over the surface at forty knots, near the highway speed limit in some places. Absurd metallic decals of cartoon characters with big popping eyes and a garish splash of the manufacturer's name festooned the sides. This was something a 1950s Hollywood film director might have used to pull some ski nymphs past a reviewing stand in his water musical. It seemed hardly the kind of craft for any mission other than to escape pursuing narcotics officers in the Caribbean. Certainly not designed to deliver relief supplies to the starving and dying, to rescue the homeless stranded in trees and on top of roofs. Either the contributors of this type of boat had been misinformed or there had been some dark money passed from one hand to the other. If our mission was anything like it had been described, I remember thinking, I might find myself a little embarrassed. The local reaction should be interesting; probably out there these waterborne rocket ships would be regarded with the same curiosity as the more educated would regard the arrival of extraterrestrials.

I was to drive one of these things.

Matt Wolff did not want the boats modified. Leave the seat and console and the cartoon decals with the manufacturer's name on the hull untouched. "The donors will want to see their boats on television. They'll see they're being put to good use," he said. We would not only be saving lives but spinning for the United Nations and its contributors as well. Over a sandwich at the airport, I suggested to him that the extra seat and console took up space needed for supplies or those we were to rescue. "Word from on high, mate, is to leave them as they were sent." For a critic of the management of relief programs, Wolff seemed very much in lockstep with those at the top.

Why not at least replace the cartoons with a stenciled *UN* on the side of the boats?

"Then you're sure to be a target, to get shot at."

"Shot at?"

He cocked his head with a look unmistakable: Maybe this guy's too much of a pussy for the job. "The UN has not got a good name in Somalia. Memories are long. Somalis considered Operation Restore Hope in 1992—an operation that restored nothing—foreign intervention, even though we were there to save lives. You know how that ended. So no need to show the flag."

"Sounds thrilling."

"Somalis are a volatile lot."

I wondered, who would they think we were, zipping over the floodwaters of the Jubba River on these obscene ski boats? Tourists?

It did not take a military strategist to see the potential of this rocket sled. Remove the extra seat and console and bolt a steel base plate and tripod on the bow for a machine gun and you would have one effective little war toy. The dream come true of every warlord: king of the Jubba Valley as well as one of the swiftest pirates on the East African coast. In the Somali civil war and the battles for territory, this kind of power could mean a lot of additional turf.

I was bent over the big Yamaha 55 outboard, wrestling with a stubborn connection, wondering what I was getting myself into but glad to have some purpose, when someone from behind announced: "I will drive this boat. Then I want to keep it."

A shirtless, wiry man in khaki shorts and flip-flops stood behind me, looking thoughtfully at the speedboat. He ran his hand over his bald head and grinned. "I have a camp on the Tsavo. You know how the UN quits a job and leaves behind all its equipment?" I nodded. But I didn't. "I can use these—I will have the only safari camp on the river with ski boats."

This was Mario, a genial, leathery bush guide of Italian descent, a self-proclaimed white hunter who, I was to learn, probably would have been more at ease tracking anticolonial rebels on the Zambezi than catering to fickle tourists seeking snapshots of wildlife. Mario, whose mother was born in Somalia during the colonial era, his father in South Africa, had a no-nonsense manner of command, apparently honed by years of employing Kenyan laborers and servants. With a quick catlike intensity, he came on as the sort who seemed eager to confront, ready to challenge.

"Yes, this one will be perfect," he announced. "Biltong?" He handed me a piece of stringy sweet-tasting leathery meat, cured, he said, from a wildebeest he had shot on the Masai Mara.

"Then this baby is all yours," I said. My needs were not great and my ego did not need the speed trip. I was not sure I even wanted one of the inappropriate go-fasts. "I'm taking it to Kismayo, probably tomorrow. You going there?"

"Haven't been told—they'll probably want me to help get the others out of Customs. Maybe even—" He looked up at a van that was approaching the hangar.

Five oddly dressed Europeans piled out. The leader of the group, a man in his early thirties with a soft, almost pretty face, introduced himself as Papa Alpha because he said we'd never get his name right: Pele, he said, like the soccer player. He and the others were the Swedish contribution to the international flood-relief effort: two paramedic firemen and three members of the *Kustbevakningen,* the Swedish Coast Guard, all young soldier types. They wore outfits that even I, of scant African experience, found ridiculous. The Scandinavians, with wintry skin the color of old yogurt, had clad themselves with all the knowledge of city boys arriving at a dude ranch. Edgar Rice Burroughs and Hollywood could not have decked them out more elegantly: freshly pressed multi-pocketed khaki pants and safari vests, combat boots and khaki slouch hats with patches on the crown that proclaimed **AFRICA SAFARI**.

* * *

THAT evening during a briefing in a private room at a hotel/casino restaurant, the upscale watering hole for most relief workers, pilots, and crew on leave, Matt Wolff spoke candidly of the security issues, acknowledging that there was some danger in the work. It was, he admitted later, all that he thought we would need to know before being sent into the field.

Standing at the head of the table, hands jammed into his pockets, he began: "For those of you unfamiliar with Somalia, the country has been in a state of civil war since 1988. It has no government, hasn't had one since their president was run out of town in '91. Somalia is divided into six major family groups that can date their histories back hundreds of years. Kids learn their ancestors' names by heart back to twenty generations. A Somali does not ask another where he is from but whom he is from. As you might imagine, these people do not like outsiders.

"These families—clans as well as any number of subclans—are run by warlords who have made it a business to kill each other. There is no longer a civil war with political goals but a deadly free-for-all piss fight between subclans and sub-subclans over territory, drugs, and control. The warlords are businessmen with armies. I suppose they are like your American crime bosses," he nods toward me, "except these guys have tanks, artillery, armored personnel carriers, all the weapons to fight a war. Many of them have Swiss bank accounts, European and American passports, and villas on the Riviera.

"Nothing in Somalia is as it seems—it is a mess. For example, yesterday, General Morgan, the Majerteen warlord of Kismayo, personally helped off-load one of our cargo planes. Today, he and his militia were nowhere around. Maybe he's been pressured—possibly a deteriorating situation."

"Who is this guy Morgan?"

"General Mohamed Siyad Hersi Morgan is known as the Butcher of Hargeisa. He is, or was, the son-in-law of Somalia's last president. It was Morgan who ordered the bombardment of Hargeisa, which was the heart of the opposition movement. Fifty thousand civilians were killed in that bombing. An upstanding human being who, at this time, is working for us. Or at least he was until this morning."

"Friends like that . . ." someone muttered.

"It is our policy that the host country is responsible for the security of the staff. Without a government, we have to rely on the warlords—we are paying him to be our friend. Now, a few suggestions when you go out to the field.

"Somalia is Muslim," he continued. "Their Fridays are our Sundays. We have to respect their traditions and behave as we would in any Islamic country. No short pants in the towns, take no photos of the women, don't give out any magazines, and PLEASE, no obvious alcohol.

"The wildlife have been displaced and all are unpredictable; snakes—green and black mambas and pythons—are a problem. So are crocs and especially the hippos. Hippos are the most dangerous animals in Africa. They have killed more people than lions. Be damn careful when driving those boats.

"There are no rules in the bush—except definitely no waterskiing. Anyone caught waterskiing or drinking beer in the boats will be sent home. Questions?"

"Weren't the peacekeepers in '92 sent in to protect the relief workers?" asked one of the Swedes.

"Yeah, they were—and to make sure the food got delivered where it was supposed to. The warlords were stealing what we were bringing in and selling the stuff to buy more guns."

"So what is the difference now?" I asked. "There are still warlords. Not stealing the food? No need for peacekeepers?"

The administrator's face darkened and I reddened.

"No one is saying it is going to be a cakewalk. But we are assured by the clans that they will help us, protect us, and make sure we get the job done. We have solid guarantees from them. Warlords, I promise you, are not going to be your problem—but hippos and crocs might be.

"Now, one last thing: We have a policy about speaking to journalists. We field all journalist queries back here—without exception. You are aid workers, not spokesmen—leave the press to us." This was especially important, he said, in these early stumbling days when the mission was being created. Mario dismissively suggested that we should "just tell the journos that everything is great and tell them to piss off," which triggered an unexpected angry response from Pele.

"We won't lie! If you ask us to lie, we leave tonight. We go back!" Silence around the table. Even his colleagues looked taken aback.

I could only imagine that the outburst stemmed from exhaustion. They had traveled for two days and they had slept little since Sweden.

This briefing on militia, on wild animals, in a posh city hotel, required a bit of realignment. To the north lay a violent and dangerous no-man's-land that we were being sent to. We listened, we nodded, we tried to take it all in, put it into some context, but I, at least, had no idea. Looking back, I could not be faulted for being so naive—this dry recital had as much impact as the reading of a shareholder's report. I had no history to place this against. So improbable were the visions it created—displaced hippopotamuses and armed militiamen—that I could not have expected such warnings to mirror the experiences we were about to face. Possibly in part because of this disassociation, I found myself taking notes.

After the meeting, one of the Swedes admitted he was scared to death to go into Somalia. I then began to realize that I might have a misshapen impression about what was out there.

* * *

THE contract with the World Food Program is a no-risk in-your-face thirty-day agreement with the United Nations. Basically it states that you obey the rules and do what you are told. Subscribers, as we were called in the contract, were independent consultants who only would be paid "subject to availability of funds." What a proviso! The U.S. had not paid its billion-dollar debt to the United Nations because Congress was worried that the money would support abortion. What about us?

Marching orders: I was to take one of the assembled water-ski boats to Kismayo on a C-130 Hercules the next day and set up the base from which to launch the delivery mission. Also, I was to report on security in the port city. I remember the odd reaction of some of the staff at the WFP office when I was there to sign my final papers and I mentioned that I was going to Kismayo; a sort of apologetic sympathy clouded their eyes. Try to get sent out to the bush, one of them suggested. "Why? What's wrong with Kismayo?"

"Safer in the bush."

Frantic last-minute outfitting with little idea or guidance what to bring: an aluminum pot and pan, a plastic plate, a plastic cup, a fork, a spoon, tins of bully beef, dried beans, rice, a liter of Kenya Cane—the local rum—towel, bar of soap, mosquito net, *panga* (machete), all hurriedly stashed into a new cheap tin-lock trunk, which, I was told, was standard kit for safari trips.

During my last evening in Nairobi, I joined the Swedes at the hotel bar. Pele, an ex-submariner, a diver, and a licensed pilot, said that he had sat on his flak jacket while driving trucks in Srebreniza to protect his balls from rolling grenades. "This is much more dangerous," he said.

"It is?"

"Much more. Then it was a war and you had some idea of the dangers. In Somalia, you don't know who will kill you.

"My government has told us that the first time the bullets are near, we withdraw, we go home. All of us are scared, and that is good or we could not have a good team."

The others related some of their own "war stories," the type of tales that since I was a child always put me in some awe of heroes—Medal of Honor winners, men who sacrificed for others, to whom war was manageable, a challenge. I had known armed conflict as did most others—from television, movies, news, and books. I had even thumbed through *Soldier of Fortune* magazine. I *am* like these people—in my fantasies. I see men with hairy arms (I am hairless) and large hands (my wrists are like gnarls on twigs) and developed biceps (I am not very strong), and I am dwarfed in their presence. A sort of middle-aged mix of Tom Hanks and Gene Wilder. Not to deny that I'm beyond a little bravura myself, at least inside my own head.

I recall that the last evening with the Scandinavians was one of laughter too quick, too whimsical, too forced. We joked about setting up a Somali water-ski school, one way to win the hearts and minds of the locals.

"If one of the gunmen points his rifle at me and demands my boat, I'll just hand it over to him," Pele announced. "I'll teach him how to drive it and even give a water-ski lesson."

The Swedes had been well outfitted by their government. Nothing had been left to chance and they would not suffer from lack of equipment. Pele took me to his room and laid out neatly on the floor were the tools of the trade. I was impressed. Despite my requests to Matt and Saskia, I had been issued no tools, told that until they could get them to me, I should find what I needed in Kismayo. In the event the outboards needed repair, or the boats sprang a leak, or something even more serious occurred while under way, I was supposed to make do. Spread out on the hotel carpet were not only shiny new tools—sockets, wrenches, a volt meter—but a satellite telephone, night-vision goggles, a flak jacket, several powerful torches, a laptop, even colored satellite maps of the latest flooding of Somalia downloaded from the Internet.

The Swedes were volunteers and were contracted by their

government. I was a consultant, contracted by the international community, and I was equipped with bugger-all. But I got paid more—possibly to buy my own tools.

"We may be forced to evacuate in the middle of the night," my host said, handing me his night-vision binoculars. "We will be prepared."

"I have no tools."

"Nothing?"

"Even forgot my Swiss Army Knife."

He reached into his pocket and pulled out a shiny red pocketknife. "Here, you take this one. I have another—my government says everything double for this mission."

The Swedes' equipment defined the seriousness of the assignment. Night-vision glasses? Flak jackets? Still it hadn't sunk in why they were taking this thing so seriously. Or why I wasn't. Their government also had issued them one very strict order: They were never to be separated from one another. They must drive the boats as a team, travel and bunk down together in the same compound, and never be out of sight of the others. Their government was watching over them, was concerned for their welfare. I was an individual contract worker recruited off the street, not a representative of any government. Still, I was certain that the UN looked after its own.

At the cargo terminal the next morning, I paused at the foot of the back ramp of the Hercules and waved farewell to the Swedes, who were assembling the little ski boats nearby. Pele motioned for me to wait. Leading the others, he joined me at the ramp, gave me a warm hug and a slap on the back. I had a feeling I would never see these guys again.

4.
The Shooter

Kismayo, Somalia

THE white four-engine cargo plane begins a slow turn and a bumpy descent through the rain clouds, over a green, well-nourished landscape that appears peaceful. In the distance to the east, the Indian Ocean spreads a hazy blue backdrop to the port city. A few tall buildings, a minaret or two, reach out of the urban sprawl. Toward the sea, cargo cranes, clawing skyward like skeletal fingers, mark where the harbor must be.

Despite the large blue UN logo painted on its tail, our lumbering Hercules, near gross with its belly full of cargo, bears the romantic suggestion of an Air America operation crewed by mercenaries flying anything anywhere for a buck. The pilot and copilot are Filipino, the cargo master Taiwanese, and the flight engineer an American from the South.

This is no clandestine delivery, however; Andrew and I, the only passengers, are the vanguard of the WFP relief mission. Our cargo, in addition to the high-speed riverboat with its big outboard, is several tons of blankets, bags of maize meal, cartons of high-energy biscuits, and pallets of Humanitarian Daily Rations—those little yellow plastic packets of instant food, not to be confused with antipersonnel cluster bomblets of the same color. The flight provides a certain feeling of purpose, a balm for our anxieties; we are arriving with supplies that will save lives.

Andrew has been assigned to create from out of the rubble something that passes as an airport. His first task is to train personnel to man the control tower and then to manage the off-loading of the future cargo flights. In his late twenties, he is an intelligent-looking Kenyan of British descent. Boyishly handsome with dark eyes that appear to be nearly always on the edge of laughter, he looks easy to get along with.

The giant Herc swoops low over the airstrip, checking for wandering livestock, errant children—who knows what is down there? A couple of camels grazing by the side of the runway gallop off into the tall grass. A crowd of people collects in front of the small white terminal and looks up at us as we roar by, our official welcoming party, I suppose.

Disembarking, Andrew and I step down into a wall of humidity and heat. The air is thick with the smells of dust, smoke, flowers, sweat, and dung. A rolling mob of curious Somalis crowds in around us, weaving and craning their heads to see who has gotten off the plane. They are a strange lot, all men and boys, some clad in burnooses and djellaba, white Arab robes, and others in ragged short pants and tattered T-shirts. Battered AK-47 Kalashnikovs, the Russian-designed assault rifle with the distinctive curved magazine, are slung loosely over their shoulders. Curved daggers with ornate hilts of horn and copper hang on their belts.

I am not sure what I expected—certainly not a brass band, nor a cheering welcome for liberators—but I also didn't expect these solemn, long-faced men gawking in silence at us as if we were visitors from Middle Earth. Andrew and I stand alone in the center of this closing circle; I can always get back on the plane. One boy not yet in his teens darts out of the mob and plucks at Andrew's fresh Levi's, then disappears back into the pack.

A gaunt white face emerges finally from behind the crowd.

"Who the hell are you?"

"We're with the UN."

"Of course you are. With who?"

"The World Food Program. I brought a boat." I realize immediately how defensive I sound, as if the delivery of the boat would make my presence acceptable.

He grimaces and shakes his head. "No one told me to expect passengers on this rotation. Bloody oath! And you?" He turns to Andrew.

Andrew takes off his ball cap, wipes the sweat from his brow, looks up at the crowding Somalis, and nods toward the airport complex.

The terminal is little more than a ruin. The big, once-proud signboard—KISMAYO INTERNATIONAL AIRPORT, in faded red paint—teeters like a seesaw above a gaping crater in the terminal's wall on the runway side, the result of well-placed incoming. The control tower above is a mere shell, its windows blown out, the interior filled with shadows.

"I'm your airport manager."

"That we can use. Well, you're here, so welcome to Kismayo," the man says, offering his hand. This is Ian, the resident UN security officer, ex–Royal British Army. He has a pale, tired, edgy sort of face. Except for the thin Sandhurst-style mustache, he hardly looks ex-military.

"So you brought that thing?" The glittering blue speedboat with cartoon bug eyes on the sides lies grinning, defiant on the tarmac.

"Yes—to deliver the relief supplies on the Jubba. I'm to set up some sort of base for the boats."

"Heard we were getting an airport manager one of these days. But nothing about river ops. That boat is just another headache—I trust you have plans to keep it under lock and key? General Morgan would love to get his hands on it." Then, considering: "We can warehouse it at the harbor. And until you go upriver," he says in a tone that brooks no question, "I suppose you can help run the operations over there. So now with you two, we are six."

"Six?"

"Right. Six Europeans." Then, sotto voce, "Read it 'white.' Six whites here in this bastion of civility and order."

There has been the odd bit of tension in town the last few days, he tells us, but then, there always is to one degree or another. "You'll find it is the way of life—you'll get used to it."

"I was also to report back on the security situation here in Kismayo," I add tentatively.

"What?"

"The security situation."

"My God," he mutters.

The glass in a window on the warehouse behind us shatters.

"Get down!" the security man yells, dropping to his knees. Rapid gunshots from the other side of the Hercules tear through the relative quiet. "There's your bloody security situation!"

Not more than a hundred yards away, a lone figure sprints across the airstrip in a crouch, firing his assault rifle at us. He runs, stops, pivots, and with gun at his hip fires off a quick burst. The flight crew takes cover behind the big rubber tires of the landing gear, the Somalis scatter, and Andrew and I, ignorant fools, stand and watch the gunman shoot in our direction. Darting across the runway toward the shoulder-high grass, he pauses again, turns, and shoots.

Above the shouts of the Somalis and the random firing, I hear, I feel, a clear, distinct bullwhip crack close to my right ear.

"Down!" Ian shouts. Another window explodes behind us.

The Somalis can't seem to unstrap their guns fast enough. Some of them return the fire in the shooter's direction, aimlessly letting rip in automatic. Spent shell casings bounce off us.

Andrew and I stare dumbly at the gunman, who returns the fire. I am too confused to be scared. It is not easy to understand. I am outside this, watching a performance. Part of me tries to convince myself that the man is not shooting at us, at *me* specifically, and I find some safety in that. So I just stand in the line of fire, not with arrogance but with confusion. It is all too sudden, too unreal, to feel fear. Only a split memory before, I was sitting in a hotel restaurant eating breakfast, surrounded by the trappings of a modern civilization. Now I stand on a runway watching these people shoot bullets at one another with the intent to kill. These are not actors dashing across a TV screen—I do not have the luxury of a couch potato to root for the good guys. My arrogant presumption of security, safety, and immunity slips away. I am now beginning to feel uncertainty, that precursor of fear. It is sharply clear that there is nothing, not our denial, not our stupidity or ignorance, that can stop us from getting shot. The UN shield, I am beginning to realize, is illusory.

The shooter disappears into the tall grass. Ian gets to his feet. His face is creased with tension, his eyes wide—I see that he is afraid. I catch my breath.

Fresh gunshots, louder, from behind us. A large gun. A Land Rover with the roof cut off roars out onto the runway in a smoky black cloud. A two-handled heavy machine gun is mounted on the back in place of the rear passenger seat. A grinning youth grips the handles and blasts away into the scrub.

The scene is chaotic. Hundreds of Somalis, with white robes flying, pour out onto the airstrip from every direction, chasing the fleeing gunman, guns blazing. They appear to shoot blindly toward the backs of those firing wildly at the lone shooter; the mobile gun sprays the bushes in front of it with a withering barrage.

An unpleasant-looking Somali dressed in a bedsheet *djellaba* approaches us from somewhere on the airstrip, his small, protuberant black eyes alive and fierce from the firefight. A bandolier stuffed with bullets crosses his chest like a Mexican *bandito,* and he carries a gun that is more ominous than the Kalashnikov. A little winded, he explains to the UN security officer: "He is just a crazy man. It is nothing."

Ian turns on him, furious.

"Nothing? You're the head of airport security! You agreed there would be no guns here other than those of your own men. Where did he come from? How could you let him in? You said you would keep those people out of here."

The clan leader stiffens. "We do not know this man. He is only a crazy man. It is *not* a problem."

"I have an airplane here! Do you have any idea what would happen if the plane were hit? If you don't keep these people out,

I'll make sure that no airplanes—no more relief supplies—are sent to Kismayo. Then we might as well pack and go home. Do you want that? I am absolutely serious, Colonel."

"This will not happen again," the Somali says.

"It had better not. I want you to go and arrest that man. No"—he pauses briefly, considers, and passes sentence—"I want you to go and kill that man."

"It is being done."

Scattered gunfire continues inside the tall grass, occasionally drowned out by the rattle from the large mobile gun.

Armed men in white robes, winded from their chase, return to our small circle under the wing of the plane and again gather around us. They seem flushed, alive, proud of their role in the one-sided firefight.

There is some commotion from behind and the mob parts. A tall "European" woman in her late twenties wearing a white dress and an outraged expression pushes through the crowd. She has rather sharp features, but her pale blue eyes framed by shoulder-length raven-black hair make her undeniably compelling. Her American accent cuts through the sound of distant gunfire.

"You promised this would never happen, Colonel," she barks at the Somali leader. Hands on her hips and her eyes flaring, she thrusts her face threateningly toward the shorter man. She is on the side of right, but he is on the side of the Kalashnikovs. From what I can observe, she is too furious and possibly too close to the end of her rope to consider her position. She glares accusingly down at the heavily armed militia leader. Her anger or her fear causes her voice to shake. This woman has courage.

He rears back, his knuckles white around the stock of his gun. His eyes widen slightly, evidently surprised he is being addressed by a woman in this manner in front of his soldiers. In Somalia, as in the rest of the Arab world, such an act of feminine truculence is dangerous and seldom goes unpunished. It is a remarkable scene. The grizzled Arab with his bullet belts and heavy gun and the young woman with her defiant eyes—both wearing white dresses—facing each other down.

On the surface, he manages a thin smile and maintains control—"We do not know this man"—but his small dark eyes tell another story.

"We are here to help you people," she pleads, cutting him off.

She turns to Ian. "How could they let that man through? What if he had hit the plane?"

"It wouldn't be the first time, Jeri," he says.

The crew of the Hercules is casually examining the skin of the fuselage, looking for holes. They've been targets in Rwanda, Zaire, Bosnia, Angola. Nothing new to them. Finished with their inspection, they huddle among themselves under the shade of the overhead wing.

The flight engineer, a taciturn good old boy from Tennessee, has seen it all. A veteran of deliveries and airdrops and too many campaigns to recall, Joe Suits scratches the stubble on his chin, shakes his head wearily.

"Been through this before, Joe?" I ask.

"Once or twice. Don't make it any easier." It's all he'll say.

The captain turns to his flight engineer: "I'd like to get out of here. Right now."

"Yep. Good time to go."

The mobile gun, called a Technical, bursts out of the high grass and speeds back across the runway. The youngster behind the big gun hangs on proudly. The old Land Rover is randomly decorated with white tape, sort of a poor man's camouflage. The tape on the left side is blood-spattered. A lifeless arm flaps limply against the side as the vehicle bounces over the potholes and out the terminal gate.

Joe hands me a cigarette and lighter. My hands shake and I have difficulty lighting the thing. "First time for everybody," he says.

A small blue-and-white twin-engine airplane skims low over our heads and I jump. My nerves are shot. It banks away and into the sun and then lands, taxis to the other side of the terminal, and cuts its motors. A strange sight; what would a private plane be doing landing in a place like this? Lost?

A few dilapidated junk cars race onto the field toward the plane. The vehicles look as if they have just survived a North Carolina demolition derby. They clatter, rattle, wheeze, and scrape onto the runway under their own steam; they are crushed beyond identification, windowless, loud, and smoky, their chassis riddled with bullet holes. Excited Somalis rush up to the aircraft and wait expectantly for the doors to open.

"That's the *miraa* plane," Ian says.

"Miraa?"

"It brings in the *qat*, the *miraa*. Every day. War or no war, gunfight or no gunfight, in any weather."

This plane has come in from Nairobi carrying bags of the narcotic grown in the hills east of Mount Kenya. It is the only freely moving object in all of Somalia with guaranteed safe passage. No one would be stupid enough to shoot down the *miraa* delivery.

"And God help us if the plane doesn't arrive," Ian says. "These people would really be out of control."

A different sort of guard, these in military uniform, takes up positions around the plane as workers unload the fifty-kilo bags. Children scrabble around them, picking up loose leaves, seeds, and stems off the tarmac.

According to a UN report, *miraa* is vital to Somalia's war economy. Militia members chew *miraa* to combat fear and fatigue. Most of the rest of the population, including women and children, use it to cope with anxiety, uncertainty, and unemployment. Militia leaders know that a steady ration of the drug keeps troops loyal and makes them a bundle of money as well.

"Happy One, Happy One, this is Bravo Delta."

Jeri McGuiness, the American Unicef coordinator for the Kismayo operations and charged with organizing food distribution to the refugee camps, is Happy One. A possibly ironic handle.

She shakes her hair out of her face and unhooks her handheld VHF radio from the belt around her dress.

"This is Happy One. Send."

"We've got a problem at the compound. There's a demonstration outside with the locals—same old story. But it is a little tense.

I suggest you keep everyone there at the airport. Has the Herc been off-loaded?"

"Roger that."

"Good. Better keep it there while I get this thing settled."

"Copy that, Bravo Delta. I'll hold it. Happy One out.

"God, not again." She looks up at us. "It might be a long wait."

Jeri explains that the protests outside the Unicef headquarters are not unusual, are frequently orchestrated by the clans, and are usually staged by hundreds of women and children demanding food. It seems the logical place to hold such a demonstration. Unicef has the overall responsibility for the distribution of food during this crisis.

The Kismayo protestors are angered that Unicef is feeding the flood victims, who daily stream out of the Jubba Valley to the city refugee centers, while it gives nothing to the locals. It might be understandable, she says, were it not that there are few starving and homeless in Kismayo. In spite of the war, there is some sort of self-perpetuating commerce with markets and shops and services.

Muddling the problem is that the refugees living in the camps and receiving much of the UN aid are of the Bantu tribe, the sub-Saharan race that migrated from southern and western Africa and whom the Somalis have for centuries regarded as no higher in the chain than domesticated animals. Traditionally the Bantu have served as slaves to the Nilotic populations of Somalia, Sudan, and Ethiopia, and even today few well-heeled Somalis would be without their Bantu. The Somalis, it could be argued, were some of the original slaveholders, long before European and American gentry ever considered the practice. It is the agricultural Bantu tribes from the Jubba Valley that are the most affected by the floods and recipients of most of the international relief effort.

I wander over to the terminal with the notion of climbing to the control tower, past militiamen who stare at me, less with hostility than curiosity. I look at them directly, grin, offer a thumbs-up, and their faces brighten with smiles and some even return the salute.

The airport, from high up in the abandoned tower, is surrounded by lush flat plains of green bush and tall grass and short flattop acacia of the African savanna. Off to the west, the encroaching floodwaters, looking very much like another sea, sparkle at the last edge of the horizon. Cells of heavy showers march across the plains, streaming diagonal tendrils of more rain. These clouds, responsible for such devastation, are not typically tropical. No majestic cumulonimbus, no electrical storms reaching forty to fifty thousand feet; merely towering cumulus that seem to struggle to no more than half that height. Yet, gray and heavy and filled with water, each deposits a torrent on an already saturated interior.

Below, the airport road to the city cuts a straight line through the scrub with a few mud-daub shanties on either side. A barricade of coiled razor wire and steel antitank crossbars severs the road. Armed sentries sit on their haunches, leaning on their rifles in the shade of a plump roadside baobab tree—the tree, according to legend, that God planted upside down with its roots in the air. Sheltering trigger-happy militiamen guarding an airport barricade probably was not part of the divine design.

It is apparent that no one enters or leaves the airport without the local clan leader's approval. The airport is territory held by one subclan, the port another, and the city itself is held by another. To raise money to pay their militia and to keep their powder dry, the control of airports, harbors, markets, bridges, and roads is worth fighting for. Without a central government, without laws, the airport belongs to whichever clan leader is strong enough to hold it. The Kismayo airport, for example, is a moneymaker; the warlord of the subclan who owns the airport levies "taxes" for its use—access to it, landing fees, protection, and a place to land the plane with the *miraa*. A small aircraft delivering *qat* pays a $200 landing fee and $12.50 per bag. This little plane arrives with about sixty bags, and whichever warlord owns this airport at the time makes around $6,000 per day.

On the business side of the airport, the Hercules waits on the tarmac like a large white butterfly ready to take flight. The four crew members, clad in their brown coveralls, wait patiently, smoking cigarettes under the wing.

It is about noon. The sacks of maize meal, the tarpaulins, the boxes of medical supplies and blankets have been off-loaded and are in the warehouse. A few curious Somalis, their guns slung over their shoulders, inspect the riverboat that has been moved next to the building. The boys from the Technical hunker in the shade of the gunmobile, plucking *miraa* leaves from the stems and stuffing them into their mouths. An uneasy tension seems to hold the midday in a delicate suspension.

I sit in the shade against the side of the tower on the asphalt roof, looking in the direction of Kismayo. Thick oily smoke billows into the sky from someplace toward the center of the town and, catching the upper winds, drifts off toward the southeast. What appears to be the spire of a Christian church rises out of the haze above the trees. I wonder what the town is like. I can't wait to get moving. The shooting has triggered some strange excitement within me, some strange thrill of danger—and admissible fear. I wonder if this is what a new soldier feels before the real shooting starts.

A shadow merges with mine. Jeri McGuiness stands above.

"Grab a seat. You from the States?"

"Philadelphia," she says, gathering her dress and sitting on a cement block.

"Far from the City of Brotherly Love."

"Further from the Main Line."

"I guess!"

She is tall, finely built, with a touch of the colleen; high cheekbones, blue eyes that seem a little weary, and a mouth slightly downturned at the edges combine to reluctantly expose some secret sadness. It is evident she does little to hide the lines of fatigue and futility. In some other circumstance, in Paris or New York, she would be regarded as attractive. But out here her appearance is what we make it. A single woman where the bullets are flying, incongruously clad in a springlike white dress. It is her concession to the Muslim dress code for women, and it does provide in these initial moments a sort of strange comfort and acceptance of this incomprehensible situation. Yet unavoidably she is herself part of this strange out-of-sync scenario. I see her thrust toward the Somali *bandito* and I look at her with something approaching awe.

"Does that occur often?"

"The gunfight? It happens sometimes. It was probably just a nutcase, like the colonel said. Still, the bullets are real enough."

"How long have you been here?"

"Four weeks. Since the operation began. Four long weeks. Without a break. At first we were welcomed as heroes. Today, less than that. And it's getting worse. Every day. Somebody is going to get hurt. God, I can't believe they're sending people to Kismayo," she says. "By the way, why are you here? I wasn't told there would be anyone on this flight. Are you with the boat?"

"I'm to set up the river operations."

She shakes her head in dismay. "Really? From here? There is no river in Kismayo. It's about twenty miles to the north. The only way you can get there is up the coast. I don't know much about boats, but I don't see how you're going to deliver relief supplies from this place. Between here and the rivers, there is an ocean. And by land you have to cross the Green Line and go through a damn battle zone. I think you've brought the boat to the wrong place."

She searches me for some other truth that I'm not revealing, some agenda I'm keeping private. She is looking at a blank page. I know less than she does. "Are you a contract worker?"

"Yes, with WFP. Yourself?"

"Permanent. Unicef—we're feeding the Bantu and Bajuni in the IDP camps."

"IDP?"

"Internally Displaced Persons—about twenty thousand of them. They are just pouring into Kismayo. And it is angering the local people, as you've heard."

"Twenty thousand—a lot of mouths to feed."

"Mostly women and children. Your flight brought in only enough for about six hundred families—the boat took up a lot of space."

This was not the last time that I would realize that while UN agencies frequently work together out of the same compound, there is a divide in operational mandates. WFP, the logistics arm, collects and delivers the emergency relief supplies; Unicef distributes them. In the field, the distinction is not so apparent, but I can imagine that the real conflicts between empires occur back in the offices. It is evident that no one from the World Food Program has told these people of the other UN agencies busy with their own work to expect us. Although I find that hard to understand—makes you feel pretty solitary.

"Happy One, Happy One—Bravo Delta."

"Go ahead, Bravo Delta," Jeri says into her radio.

"We've got a killing at the compound. Don't let that bloody plane leave!"

5.

Help Us, Don't Kill Us

THAT strength and control that I so admired in this woman has been replaced by a sort of cornered wildness. "A killing at the compound! Who, for God's sake? One of theirs? One of ours?" She jams the mobile radio back into the holder on her belt and steals a quick look at the airplane below.

I cannot imagine what is occurring in town, but from the look on Jeri's face, I should be worried. I search for some answers; over to the city in the haze, down at the airfield—for what? An attack? Angry stone-throwing mobs? There is no sign of any activity. Maybe that in itself is an indication. On the grassy strip next to the tarmac, the boys sitting in the shade of the Technical continue to pluck and chew their *miraa,* and nearby, others lie curled up against the warehouse, no doubt dreaming of the *houris* who await them somewhere in the Great Beyond. On the airstrip, the large white cargo plane with the UN logo on its tail, an object that we equate with movement and power, gleams cold and lifeless. A few Somali gunmen, rifles strapped to their backs, squat in the shadow of its giant wings, looking up in fascination. Getting back on the plane is not a thought that I am consciously aware of. It is more of an instinct.

I follow this suddenly energetic woman down the wooden stairs two steps at a time, past two bony old workmen who are slapping cement into a shell crater in the wall. They are reluctant to move aside on the narrow stairway, and it is only when Jeri barks something sharp in Somali that the two men, hand trowels heavy with wet cement, let us pass. I wonder if they will toss the mud at us as soon as our backs are turned.

We join the UN security officer and Andrew outside the terminal building. "There has been a shooting in town—at the compound," Jeri reports. "I don't—" She stops in mid-sentence when the subclan leader berated earlier this morning approaches us. He is backed by four men who don't look old enough to shave. With unaffected insouciance, they cradle their Kalashnikovs, fingers just off the triggers. There is a new arrogance in the colonel's manner, an authority restored. The brief firefight near the Hercules is long forgotten. This is a Somali militia leader and we are interlopers, and for whatever reason we are here, we are here at his sufferance. I observe him intently, wondering if he knows about the incident in town.

"Why is that airplane still here?" he demands of anybody.

Jeri is the quickest, her voice now respectful. "It's raining in Nairobi, Colonel."

"Rain in Nairobi?" he repeats in disbelief. He looks us over with dark, suspicious eyes. "Yes, all right." The Somali turns and walks away, apparently satisfied. A nice piece of diplomatic footwork.

Later in the day, the radio voice of Bravo Delta gives us the all clear: "We'll meet with the sultan and try to figure this one out. Tell the Herc it can go back to Nairobi but to monitor the normal high-frequency channel in case we need him back here in a hurry."

With a roar of its engines, the lumbering aircraft turns and taxis down the apron. It doesn't pause at the runway; there's no revving of engines, testing of flaps, a cautious look both ways. The pilot doesn't appear to consider wind direction when taking off. As soon as he is on the runway he just gets the hell into the air without looking back. There is no doubt he's glad to see the last of Kismayo on this day. Our lifeline becomes a disappearing mark against a nacreous sky.

Andrew and I squeeze into a UN vehicle between two young Somali militiamen in sunglasses whose AK-47s stick menacingly out the windows. Ian is sandwiched between driver and guard in the front seat. Two other gun-toting youngsters ride atop the roof. The Technical escorts us slowly down the pitted asphalt road to town, the long barrel of its gun sweeping from one side to the other. The blood on the old Land Rover's dirty white tape has dried and turned into caked streaks of brown.

Our small convoy draws up at the closed barricade that I had seen from the tower, an impenetrable barrier of concertina wire and steel crossbars. The man behind the gun on the Technical shouts at the armed sentries below to let us pass. The keepers of the gate respond by quickly unslinging their automatics and leveling them at us. Soldiers on both sides begin screaming at one another. The sentries hastily backpedal, putting some distance between them and the vehicles, a move I recognize later as the first step in a possible shoot-out. They jerk their rifles skyward, motioning the driver of the Technical to reverse back to where he came from. One of the men on the mobile gun pulls back the cocking lever and lowers the muzzle toward the sentries.

Our boys, rifles in hand, spill out of the car, jump off the roof to join the dispute. First they remove their sunglasses, then they cock the guns. I wonder about the sunglasses; is it the eye contact? The loaded and cocked guns point at one another, and the angry jabber continues. Inside, wet heat runs down our faces into our shirts. In this tropic swelter, we wait while the armed Somalis bicker in a language of strange, sharp guttural sounds. The argument is something abstract. It appears they are ready to shoot one another.

Without turning his head or moving his lips, Ian says in a low voice, "No sudden movements. Just stay here like you are." Then he adds quietly, "The blighters probably want some money to let us pass."

"And?" I croak. "We give them money?"

"No. These are all General Morgan's men. Different subclan

but still his men. We pay him for the security. Not every bloody roadblock in town. It appears, gents, we are at daggers drawn."

Our guards return from the barrier. One of the boys, grinning victoriously, crowds back into position next to me, winks, gives me a thumbs-up. I hear the two lads clamber back up onto the roof. The sentries angrily drag the coiled razor wire off the road, kick aside the tank traps, and hurl Somali abuse and clenched fists as we motor past. Our driver attempts to whistle some tune. Not far down the road, a metal sign, as bullet-riddled as any on the Pennsylvania Turnpike during hunting season, remains defiantly cheerful. Its message in Arabic, Italian, and English is barely legible: **Welcome to Kismayo.**

The road to the city passes communities of wattle shacks and vacant *boma*, round corrals made of thorny branches. A lone camel rubs its withers against a baobab and gazes at us with sleepy half-lidded eyes as we drive past.

"During the UNOSOM days, there were five hundred blue helmets along this road to protect the food convoys," Ian says. "Now we have some boys with guns."

"What about the riverboat—think I'll have any problems getting it to the port?"

He shrugs.

The UN compound appears impenetrable. I am not sure what I expected—not necessarily a city office building, but certainly not a desert fortress. High bilious-colored cement walls defaced with graffiti in Arabic and nibbled by bullets rise out of the dust like sheer cliffs. Six yards tall, the thick walls are topped with sandbags and concertina wire. It reminds me of a state prison.

The only vehicle entrance into the compound is through a large blue solid-steel door; an attached cement guardhouse with a smaller door and narrow observation slots anchors the big gate. Unicef guards—locally hired Somalis distinguished by their loose-fitting baby blue uniforms that in a normal world would be mistaken for children's pajamas—admit walk-ins through this small portal.

A mob of Somalis mill in front of the entrance and turn to face us as we approach. It's hard to know what is or is not normal in this place, but it doesn't take an old hand to feel the tension, to realize that the crowd is on the brink of challenge. It is apparent by the atmosphere, sullen and malefic, that despite our good intentions we are regarded no better than foreign intruders.

Our escorting militiamen sweep their guns over the crowd to clear a path. The big gate swings open slowly, just wide enough to let us through, then slams shut. Only the UN vehicle has been permitted inside. The Technical and our roof guards remain on the other side.

"One day they protect you, the next day they want to shoot you," Ian mutters.

Within the walls: a two-story office building of yellow cement, several outbuildings, and a dusty parking area. On the roof of the main building, a blue-uniformed Unicef guard leans lazily against a battlement of stacked bags of sand, monitoring activities below. There is an empty slot for the barrel of a machine gun, but the only weapons allowed are those carried by the Unicef blue pajamas. A UN flag hangs impotently in the still air from atop a tall mast next to the makeshift pillbox.

If there were tensions outside, you would not know it in here. A few day laborers sit in the shade of a scraggly gum tree in the center of the parking area, chewing *miraa*. Under a thatch-roofed shelter nearby, two men on prayer rugs bow to the east, heads down, bums up. Perhaps it is the sight of prayer that offers this place a sense of peace. I wonder, however, when, how, and what event caused the main building to be so splattered by bullets.

Upstairs, Brian Devenport, the UN Development Program project officer known by his radio phonetics as Bravo Delta, sits alone in the middle of a threadbare couch in the lounge area, staring off into the distance. In his early forties, he is unshaven and his graying hair needs a trim. He wears a faded green T-shirt, jeans, and old running shoes. A fishing captain from Perth with years of administrative experience for the United Nations, he is in charge of all UN operations in Kismayo. In uniform and scrubbed up, I imagine he would cut quite a figure.

Bravo Delta says he will meet with the sultan in a few minutes and we are welcome to sit in. "Might give you blokes an idea of what Kismayo is about." There is not a lot of enthusiasm in his smile. "I've got one of your boats in the lot if you want to check it out. They tell me you've got some sea time."

"Worked merchant ships, towboats, fishing in Alaska, yachtie." I try to be dismissive. I'm a little embarrassed.

"Fishing? Commercial fishing? We'll have to compare notes. And you've got a yacht as well. That's my dream. One day I'm going to buy a boat—to sail around the world," he says wistfully, and then with sudden brusqueness, "You can help run the port while you're here until you start your deliveries. Oh, sign up for a radio—you'll be Juliet Bravo."

The boat that arrived the day before rests on cement blocks in the dust next to the makeshift mosque. I assume that there are others worried about the Somali reaction to this flashy obscenity, for it has been well covered by a heavy gray tarpaulin. Or maybe someone was just protecting the shiny blue toy from bird shit.

When I join the meeting upstairs with the sultan, Brian and Ian are sitting together on the couch, wearing expressions of truant schoolboys caught smoking behind the barn. They are not big men; Brian is stocky, more rumpled, blondish, and Ian, the ex-military man, is of average height and thin and neatly kept. Neither of them looks like they'd take any crap, yet they look less significant next to the powerful-looking balding Somali with a small gray mustache in the lounge chair across from them.

I had imagined that sultans wore turbans, white robes, and gold daggers. Not this one. This grand poobah is dressed in a blue-and-white-checkered wraparound sarong. His bare hairy chest appears the size of a forty-gallon drum and his gut about the size of a sack of maize meal. He wears matching blue plastic sandals and brown socks. His limpid eyes avoid any direct contact and he speaks softly but with authority:

"We know how important it is for the United Nations to be here," he says slowly through a translator. His oleaginous tone is soothing. "You have helped our people and this is well known. You will be our friends always. The work you do to help Somalia will never be forgotten. You will always be welcome here as our friends."

Brian and Ian look up, try to smile in appreciation. I notice Brian seems to purse his lips frequently. Is it a tic?

"You are here to feed our women and children," the sultan continues. "You are here to feed them—not to kill them."

I am not sure I heard correctly. His statement has no meaning. I look to Brian and Ian; they nod as if being scolded.

"United Nations shoots our people without provocation! Your security men—they kill our women and children."

The UN does not kill women and children and I expect some protest, some denial, but they remain silent, waiting for the sultan to continue.

"The UN, Unicef, WFP, they are all very important to us, but this situation is not acceptable." The sultan's tone is low and deceptive. He furrows his round face in concentration as he chooses the exact words. He does not need to raise his voice. "My friends, I know you would not order your guards to kill our people. Yet they have done so. You are here to help us, not to kill us. I know that. But now my people do not know that.

"I know you are here to help and that is good. But I cannot accept such killings. My people cannot accept the murder of our citizens, of our women and children. Your guards—Unicef guards—shot our people, who came only in peace. This is not acceptable."

I find myself holding my breath.

Ian rubs his mustache with his forefinger, his voice low with sadness and contrition.

"Please tell the sultan that we will investigate the shooting thoroughly," he says to the translator. "It is too early to know exactly what happened, but we very much regret the violence at the gate."

"I am happy you will investigate," the sultan says in a tone of mild reproach. Something is out of sync here; I would expect the sultan to be furious, but he doesn't sound very upset.

"Please tell the sultan that during our investigation we will hold those men responsible."

"Yes, that is good." He pats his heavy lips with a white lace cloth. "My dear friends, I am worried. My people are not happy. They are very angry. And this is a worry." He raises his heavy brown eyes, offers an insincere smile. "I am confident you will find a solution and that we will work peacefully together. I say this again to you. You must not shoot our women and children. My people must know that this will not happen again."

"We thank the sultan for meeting with us, for helping us," Brian says. "Please extend our sympathies to the families of those shot. We hope that the sultan can help us find a solution. As the sultan says, it is very important for us to continue our work here, and we hope that he will give us the same cooperation he has in the past."

The meeting adjourns and my mind reels. Unicef guards shot into the crowd? Women and children?

"Yeah, the wankers shot into the demonstrators and hit a woman and a schoolkid. They were throwing rocks, sticks, mud, anything they could get their hands on, and the guards fired back. The woman was pregnant and the schoolboy—he was about ten or eleven. Shit!" Brian slams his fist onto the table. It now is apparent how much control he had managed during the meeting. After a moment, he looks up. Calmer: "I guess you've come at the wrong time, eh? Let's just hope the sultan can keep the lid on."

Andrew, Ian, and I are driven to our quarters on the other side of town, each of us with his own thoughts. The armed guards next to us sit quietly, leaning on their guns. What are they thinking? Are they angry? Do they care? I cannot seem to focus. Killing at the airport. Killing at the gate. Sultans, warlords, desert fortress, Arabs with rifles. This is all fantasy—it must be, for real life is not like this.

Our compound is up the paved road that leads to Mogadishu

in the north. There appear to be very few operating cars in this town of sixty thousand people, and the streets are available for women in colorful veiled chadors, children, chickens. Stooped old men shamble beside their wooden donkey carts, pulled by plodding beasts with great sullen heads and long flicking ears. We veer around a cart on truck tires pulled by a young barefoot boy with cracked heels and splayed feet. Unattended goats and dirty white cows with camel-like humps wander without evident direction down the road. They cannot be hurried or directed, and we slow down or stop and wait. The long, gently sloping road evokes a basic need: How desperate I am for a run—haven't jogged in weeks. It looks like an interesting run; maybe I'll try it in the early-morning hours before the heat. Although, on second thought, it might not be such a good idea.

From the street our quarters appear similar to the Unicef compound: high walls, sandbag battlements, big blue steel door with peepholes. But inside, the similarity ends. While a tension hung over the Unicef fortress in town as if it were always under siege, and a dusty air as if it were always temporary, our base within the walls looks and feels positively Elysian. Well-kept graveled walkways, lined with planted basil, oregano, chili pepper, and poinsettia plants, connect the three buildings of the compound; flowering bougainvillea, frangipani, and mango trees in the yard give the impression this could be an inexpensive but well-kept little tropical hotel. It's evident that somebody puts effort into this place.

During Operation Restore Hope it had been the headquarters of the UNHCR, the UN's refugee agency. Because of its location this far out on the main road toward Mogadishu, it is apparently seldom a target and few locals bother with it. All demonstrations and manifestations of anger are held traditionally at the Unicef compound, not only because it's more convenient but because it is Unicef that has the high-profile job of determining who gets the food.

The three of us gather under the thatch-roofed open-air dining area; serve us a piña colada with a little paper umbrella, add a soft melody from some steel drums, and we could be in some cozy Caribbean hideaway. Tropical birds sing sharply in the late-afternoon sun. Gunfire echoes on the outside. Ian pours the tea.

Two of our blue-clad guards did fire into the crowd, the security man says finally. "The idiots shot first."

"Why?"

He shrugs. "Tribal feud, perhaps; we'll never know. The pregnant woman died on the spot," he says, heaping sugar into his cup. "The schoolboy is at the Médecins sans Frontières hospital in town. He'll probably die by dawn."

"Wait a minute," I say. "Let me get this right—our guards fired their guns into a crowd of people who were demonstrating for food? And they killed a pregnant woman and wounded a schoolboy?"

Ian nods.

"Unicef was created to protect children, not to . . . This is insane. In the States, Ian, Unicef sells Christmas cards, collects money during Halloween, makes Easter appeals for children—how is it possible that the agency known to the world and to God for its good works is responsible for killing a pregnant woman and a child?"

"No one was firing at us?" Andrew asks. "We weren't returning fire?" His good-looking boyish face reveals his disbelief.

"No and no."

"Women and children—the two objects in the Western world that are held most sacred," I say quietly.

"That's what happened. But then, this is Somalia."

Even with all the talk, it doesn't sink in. How could it? It is just too damn preposterous. I should be shocked. Yes, certainly, I am shocked. But am I really?

"What's next, Ian?" Andrew asks.

"We keep our heads down. May have to stay in our compounds for a day or two until this gets sorted—and the families get paid."

"Paid? For the killing?"

"Blood money. The families will demand retribution and they'll get rich. Thank God it wasn't a camel. Then we would have serious problems. A woman and a child are not so important to these people, at least not in death. They are dealing with Westerners, so they are playing their hand. But camels are far more valuable. They always have been."

"What is the price of a life? A pregnant woman worth more than the schoolkid?"

"Other way around. The schoolboy was male; he'll fetch more. Probably the price of a few dozen camels."

"What's going to happen to us?" Andrew asks. I think we are both guessing that if this happened in Los Angeles, Detroit, or even Nairobi, the cities would burn down.

"As long as the sultan and General Morgan keep things under control, we'll be okay." Ian pauses, stares into his cup. "But it could blow. I've been warning Nairobi that something like this could happen. We've got to put together an evacuation plan."

In the empty dormitory-style sleeping room, I rig the mosquito net above my bunk. My mind is cluttered with facts, faces, vitiated by events unrelated to any nightmare I could have conjured. I try to catch up. I've been in Somalia for less than five hours, haven't even unpacked my bags.

I find I am curiously exhilarated. My nerves taut, my senses alive, my stomach in a knot—not from stress but excitement. I think I am enjoying this. Not far from the surface is a nagging frustration expected of a former reporter. Being on the scene when it happens. *This is a story,* an event that should be covered: UN guards kill a pregnant woman and schoolchild. I doubt that news of the shootings has made it to the outside or that anyone beyond Somalia will ever hear of the shootings. It is breaking news, but there are no journalists here. Certainly I cannot report the event, not only because I am so isolated, but my consultant contract with the UN is pretty clear on the matter: I cannot disclose anything that occurs out here while "in the course of performing (my) obligations." And really, what does it matter? I recall a CNN promo in which one of their cameramen says: "If there is no picture, there is no story." Something like the sound of a tree falling in the woods. It makes no sound. No woman, no child shot. There is no story.

Such frivolous thoughts seem to be a way to skirt the real issue. Sitting on the bed under a creaky fan that does little to dry the sweat, I try to come to terms, or at least to make myself feel the anguish of these events. A woman, a child. But how am I supposed to react? I let it go; I wasn't there. I didn't see it happen. I find release in my abstention; I am trying to demand too much from a tarnished soul.

The daily staff briefing with the four other internationals is scheduled at 1800 hours at Unicef. Our vehicle bounces down the street toward the compound, blue UN flags fluttering from the fender poles and assault rifles poking out the windows both front and back.

It is dusk and the lighting is not good. As we approach the Unicef base, a mournful keening, a sort of shimmering sound, rises out of the dust ahead.

Turning the corner on the road leading to the compound entrance, we stop with a screech at a barrier of boulders the size of basketballs loosely stacked as a wall. Our cheerful young driver, named Harun, tries to drive around the blockade. Ian and Andrew both yell out, *"Stop! Stop!"*

Half a dozen impassive youths standing shoulder-to-shoulder behind the stone wall point their assault rifles at us. Our guards jump out and begin arguing with the militiamen.

In front of the entrance to the compound, a thousand veiled women, an undulating mass of colored and black robes, sway as one like sea swells from an approaching distant storm. The woeful ululating of the cowled women, a haunting mournful cry, rolls through the air.

Our guards return to the car, subdued.

"Sasa, sasa!" they order the driver. "Go back!"

Harun backs out cautiously and the youths on the road lower their guns. The frightful wailing recedes.

Back at our own compound, over the handheld radio Bravo Delta tells us that his people are now surrounded on all sides by militia forces armed with recoilless rifles, RPG-7 grenade launchers, heavy machine guns, mortars, and, he reports, "more fucking firepower than I've seen since Mogadishu." The agreement reached earlier with the sultan isn't working.

The dead woman's subclan is demanding the UN hand over the guards responsible for the shooting. The elders say they want to deal with these killers according to Somali tradition, which I suppose is beheading. The subclan of the shooters is demanding it hold their own boys overnight to protect them from the woman's clan. In the meantime, the militia leaders are wondering why the UN guards have not yet been formally arrested. The two sides are about to shoot it out, and Unicef is being blamed for all of it.

Ian admits this is about as serious as it has ever been. "If the boy dies tonight, then I hate to consider the consequences."

Within the relative safety of our quarters, I am chilled by the lament of a thousand women, a thousand mothers, their taunt of everlasting torment upon those of us who have committed such evil. This wail of accusation is damning within and upon my soul because I know that we are the accused. Their trolling chant drives out all other thoughts. I have a perverse, near-desperate need to hear more.

We are cut off from our headquarters and our colleagues; four of them are there and we three are elsewhere. They are being held prisoner, their compound under siege. We are unable to help. If any nation's citizens—Israelis, for example—were in a similar situation, separated from their colleagues, imprisoned at gunpoint, they probably would be rescued immediately.

They must be scared shitless. Is this not serious enough to get the hell out before someone gets hurt? I catch myself in mid-thought, for already I am dismissing the dead Somali woman and dying child. "Someone" means one of us, not one of them.

"You've been asked to report on the security situation, and now is your chance," Ian says, pulling a satellite phone out of his briefcase. "Perhaps you will have better luck."

During this flood emergency, the Nairobi WFP/Somalia security office is to be manned, according to Wolff, twenty-four hours a day. But no one answers my call. Finally, during a third attempt, I raise a sleepy *askari* at the office gate. In a mixture of Swahili and broken English, he says he is merely the guard and to call back in the morning.

Ian disappears into his quarters for a bottle of whiskey. Andrew and I rummage around the kitchen area and find some dirty glasses. It is dark now, and the one dangling lightbulb in the outside dining area attracts the flying critters of the tropics. A large bat swoops just above our heads.

Ian returns with a bottle of Glenfiddich and pours each of us a hefty shot. "Well," he toasts, "If we 'can fill the unforgiving minute' . . ."

" . . . 'with sixty seconds' worth of distance run,' " I add a little uncertainly. "Kipling." I feel foolish. I don't know if Ian's statement is a traditional British toast or his comment on the times. Or if I am sounding like a smart-ass.

"That says it all," Andrew adds, lifting his glass.

Ian tips his glass in my direction, smiles broadly—it is the first time I have seen him smile. "Well done! And for a bloody Yank." A quick burst of gunfire outside the compound concludes the toast.

"Where do these people get so many guns, so many bullets?" I ask, breaking the silence. "Everybody seems to own an AK-47."

"Nearly everyone does. The guns come from Yemen and Pakistan, originally from China and Russia, paid for by foreign aid from the Libyans. Ethiopia sells guns to one faction, Eritrea to another—you would never guess there's been an arms embargo on Somalia since '92. The militiamen for the most part are given their guns by the clan leaders. It is up to the shooter to buy his own bullets, and they are expensive. Each bullet costs about twelve cents U.S., a lot of money down the barrel for these people if the gun is on automatic. Sort of a way to keep control of the boys: We give you the guns but you pay for the killing. The shooting won't stop until they run out of bullets—which won't be anytime soon. By the way, if the big gun goes off next door, we've got trouble."

"Shooting at us?" Andrew asks.

"No, no. General Morgan's headquarters are across the way, and he's got some artillery. It may mean a new clan war—the Marehan trying to take back Kismayo."

"Apologize for my ignorance, Ian, but what is this thing with the clans? I've heard talk of subclans, even sub-subclans."

"There are basically five or six families in Somalia, each with its own turf. When the government collapsed, the country was left in the hands of the clans, and most of them fought for the ports, airports, main roads—wherever money could be made. They run import and export activities in narcotics, charcoal, and guns. Many of the clans print their own money."

"The militia are the clan soldiers?"

"Not always. Militia are often independent of the clan elders, especially here in the south. They are the unknown—unpredictable and powerful, too powerful, with the ability to disrupt. The clan elders can lay down an edict, but it is the irregular forces, the militia, who rule, who because of their guns have veto power over legitimate clan activities. Those guys are the wild-hairs, the troublemakers led by small-time gang leaders. I suppose it is something like Mafia families, families within families."

"That shooter at the airport. What was his story?"

"Don't think we will ever know. Strung out on *qat*. Or angry over some family feud. Or angry with us."

Andrew mentions that we weren't given any indication back in Nairobi there was clan trouble in Kismayo.

"Don't they know there are problems out here?" I ask. "I mean, isn't there any communication between here and there?"

"Yes, on both counts. There are comms between here and Nairobi, and they know. We have contact with them by long-distance radio and by the phone," he says, nodding toward the aluminum attaché case. "They know there are problems in the field."

"I don't think the WFP knows."

"Well, Kismayo *is* a Unicef operation. But I would be quite surprised if the WFP doesn't know what is going on out here. They get the daily and weekly reports from the field."

"It rather feels that once here, we are forgotten," Andrew says. "Almost abandoned."

"I was told that Kismayo was safe," I say.

"Right."

"What an unholy mess—you know, I'm not even sure what I'm supposed to do here. I've got some boats, but I am told there is no river."

"That's right, not here there's not."

"I'm told to report on the security situation, but no one answers the phone." I am not a scotch drinker, but this is going down remarkably easy.

Andrew was in Mogadishu briefly when the UN peacekeepers pulled out in 1995. He has seen some war. "I didn't expect this. I'm a bit nervous."

"Understandable. It's smart to be. You never know whose name is on the bullet."

Andrew and I catch each other's eye. I wonder if I look as anxious as he.

"Last week," Ian says, "the militia tried to shoot down one of the relief flights. My own UN rig was fired upon en route to the airport the day before last." Here is a person who has been ambushed and presumably nearly killed. This news now brings it home.

We sit quietly, waving off the mosquitoes and ducking the large black june bugs that bounce off the overhead light and tumble into our laps.

"What's considered a serious enough incident to pull the plug?" Andrew asks.

"Well, it hasn't happened yet. It will take a lot more than this before Unicef and WFP consider pulling out."

"How much more?"

Ian responds with a lost gesture, adds nothing.

"Why?"

"Politics. If Unicef and WFP weren't here, where would they be? They need these 'emergencies' to keep the system working, to keep the bureaucracy going. I seriously doubt your people in Washington or even ours in London know what really is behind all these emergency humanitarian relief efforts. Certainly not this one.

"We never were invited into Somalia for this crisis. Few people know that. We never were asked to come to help these people. Of course, it must be said that this country has no government to ask us to help, but had there been, I'm not sure we would be any more welcome than we are today. Few anywhere particularly care what happens here—how many mouths are fed, refugees sheltered, lives saved; not in London, New York, Rome, or Geneva. Certainly there is no local interest."

I find this cynical remark a little extreme and call him on it.

Ian raises his voice: "You don't think the local elders, the warlords, even the sultan really give a shit about helping the flood victims? They couldn't care less—it is not their people. They permit us to save lives because we pay them to let us do so." Ian tops up his glass and, not wanting to appear that it is getting personal, fills ours. "The ultimate protection racket."

We listen to the night, the crickets, the frogs, the gunfire. I am taken aback by Ian's bitter honesty; this is a UN official—he should be toeing the company line. I wonder if he has got a proper perspective on our mission.

"We are needed and we help, there's no question," he continues, a little affected by the whiskey, "but when you begin your deliveries on the Jubba—if you ever get there—you probably will see very little famine, disease, or death. These people are in trouble, but is there an emergency? Famine in the Sudan—that is an emergency, but here in Somalia? There have been floods in Somalia for centuries. Look at the maps. For the Jubba Valley there are two sets, one for the dry season and one for the rainy season. During years of serious floods, there was never outside help. It is our Western arrogance that presupposes we must step in and save lives, whether or not we've been asked. And we present to the concerned world this farrago of half-truths, and the money is raised—not without difficulty, but it is raised."

"What about us here in the field? Does anybody know we are out here?"

"In Nairobi, of course. You say there are some Swedes going to the river? Then someone in Stockholm knows and keeps track of them. They are on contract sent by their government. But those of us who are permanent are sent where we are told. We are doing our jobs and we accept that. And it is our risk. But our security—and I am a security man—is not of paramount consideration."

"We almost sound expendable."

"You might say that."

"I was joking. No one is expendable."

"Well, we are. To a point."

"Why weren't we told? Those Swedes—they think this is going to be worse than Bosnia."

"Possible."

"But that was a war."

"This is different. This is not a war, this is just a big secret. In Bosnia, you had peacekeepers, authorized by the so-called international community—the eyes of the effing world. Here—there is no one here but us. It was up to you to know what you were getting into. They won't tell you. How would they get people to do the job?" He takes a deep swallow of his scotch.

"This is classified as a Phase Four operation," he says, "indispensable personnel only. But here in Kismayo, it is Phase Five, and I have been trying to shut us down. I fax, I message, I call the Unicef director personally, urging him to close the shop. But he won't do it, no matter what happens. He has got to hold on to that bloody little empire." Ian fiddles with his blond mustache, short nervous scratches—while I wonder how in the hell they could send us out here when they knew that the security officer at the time was recommending pulling out.

Ian disappears for a few minutes, returns with some papers.

"WFP didn't know about the security situation? This is the UN Country Team report filed last week:

SECURITY UPDATE

KISMAYO: The security situation in Kismayo and its surroundings remained quiet but tense. On 13 November, at least one person was killed when two militia groups fought near that town's airport following an internal dispute. The situation was later resolved by

> the elders amicably. On 15 November, a lone gunman fired several shots at the Unicef compound in Kismayo during the loading of eight trucks with relief supplies meant for the flood victims in the valley, north of Kismayo town. The guards of the compound returned fire and disarmed the gunman. The motive of the attack was not clear."

He reads us a memo he wrote to the head office nine days earlier. In it, he recommends abandoning the operation and evacuating the staff from Kismayo.

"Even if we did pull the plug, right now I'm not sure we could get out alive. The local militia, the sultan, the warlords—General Morgan and the others—they're all getting fat off the UN. It is the only business in town. If it is any comfort, that is why they don't want anything serious to happen to us. That's not to say it won't just explode and one of us get killed by accident—or intent; it has happened before. But you can take some comfort that the local authorities, such as they are, don't want anything to happen to us, because they know that would be the end of their gravy train. Trying to get out is as suicidal as staying.

"And now"—he stares into his glass, rubs away a mosquito boring through his sleeve—"we are bloody well in it. No, mates, we are simply jobs for the boys. Jobs for their boys, jobs for our boys. Everyone who doesn't return in a body bag is a winner. Evacuation." He raises his drink and, with a smile that appears lost and spiritless, salutes us.

A strange inhuman moan drifts in from beyond the compound walls, a sad, deep-throated cry from somewhere in the distance. The thrilling sound is joined by howls of desperation, a wail that intensifies, stops conversation, and sends a chill.

"Hyenas," Andrew says. "Haven't heard them for years, but that's what they are. They're close."

"Driven here by the flooding," Ian says. "The water comes closer every day. First time I've heard them this close. Might give the Somalis something else to shoot at."

"I thought hyenas were supposed to laugh."

Ian snorts. "Not tonight, not in this place."

Ian speaks more to himself than to us. "I have never told anyone to kill someone before. I did today. God." He stands, a little unsteadily. "Good night, gentlemen."

Andrew and I walk outside toward the room we share. I look up at the stars that sparkle in the blue-black African night. It is a low, all-enveloping consuming darkness; white pricks of diamond light, impersonal and cold, confer a clear, inviolate truth. Andrew, a city boy, raises his eyes to the night. Far away, gunfire rattles. The hyenas howl.

"You don't see a sky like this in Nairobi. It's beautiful."

6.
Planning Our Escape

IAN is oddly quiet this morning. Joining us for breakfast, he proffers a cursory greeting but then seems to brood. Maybe it is because the stove ran out of gas and his tea is cold. My breakfast is equally disappointing; it is whatever I had thought to bring when I left Nairobi: several cans of tuna fish, Snickers bars, some processed cheese, instant coffee. I had forgotten about breakfast. Ian offers his supply of Weetabix, a sort of shredded wheat, and UHT milk.

"I won't be needing them. I'll be gone in a couple of hours."

Andrew looks up and over at the security man at the far end of the table. Ian seems more diminutive in this light.

"You just make that decision?" Andrew asks. The sharp tone leaves no doubt about his feelings.

"I've been here five weeks, gentlemen. I am scheduled for leave. Time to go."

That is all he will say. No reference to last night's discussion, no desire to keep talking. Perhaps his candor then was whiskey talk. Although he didn't seem the sort who would say something drunk that he would not say sober: He showed us his memos to the front office suggesting evacuation; he revealed his cynical take on our mission. So I can't help but also feel a little resentful, as if we are being deserted, left to the wolves. It shouldn't matter to us whether he stays or goes. But we are surprised, disappointed, and, more than that, almost betrayed; why didn't he tell us last night when he was being so honest?

He doesn't owe us. He is the security man for southern Somalia, with a burden of responsibility I would hope never to have. He has a few more things to worry about than the ruffled feathers of the two new birds in the coop. Still, we can't afford him the opportunity of denying us our place in this strange dream. It now will be just Andrew and myself, and that is disconcerting, for we are without the experience that might help put this insanity into perspective.

Bravo Delta radios us that as a result of meetings all night long with General Morgan and the sultan, the troops will be withdrawn by noon and we can proceed as planned.

Later, when we arrive at Unicef, only a few of our rifle-toting blue pajamas are guarding the gate, and they are sitting in the shade of an old mango tree nearby. No angry crowds, no shrieking women. A half dozen little boys in threadbare clothes throw rocks at a whimpering piebald mutt, bone thin and stupid, which despite the stoning tries to return to their arrant friendship.

Inside the headquarters, there are faces I have not yet seen—European, Somali, and darker sub-Saharan members of this humanitarian effort. Joel is the French-speaking Belgian, a container-ship captain who is currently running the port. He will be leaving within a day or two, and while I set up the delivery base, I am also to take over the port until he returns. Mwalimo, the Tanzanian procurement officer, is keeper of the keys—that is, he fuels us, feeds us, and, I am told, if necessary will kit us out with peacekeeper combat helmets. There are a number of random Somalis: drivers, cleaners, secretaries, and cooks who keep the compound running. Despite being held hostage, surrounded by Technicals and heavy weapons and probably kept awake all night, none of the "internationals" seems the worse for wear. No signs of exhaustion, no short tempers: These people are going about their jobs as if it is just another ordinary day at the office.

I sign my life away for some bottles of drinking water from the kitchen, the cost of which I am told will be deducted from my paycheck.

Andrew and I take our places inside the Land Rover for the trip to the airport to pick up the boat. The unspoken rule is that we are always to be sandwiched between loaded guns. Never, it seems, will it be possible to grab a cooling window seat. The car doesn't move more than a few meters inside the fortress before it is stopped at the steel doors and we are told that the compound once again is surrounded by troops and Technicals whose heavy guns are aimed at the gate. The militia has orders not to let us in or out. The agreement has collapsed.

The ruckus on the other side of the wall is clearly audible; it is unclear who is doing all the shouting—I suspect the militia and the locals are yelling at our guards. And for what purpose? Demanding to let them in to kill us? Perhaps it was one such incident in another era that decorated the inside building with bullets. Despite the garbled angry sounds of whatever is going on out there, it remains peaceful inside. No gunfire yet. Gunfire appears to be the standard to gauge the tension. While there always seems to be shooting, day and night, distant gunfire, at least, no longer seems to make much noise.

Outside the car, Harun, our young driver, leans against his door, chewing a stick of *mswaki,* a twig from the toothbrush bush. Western-style toothbrushes and toothpaste are not found here, and this is the traditional way of keeping teeth clean. It is very effective.

"You captain of port?" he asks.

"For a while. You my driver?"

"Shua, I am your driver now, Captain." Harun's smile is unaffected and cheerful.

"Sure?" I am not quite certain I got the word right.

"Shua, Captain."

Harun shakes my hand in the East African tradition: the palm, then the thumb, then the palm; it is far more expressive than our Western handshake. Introductions made, I realize that I need to learn some Somali if I am going to be working with these people, and the first phrase is "good morning." *"Subah wanaqsan,"* he offers. I try to repeat it and make a mess of it. He and his militia mates, with their assault rifles slung over their shoulders, find my efforts hilarious.

Harun wears a tattered New York Yankees baseball cap back to front and a frayed pair of Reeboks; his slightly pocked face is unshaven, his eyes are clear, and he is quick to smile. There is something personable about him, something immediately sympathetic—and very individual. Appearing more solid than the others, he wears a thoughtful self-assurance. I take an instant liking to the man.

I return to the lounge upstairs. It is the kind of place that you might expect of a headquarters in a no-man's-land: cracked windows that front onto the dusty parking area below, walls of different colors crumbly from the dry heat, collapsible rusting chairs and unsteady tables, cushions eaten by moths and silverfish. The place is well used and well ignored and a fitting statement of our eternally temporary existence.

A *Time* magazine and a *Nation,* the Kenyan English-language newspaper brought in on a recent rotation, offer some reassuring link, however tenuous, to the Outside. There are a few paperbacks on a shelf: forgettable dime novels and one curious volume, water-stained and faded: *Canto XVI, The Divine Comedy, Hell* by Dante, published in 1949. It doesn't appear that anyone is reading it, so I slip it into my pocket in case I get bored.

In a corner near the kitchen, an old Somali dressed in a white apron sits before a small color television and video recorder, angled intently toward the screen like a frail tree in a blow. So close is his face to the television that reflections from the tube dance on his dark skin. Before him on the screen, a man in a dark suit, clutching a name card and microphone, paces in front of a studio audience, the soothing voice of reason. The camera switches to two jowly women who overflow their stick-back chairs. They are apparently twin sisters. Between them, a scrawny guy with earrings in his nose looks worriedly from one to the other. One woman barks: "You couldn't get it up with me, so why do you (bleep) think you're going to be able to (bleep) her?" The audience cheers. The Somali, who I imagine commands no more than a few basic English words, giggles quietly.

In the conference room below, Brian, Ian, and Jeri negotiate for our release with the sultan, General Morgan, and his aide-de-camp Major Yeh Yeh, a reed of a man with a sharp goatee and a red-checkered kaffiyeh atop his head. Yeh Yeh is the appointed "protector" of the UN contingent.

Was it like this during the early days of the Iranian hostage crisis? Was this the way it began and the way it felt for those trapped inside? There is one significant difference: Then the world was watching and waiting. There had been a certain amount of posturing for the cameras, and the media milked the situation for every entertaining drop of blood. Now in Somalia, the media world doesn't know we are out here. There is no geopolitical agenda here in this run-down land, no reason why anyone should care. Certainly these events are not important to a nation's pride or ego. To our advantage, however, being away from the public eye permits men to negotiate on a one-to-one level as human beings without seeking the approbation, the huzzah of a public that has become so involved through instant news reports. Egos remain localized, and while it appears that offended Somali pride can result in instant death, the natural relationship between human beings of conflicting cultures is based on a grudging respect. Ironically, in this unknown little place on the planet where the value of life is measured in camels, the foundation of reason is still the prevailing modus vivendi.

Last night's discussion still sticks in my craw. We do not belong to any one nation, we are neutral, internationals without specific identification; we are with the UN, a monster of an organization with offices flung over the globe, of varying missions, nationalities, empires, large and small. We are the people on the ground, in the field, moved, shifted, arranged according to the needs of those we must help and according to the needs of the slaves to their own measures of importance, those builders of empire. Does anyone care what happens out here? I would like to think it is because no one has been told and so no one knows. I heard that the executive director of the WFP, Catherine Bertini, had made an inspection trip to some secure village on the river a few days ago. I am told she saw what she wanted to see, patted a few children on the head, clucked at the apparent misery, and that evening, back at some embassy function in Nairobi, the discussion probably turned to another humanitarian crisis, another humanitarian opportunity. Security for those in the field is apparently not much of an issue, and I am beginning to think that nobody takes much interest unless one of us is shipped out in a body bag. A murdered relief worker does not warrant the same attention that a well-armed soldier gets when killed fighting for some nation's military and political policies—and declared a hero. There are the others also not worth the attention: a pregnant woman and a schoolkid. We are dickering over the number of camels.

Brian and Ian return from the meeting with the Somali leaders, and I can tell by their long faces that the discussions did not go well. The seven internationals are called quietly together in the lounge. The local staff and our Somali overseer Major Yeh Yeh, who I am told are usually involved in staff meetings, are excluded. Brian wants to discuss our evacuation.

The airport as an escape route is out of the question. We could never run the gauntlet, the roadblocks and checkpoints. Ian reminds us of the time he was shot at on the way to the airfield. I suggest that if I can get one of the boats operational, we could escape by sea. That presumes I can get them delivered to the seaport—thus far a nonstarter. Brian wryly suggests we find ourselves some fishing rods.

Last night in bed, staring up at the noise of the revolving fan, listening to the tree frogs, the hyenas, and the occasional gunfire, I had rehashed the conversation with Ian and found myself planning my exit. If escape from a city were necessary, I would be the first one trampled by the masses. Out here, close to the sea, I know I can survive if I rely only upon my own wits. I don't know if I'm being selfish or cowardly, but I am beginning to think that soon—minutes, hours, days—it will be every man for himself.

"You come up with a plan, then," Bravo Delta says. It is not a suggestion, it is an order.

Two and a half hours later, word is sent into the compound that we may go about our business. Where this word comes from is anybody's guess. There were no further negotiations for our release.

Andrew and I hop into the car and are cheerfully waved out of the compound. There are no militia, no Technicals, no one other than the normal few locals looking for jobs or handouts. The stone-throwing boys are gone, and the dog lies asleep in the shade of the fortress walls.

At the airport, a flatbed truck is parked next to the boat, engine running. The boat keys left in the ignition by Mario when it was loaded onto the plane ("We can leave them in. What could happen between here and Kismayo?") have been stolen. I should have insisted on keeping the keys since the boat was ultimately my responsibility. It is going to be a pain in the ass to hot-wire the theft-proof ignition. God help us if the boat is needed at a moment's notice. I do have a key to the lazaret in the bow, but the door has been forced open: The medicine chest, including the painkillers and, most important, the chloroquine for malaria, has been looted.

The colonel in charge of airport security arranges for the boat to be loaded on the truck, and it is done with remarkable efficiency. The truck and gun-mounted Technicals leading and taking up the rear form the convoy to the port. In a feeble attempt to hide the hideous-looking boat from the idle masses in the city as we motor past, I have strapped a gray plastic tarpaulin tightly around it. The tarp is emblazoned with a large logo of Uncle Sam's clasping hands and **Gift of the People of the United States of America.** I wonder if I am not making a mistake by parading the Stars and Stripes. Is this symbol of American aid so common that they no longer see it? Or is it a red flag that triggers an instant response of resentment and hostility? It wasn't so long ago that Somalis dragged the corpses of American soldiers through the streets of Mogadishu, members of the peacekeeping mission assigned to protect UN food deliveries. As this symbol of American generosity is unintentionally displayed, will they assume that we relief workers with a neutral UN are an extension of American foreign policy or that we work for the U.S.?

For all my efforts and concern, the armed militia boys riding shotgun on the boat take off the tarp shortly after we leave the airport and stand proudly for all their people to see. One young rifleman, gun on his hip, his leg cocked on the boat's swim ladder, stands like a dashing frontiersman in a Frederic Remington painting, a proud young hunter over the carcass of his dead buffalo. Briefly in their lives, this fancy Western boat is theirs and they flaunt it.

A causeway leads to the harbor and the wharfs, warehouses, and the port's administrative headquarters. The harbormaster's office is little more than a bomb- and shell-ravaged two-story cement building. Shadowy figures inside stand before the dark window cavities and stare out at the convoy. A helicopter landing area, the departure point for the fleeing UNOSOM peacekeepers a few years back, is painted in front of the building, an X within a circle on the pier.

A barnacle-encrusted fishing float rides the slight swells beside the wharf. It marks the graves of two Soviet-built warships, frigates sunk during some battle for Kismayo years before. These vessels, visible through the clear water, rest on their sides, their missile tubes and guns pointed toward the surface in constant state of battle. Brightly colored tropical fish dart in and out of the portholes.

A small group of women in colorful chadors huddle around a clay charcoal brazier in the shade of the port office building. It is impossible to know the beauty or the age of these women, for only their dark eyes sparkle through the opening in their veils, the only part of their bodies open to the public. A fire-blackened earthenware jug with a long neck nestles amid the white-ash coals.

A row of boxy warehouses stand like Monopoly properties at the far end of the wharf toward the entrance to the harbor. Scrawled on the face of one wall in English:

THE GUN IS NOT A TOOL OF UNITY
SUBCLANS ARE NOT THE PATH TO NATIONHOOD

The other boat that had been in the UN lot has been delivered, and it rests on a flatbed in front of a warehouse.

We pull up to the harbormaster's headquarters. Part of its front wall is missing. This nearly empty building has no electricity or running water, and I am to discover later that the building's one toilet is just a hole hammered through the concrete foundation into the earth and overfilled with excreta.

Ali, the port manager, has his office on the top floor, and it looks down on the harbor and our truck below. He oversees the infrequent ship traffic in what once was a vibrant commercial port. He has offered to help me arrange the off-loading of the boats and set up a logistics base for the river deliveries.

In this land of crossed communication, misunderstandings, slights, and insults, Ali, blessed with a quiet sense of his own dignity, offers an open and trusting hand. Over *cha,* syrupy-sweet Somali tea, he reminisces. "We once had a very beautiful port. That was when we had a government. It was a very beautiful place. Very busy.

"One day there will be no more war. No more killings. One day a government will come. Someday."

Down on the wharf, the delivery of the two boats has caused quite a stir among a large crowd of expectant laborers. They press in on the craft, partly out of curiosity, partly, I discover, to be first chosen for the work of off-loading. It is a ragtag bunch, poorly clothed, teeth stained from *miraa*. Many are holding hands, not unusual in this part of the Arabic world. They are not hostile, these people of long narrow faces, high cheekbones, small mouths, small eyes, and strong Roman noses—handsome people. They look up at me with expressions of hope that they will get a job.

I feel honored, thrilled to be with these men, to work among them. My excitement easily overrides any discomfort I could feel. I look at them not consciously superior, just comfortably different. I wonder if this isn't what a missionary might have felt a hundred years ago faced with unknown challenges. At this moment, oddly, I feel less fearful than when I am in town.

"Subah wanaqsan! Subah wanaqsan," I say to anyone interested. I use up the only Somali I know. The men laugh, return the phrase, some even translate in barely decipherable English: "Good morning!" The ice is broken. I appear to relax. They appear to relax.

"Ali, I will need at least ten men per boat to slide them off the trailers and into the warehouse," I say as I climb onto a flatbed.

There are about a hundred or so eager faces, and they look to me for selection. From above, I expect to select the men. There are problems. Many more men than are required are looking for work, and there is some tension. I point at one, then another. Immediately, the selection process falters as the arguments begin. The port guards, identifiable not by any uniform but by their loaded guns, stand off to the side and watch the longshoremen squabble among themselves. Voices are becoming louder, more strident. One man shoves another. Angry jabs of fingers and furious faces. A punch is thrown, a face is bloodied. Someone is kicked, a wet sound as another fist connects.

Ali sees that I have lost control of the situation and asks my permission to choose. Ignoring the simmering violence, Ali selects this one and that one without obvious favor. Those chosen whoop in delight. I can't help but wonder at the criteria for selection, possibly membership in his own subclan. Thirty, ten more than necessary, are given the jobs. The winners laugh, joke; those rejected skulk off to the side, raise their fists, and threaten revenge.

Inch by inch the men slide the heavy boats off the flatbeds. I wedge myself between sweaty Somalis and, with some authority, repeat their cadence: *"KOH, LABA, SADER, HOEK!"*—One, two, three, STRONG!

The men opposite and next to me grin broadly as we slowly ease these half-ton rockets off the trailers and into the warehouse. We applaud one another's achievement. *"Ficaan, ficaan."* Good, good.

A feeling of fellowship shared briefly with these strange people, my first contact with Somalis not on the UN payroll and not members of the militia. They are laughing with me and at me and at my silly attempts to learn their language, and they seem to enjoy sharing a bit of sweat and a bit of success, however small. I delight in their easy laughter; it is open and honest, and when these guys finally laugh, it feels sincere and spontaneous and without reservation, an indication perhaps of their exhaustion from the state of continual war. I congratulate them for moving these heavy boats, and they cheer. It is evident they are just as ready to laugh as they are to fight. After the recent tensions, I laugh hard and enjoy these moments of levity. Just as desperately.

Joel, the Belgian, joins me in the warehouse to help commission the boats. I had borrowed some tools from Joe Suits, the loadmaster of the C-130, and combined with Joel's personal set, we are able to get one of the boats nearly ready to launch. A small crate from Nairobi in the corner of the warehouse contains some of the essentials: outboard oil, two liters of hydraulic fluid, jerry cans, and a tangle of thin plastic rope, which I suppose is to be used for anchoring. There are no anchors. Digging through the box, I can't resist a feeling of resentment toward Matt Wolff for sending me out here so poorly equipped.

Despite stern warnings from far away, we rip out the extra seat and the console. We strip off the silly cartoon faces plastered to the hulls. Looking-glass mad the UN may be, but out here the reality is other. I do leave the manufacturer's name on the side; maybe they will get another contract after the cameras focus on the boats.

Outside the open warehouse doors, the clamant bickering continues. Small groups of men fight among themselves. The guards try to separate the combatants. Older men stroke the goateed chins of the angriest; a traditional soothing gesture or a provocative one? It seems a very long time to keep up such anger, to still argue about who should have been hired. The conflict seems to have evolved into a greater feud. Suddenly, a gunshot. I jump nearly out of my skin. My nerves are already frayed from the sound of too many guns, too many threats. A sudden noise now takes on a new meaning. It doesn't help that the report of the gunshot is amplified tenfold in the nearly empty metal warehouse. My ears ring in the silence. I have ducked behind one of the boats. Joel is crouched next to me.

I look around for death. I am alive. Everyone seems to be alive. Outside, one of the guards, the stock of his Kalashnikov jammed onto his hip, finger still on the trigger, has fired into the air. The surrounding crowd of angry men simply stares at the man and his gun. Like crickets after a summer storm, the babble of angry voices begins tentatively, then rises in crescendo without restraint.

Another guard snaps his bayonet onto his rifle barrel and jabs it at the mob. At the outer edge of the pack, a youngster no older than thirteen or fourteen kicks an old man leaning on his walking cane squarely in the middle of the back, sending him sprawling onto the cement. I can't imagine why.

"Quick, you must leave here," Ali says, taking me by the hand. "Please, you call on your radio, the UN to take you away. You must not stay here. There will be trouble."

Couldn't we go to the other side of the port out of harm's way and wait until things cooled down? With my thoughts on escape, I know I must get one of those boats ready to go today. He agrees, but he is not happy with my request.

"Yes, all right. But now you must go or you may be killed."

We have to walk out of the warehouse and through this angry crowd. There is blood on some of the faces. A guard presses his bayonet tip against the chest of one of the men, waiting, it seems, for him merely to breathe hard. There appear to be two factions of armed men; each points guns at the other. Grudgingly, they slowly move aside as we walk past. Our backs to them, there is now only a resentful silence, and that is even more frightening. My legs, weak and shaking, have a will of their own.

Escorted by two armed militiamen, I look for a place to run when the bullets start to fly. There is a shipping container nearby, but I don't think we can get behind it fast enough. Behind us, the low rumble of anger increases like a slow-approaching train.

A few minutes later, Joel and I sit quietly on the riprap of the breakwater behind the warehouse area. A school of multihued wrasse swims lazily among the rocks at our feet. Across the bay, a heavy shower dumps rain on the low hills where the airport should be. Here the sun blazes without obstruction.

We discuss our escape plan. His idea is to take one of the two boats and speed out to the shipping lanes.

"There is a ship to and from Mombasa every six hours," he says in a thick Belgian Walloon accent. It is a clever idea, but it is doubtful that a tiny boat bobbing in the ocean swells could be spotted by a passing ship. Or, if found, that any ship would stop to pick us up. The officer on the bridge would assume that anyone approaching his ship on boats like these were pirates preparing to attack. Additionally, only a few of our radios are equipped with any of the marine frequencies.

My own suggestion is to load fuel and water onto whichever boat is properly commissioned and attempt the 147-mile trip down the coast to Lamu, Kenya, where there are resorts and cold beers and relative peace. Joel doesn't think the small boats would survive the voyage. Privately, I agree, but that won't stop me.

Later, back at the warehouse, there is no indication of the fighting of a couple hours earlier. Most of the combatants sit in the shade of the warehouse, chewing *miraa*.

Spurred by the recent violence, I load the forward lazaret of each boat with plastic bottles of water and ten emergency food packs, certain now that I'm doing something to save lives, even if they are our own.

A Unicef guard in blue pajamas rushes up and in broken English explains that I am wanted urgently in the port manager's office.

Sweaty and grimy, wearing an oil-stained sleeveless T-shirt, and looking more like those I work with than a UN supervisor, I climb the circular stairs to Ali's office two at a time.

Ian and a new international sit in hardback chairs in silence at one end of a long table. Opposite, some puffed-up Somali officials I have never seen before sit staring straight ahead like Easter Island stones. Apparently, I've kept them waiting.

The man at Ian's side is unexpected and a mystery. Broad shoulders, craggy handsome face, and short white hair, he sits patiently without expression among these dusky Somalis, one hand clasped atop the other in the pose of a preacher at the Eucharist. Dressed in a long-sleeve blue shirt and jeans, he can't hide that he was born in a soldier's uniform. I watch him observe me as if I were something unidentifiable his bird dog once rolled around in.

"Captain," Ali says with a wink, "we are glad you can join us." He, at least, is enjoying himself. I flip a brief salute. One of the corpulent port officials laughs. The new international at Ian's side looks shocked.

After introductions and some compliments by Ali, I'm told I have a serious problem. The port guards, he informs me—as if I were the boss—are demanding payment for providing security for my boats and me. I say nothing. Considering the tensions earlier, I hope they pay them anything they want. Ali is assuring me that, of course, in Somalia there is always a solution.

They are talking to the wrong man. I deflect the problem/solution to Ian. Ian, expecting to be on the next rotation to Nairobi, passes the problem/solution on to his apparent replacement, who fields it deftly with the logic of the day with which all such issues are handled.

"Security is arranged through General Morgan," the new man says. There is a hint of a drawl in these first words. His tone is deep and commanding and his words are slow and measured. His cool gray eyes scan those at the table, apparently measuring his audience. He unclasps his hands and jams them into his pockets and leans back. There is time enough to note that on his right hand there is only a stump where his thumb should be. I wonder. Had he been covering his hand to hide it?

"Unicef pays the general, and we understand that he takes care of the port. Our security here and at the airport is his responsibility and I would suggest that he is the one you should talk to."

But the port officials appear mollified when the new security man agrees that we will pay for additional security once the small boat jetty is completed and my little go-fasts are permanently in the water.

Outside, Chet Sloane, a former U.S. Special Forces colonel, offers a reluctant hand. Juliet Bravo, meet the new Sierra Sierra, the top gun, the head of UN Security/Somalia. What a job that must be. Head of security for a nation ripped apart by civil war. Something foolishly contradictory here. Like putting out a forest fire by pissing on it.

Sloane is a stern, aging bull from New Orleans, a security consultant during the Somali fiasco in '93–'94 who at one time operated a "security" (read "mercenary") business with assignments in various parts of Africa. He is a soldier of fortune kind of man. He will bunk with us at the UNHCR quarters. It should be interesting.

At the evening staff meeting, the new Sierra Sierra gets updated by Brian on our current security situation. I suspect that is the reason for his posting—to determine if Ian's assessment is accurate. Or whether his colleague was buckling under stress and just needed a well-deserved break.

The elders of each subclan, Bravo Delta reports, are satisfied that the two guards guilty of the shooting are under protective arrest; still, the sultan, on behalf of the families, is demanding one hundred fifty-six camels in total for both the dead woman and for the boy, whose brains, we are told, are permanently scrambled.

"We are balancing on the head of a pencil here," Brian says. "It's all right now, but in ten minutes it could go to shit. If the Hercules is at the airport and if some of us are out there—like Andrew and anyone else—well, that will take care of one or two. But that won't help the rest of us. If we're not at the airport when we have to leave, then we will never get out."

His thinking is that I should have a vehicle ready at all times and spend most of my waking days at the port. The urgency to get the boats ready for the water is not to save some lives upriver but to have them available when we need to flee. When we are radioed the evacuation order, I am to take one of the boats to a designated spot on a beach and collect the remaining staff. It saves them risking their lives trying to run the roadblocks that are between them and the obvious exits of escape, the airport and seaport.

"When will you have the boats ready to go upriver?" Chet asks.

"One of them possibly tomorrow. By the way, I have no charts of the area, not of the harbor or the river entrance. We have any?"

Brian snorts, shakes his head.

"No charts? You got any equipment?" Sierra Sierra asks.

"Equipment? What equipment?" I respond. I had sent with Ian a note to Matt and Saskia requesting tools, more outboard oil, hydraulic fluid, a high-frequency radio for each boat, replacement painkillers and malaria medicine. If I am going to be running around some Somali river, possibly alone where they are shooting at one another, then I sure in hell am not going without the gear. "The rope that I do have is a plastic clothesline that wouldn't hold a wet T-shirt, and there's not much of that. I have no long-range radios, so once out of sight my boat drivers will be on their own with no communication. There are no anchors, but I can use cement blocks. The only tools are those that I borrowed from one of the crew of the Hercules. We have been promised satellite navigation sets, but I suspect they're still in some bonded warehouse in Kenya."

"What the hell do you need GPS for?" Brian asks. "You'll know where you are, where you're going—doesn't take a genius to follow a river."

Before I begin to take affront at Brian's question, Chet explains: "He needs them. It is not to keep the drivers from getting lost but to call their location to a helicopter in case they run into trouble. Don't worry, son, I won't permit you to go upriver without a full set of comms and navigation equipment. You can use my set until yours arrives. You are the one who needs it." He opens a briefcase and hands me a small handheld GPS.

"We may have our problems here," Chet says, "but you could just walk smack into it when you begin your delivery runs on the Jubba. They have been known to shoot across the river at one another."

"The river I'm going to be on?"

"You got a clan on the east side, another on the west. We're trying to get some guarantees; we won't let you go up until we get permission from both sides."

"I'm going to be some moving target?"

"Why, I sure in hell hope not."

"We have flak jackets?"

"I'm not sure. Mwalimo?"

7.

Me, I Wouldn't Fly It

I am dreaming that Jacqueline and I are on the *Unicorn,* anchored in a quiet cove in the Chesapeake Bay, when I'm awakened by a thunderous explosion.

I have no idea where I am, not sure whether I actually heard it or whether I just carried it out of my dream. Another explosion and the windows rattle. Andrew bolts upright on the edge of his cot. The noise is metal on metal—*thunk!*—followed by a ground-shaking boom. I have never heard artillery but I think that's what this is, and it takes a minute or two and another two rounds to determine the direction of fire. It is the general's big guns nearby—outgoing. I wonder who the gun is shooting at—some clan trying to take the airport? The seaport? The town?

A muffled explosion rumbles in the distance. If they are firing from here, won't there be incoming? There are three options in an artillery duel: outgoing, incoming, and bull's-eye. Fucking hell! A big explosion. Not the clear-cut report of outgoing. This is a roar without definition that envelops everything, a sound I feel to my very core. The ground grumbles like an earthquake. A piece of glass from the broken window splinters to the floor.

I scramble under my bunk. My roommate remains on his.

"Andrew!"

He rolls under the bed as another explosion shakes the building.

There comes a sudden silence. On my stomach, face pressed against the grimy floor and my hands clasped over my head, I turn toward Andrew. Our eyes meet but there is nothing to say. We remain under our bunks for the next few minutes, clawing out only when we hear the birds start to sing.

By the time we emerge from our cheerless sleeping quarters, Chet has already left for the Unicef compound. I radio Brian, who says he had been asleep and didn't hear the exchange but, as of late last night, there were no reports of a new clan war or any unusual military activity. As far as he knows, the airport and the seaport remain in the hands of the Butcher of Hargeisa. But then, we will find out when we go to work. Andrew, who is normally cheerful and takes matters less seriously than I do, looks a little unsettled.

Over coffee, he manages a smile: "God, and it's only our first week."

Armed with my borrowed bag of tools and Andrew's small, boxy high-frequency radio with which to talk to arriving aircraft, we drive to the office.

"War?" I ask Harun.

He turns back and grins. "No war, Captain. We have peace now."

On the streets, there are no more gunmen than usual, no obvious signs of concern by the hundreds of Somalis going about their daily lives. There is no evidence of damage or even that shells landed anywhere near our compound, although the area is so pitted from what look like previous exchanges that I don't suppose there would be much difference. There were three outgoing, two incoming. Perhaps General Morgan's Majerteen soldiers were just practicing. And the Marehan on the other side of the Green Line were practicing back.

I am embarrassed by our procession down the crowded road where so few cars are ever seen. I wedge myself deeper between the guns. We could not be more conspicuous: white Land Rover with the big blue UN decals pasted on the sides, UN flags snapping from the fender, and Harun, leaning on his horn, driving like a man possessed, ignoring pedestrians, goats, donkeys, and cows, which, at most times, consider the deserted road as inviolate as a garden walkway at an old-age home. Considering the tensions of the day, such a display of bravura is the very last thing our foreign mission needs. I don't think Harun wants trouble, but his driving sometimes reminds me of a show-off teen who just got his license. Does Harun even have a driver's license? Unlikely. There is no authority to issue one.

We screech to a halt before a crowd of armed locals in front of the blue steel gate. The gate opens slowly and I catch my breath; there seem to be more Somalis inside than out. My first impression is that they have broken in, attacked the compound. Yet there is no violence and little sense of tension, just a crowd of locals milling around in the dust outside the conference room.

Brian, Jeri, and Chet sit at the head of a long table in the darkened chamber facing the sultan, General Morgan, clan and subclan elders, and various officers of militia groups. There is no electricity in the room for some reason, and the gloomy light from the few high windows and from the open doors underscores how very alone my colleagues are. Although I have my own challenges, I feel an affectionate compassion for them. It is evident by their expressions, somber and rigid, that they are getting another berating and that there is yet another crisis to defuse.

It is nearly as serious. Sierra Sierra says during the break that the BBC is reporting the Unicef killings on their Somali Language Service. In an interview translated into Somali, some Unicef official in Nairobi is rejecting charges of Unicef responsibility, even denying that they were our guards who pulled the triggers.

The BBC Somali Service has profound universal influence here, as widespread as the commerce of *miraa* or the distribution of bullets. Somalis, who have only had a written language since 1972, hold a strong oral tradition; they are said to be among the world's best listeners. According to one Somali journalist, "If it has been broadcast by the BBC, that is the final proof that something is true." The warlords, who had already received an admission of culpability from our people here in the field, are outraged and newly suspicious that our bosses are denying the UN's role in the killings.

Chet is furious. The stress he is under is evident. "Christ, if he could only have kept his damn mouth shut. Or told them that we're investigating the incident. Those guys behind the desks have no idea what they get us into—it's not their nuts that are in the cracker."

Brian and Jeri, ever under a constant barrage of charges and threats to our lives, have remarkable stamina. Their mission is not to put out fires or keep us from getting killed but to feed and house displaced refugees and help me get supplies to the flood victims on the lower Jubba. While the floodwaters rise daily and people flee for their lives, we in Kismayo, the center of operations, are daily under siege. There must be a better way. Not involved in the meeting, I head off for the port.

* * *

THE airfield has one sub-subclan and the seaport has another, both under the control of General Morgan. Andrew—Alpha Kilo—is worried that the spasmodic violence and threats of violence at the airport will one day suddenly get out of hand.

"I'll shut down the airport," he warns. But it is not a serious thought. The controlling subclan of the day that rakes in the money from the UN mission won't permit it. And the *qat* plane must come in.

The combatants of one subclan know the combatants of the other, and they are often related and all are ready to kill one another. It is, I suppose, like any grouping, like football teams, perhaps, the Patriots on one side and the 49ers on the other—all know one another personally, but on the field of combat, *à nous deux!* Some of the players are motivated, others are not; some have discipline and others do not. So it is with these various subclan militia, the irregular armed forces, teams of boys with high-powered guns. Some are easier to control and are less trigger-happy and are more responsible. At the seaport, I think I have the home team. I've got the players who do their job protecting me from the other armed players.

It may be that the port is a little more secure because there is an international on the wharf, sweating, pushing, lifting, physically working with them. And joking and trying to learn their language.

Andrew, unfortunately, spends most of his time in the tower. Burdened with changing flight schedules, loading and unloading, cargo manifests, impatient pilots, he admits he has little time to commune with the locals. Or to make a fool of himself.

At the port, I wear a baseball cap and torn cutoff jeans above my work boots, pack a radio on one side of my belt and a utility knife on the other. Maybe I look like some western gunslinger. Or a telephone repairman. My white-blond hair comes down to my shoulders. They make fun of my long hair and guffaw when I make like putting it in a ponytail. It is obvious to them that I'm not young. Those who speak Swahili call me *"Mzee,"* an honorific used for a respected village elder. At my age I don't mind a title now and then.

I've begun teaching the men, many of whom hold themselves stiff and unsmiling, how to high-five, the unique hand slap that ends with a little boogie, a little shake of the hips. I use this silly American gavotte to break the ice, to get them to laugh with me, at me, a communication, a relationship. It seems to work, and they laugh freely as this slightly wizened fifty-year-old gyrates his money-maker.

One port guard sits back on his haunches in the shade of the warehouse, leaning onto the barrel of his Kalashnikov. I see him observe me darkly under the brim of an old floppy hat made of plaited palm fronds. Rangy, thin, finely muscled, he has a chiseled face, creased deeply, sharp nose, deep eyes. He wears a clean but frayed red-and-blue-checkered shirt, threadbare brown trousers, and plastic flip-flops. His skin is jet-black but he is not Bantu; he wears his Somali heritage proudly. I am compelled by that expressionless yet distinctive face. He appears fierce and unyielding, yet

I sense something inside those corvine eyes, an intelligence, a sensitivity. I smile at him and get nothing in return. Yet I am certain there is a personality in there—somewhere.

I struggle with the large steel warehouse doors and he rises to help.

"Maha samid," I say. Thank you.

"Isa," he says, tapping his chest with his fingers.

"Isa." I take a chance. "Isa," I say in simple English, "I teach. Give me five! Here—your hand."

He shies away as if I were a spitting cobra.

I offer my upturned hand, reach for his hand, and slap it. I give him my hand and have him slap it. I instruct him to raise his hand in the air and I slap it. He is quick to learn, and on the second go we raise both our hands in high-five and slap them together and gyrate. "Yeah!"

That is, I gyrate. Chin thrust forward, he watches suspiciously as I give a little shake of my booty. Eyes widened in dismay, he looks at me as if I'm crazy, maybe even dangerous. Or worse, insulting. There is no humor in those sunken eyes. His countrymen are laughing so hard they are nearly doubled over. I want them to stop. What a stupid egotistical thing I've done. I always go too far. The man turns, picks up his gun that he had set against the wall. He glares ominously at the men and they fall silent. Then he glares at me. Suddenly he breaks out in a wide toothy grin, shakes his head at this crazy *gal*—white man—and walks away.

I'm nearly pissing myself.

A short, swarthy Somali with a goatee and a rifle draped over his shoulder approaches me inside the warehouse while Joel and I are working on one of the outboards. I can tell he has some authority—his gun is bigger. He introduces himself as a colonel. His English is ragged but understandable.

"I see your keys, keys to boats."

"Where are they?"

"In town. Some boys have them. You want?"

"Of course I want. They were stolen. Can you get them back?"

"In Somalia, always solution." He grins.

I recognize the word. "What is the solution, Colonel?"

"The boys want thousand dollars for each key. I tell them no." He shrugs. "But that is what they want."

"A thousand dollars?"

"Ha ha!"

"Ha ha?"

"Ha ha!" He grins. Something is missing here.

I turn to Joel. "What is this guy, an improv comedian?"

"*Ha ha* means yes in Somali," he says.

"*Ha ha* means yes? No shit." I turn to the Somali. "NO *ha ha*. Tell them absolutely no *ha ha*." I walk away. Screw him. I've already hot-wired one of the boats.

My handheld VHF crackles. Alpha Kilo is telling Bravo Delta that our Hercules in from Nairobi has just backed into the warehouse, wiping out parts of the metal roof and wall with its tail. "And there's damage to the aircraft."

"Oh, God." I hear the despair in Brian's voice. "How serious?"

"Well, it can't take off. Part of its tail is missing. Might be days before it can get back into the air."

So much for one escape plan.

Apparently this is on Brian's mind as well. "We've got to get that aircraft operational, Alpha Kilo. Immediately!"

"The pilot says he is going to try to get a mechanic out from Nairobi to see if it can be put back together."

"What do you think?"

"The Herc can take a beating, but me, I wouldn't fly it."

* * *

I am alone at the port now; Joel has left to catch his flight for the relative sanity of anywhere else—on a smaller single-engine cargo plane. I want to get one of the boats into the water and ask Ali to arrange a crane. Then comes the dreaded selection of longshoremen to slide the boat out of the warehouse to the pier's edge. I know of no clan affiliation and so I select men randomly—those who I don't think have worked before. I am very alert, very nervous, and I try not to show it. The pushing, shoving, chin-stroking is merely a threat today, more restrained possibly because they don't know how far to push it. The crane on the edge of the pier slowly lowers the boat and finally, for the first time, it touches the water. I feel like breaking a bottle of champagne over its pointy little bow.

I have wired an old car-ignition switch to the boat's electrical system. With some apprehension, I turn the key and she roars to life. The Somalis on the wharf above cheer, slap one another on the back in mutual congratulation. I grin and toss them a thumbs-up. I have an undeniable sense of fulfillment. It is not just that; I have hope.

After testing the controls, I toss the lines and ease the boat out into the bay to break in the engine. I am in my own world. I feel like a schoolboy exploring the neighborhood with a new bicycle. I motor toward a bombed-out patrol boat that lies awash in the middle of the harbor on a mudflat, its rusted hull streaked white with the guano of seabirds. Following the shoreline, I am careful to stay out of the shallows, where, according to Ali, wrecks by the dozens lie scattered just below the surface. On the back of the engine manual, I sketch rough contours and landmarks of the bay, recording coordinates of latitude and longitude of the harbor entrance from the GPS. I note the waypoints of locations on the beach that are accessible from the water and, I hope, from the road. I am flushed with success and accomplishment.

At the evening briefing I am met with a communal gloom. But I have a boat in the water—working!

"That is great, Juliet Bravo," Chet says. The news is greeted with dead eyes by the others.

"Well, I guess *you* will be able to get out," Happy One says testily. I am surprised and a little hurt by her remark. I don't know what I expected, but after days of repairing, rewiring, rebuilding, organizing, and ducking a few flying bullets and a little bloodletting, I suppose I expected something more than Jeri's liverish grumbling. But I don't take it personally: We are all wiped out from the heat, from the tensions, from the work that runs from dawn to eight o'clock in the evening, fourteen-plus hours of futility and fear.

Brian drones that we've contracted out installation of water pumps and some rain collectors in what remains of a local school. Andrew describes briefly the damage to the cargo plane. I have trouble keeping my eyes open. It is the same for the rest of these stressed-out nodding humanitarian mercenaries. These are not hardened veterans but mere fellow citizens who hope they will be able to get the job done and get out of here without getting killed. I think every one of these permanents is more surprised and frustrated than I that things are going so badly.

They are a strange lot. As I look across at them I can't help but wonder who these people really are or why they are here. Are they married to the UN, to the adventure, the altruism, the money, the loneliness, the independence, the adrenaline? Each one possesses that vague, private air of a loner; each one, I have learned, is a virtual stranger to the others. They have so little in common, not even from the same countries. They find no succor even in that most essential bond from working for the same outfit. Each is a representative of a different agency—WFP, Unicef, UNDP, UNHCR—with different bosses, different instructions, different and sometimes competing methods. Jeri, an attractive woman, wearily sweeps the hair out of her eyes, and I wonder whether she has any kind of life on the Outside. Does she have a husband, a lover waiting for her return? I have not had the chance to ask, probably won't get around to it before they send me upriver. Andrew, not a permanent, has his girl waiting for him, and I hope I have Jackie. But do any of these permanents who spend so much time in the field have a long-term relationship—families, lovers—waiting for them back home? How could they maintain any kind of a relationship? They, we, have so little in common with anyone not here. It is not unlike returning to the mainstream after crossing an ocean on a small boat; the eyes of friends glaze over when I try to tell them of my adventures, as do mine when they tell me of their day-to-day lives. How can you tell your partner about Somalia? A soldier goes to war, gets shot at, suffers the traumas of combat, goes home. Who is he going to talk to?

We are too exhausted to report in much detail our day's

activities. Happy One, however, seems to find some energy. Tomorrow she will try again to distribute food to the local Kismayo camps of twenty thousand flood victims. This will be the first delivery since the one a few days ago that resulted in the shootings. She is not optimistic:

"Every time we take food to the camps, the militia comes during the middle of the night and robs the refugees, and the next day the food we have distributed is sold openly in the markets in town. It just cannot go on like this. What are we doing here, for God's sake?" she says, rubbing eyes sunken with fatigue. Happy One looks finished.

The difficulties are not unexpected. In 1992, nearly three thousand people, mostly the elderly, women, and children, were dying daily from starvation. Despite this human calamity, eighty percent of the emergency relief supplies were looted, which was one reason for UNOSOM military intervention.

Mohamed Sahnoun, UN special envoy to Somalia in 1992, wrote: "High-quality items such as sugar, rice, flour, cooking oil, while very much welcome, have many times caused unnecessary deaths and injury because, by and large, they invite looting and consequent fighting." The port of Kismayo, he reported, "is so important for emergency relief in the south that any delay in ensuring security there is to be strongly denounced." This vital seaport, through which most of the relief supplies for southern Somalia were delivered from the outside, "changed hands so many times and presented us with serious security problems." Things haven't changed much.

Cold showers, a change of clothes, and under the thatched roof of the HCR compound we try to unwind. Chet, our new compound mate, is nothing like his predecessor. Not a man of many words, not a man with a responsive smile, not a man who offers information easily. During our staff briefing, he gave the impression that if you worry about your safety, you don't belong here. I wonder if he is going to forget that we are not his soldiers. Whatever the initial impression, he makes two instant friends when he puts a couple six-packs on the table.

Andrew's account of the Hercules accident is a mirror to all our frustrations. Engines running, props pitched in reverse, the Herc was being directed back toward the warehouse by one of the crew who couldn't see the top of the forty-foot tail in relation to the building.

"I was standing in front of the warehouse and I could see what was going to happen," he says. "Once it starts backing, it is hard to stop. I ran in front of the plane, screaming like a bloody madman trying to get the pilot's attention, but he was looking round at his engineer. And the engineer had no idea—he was looking at the wing, not at the tail. I should have realized what was going to happen."

"They can fix these things?"

"Sure. I am not sure how, but yes, it can be done, so they tell me."

The subclan leader, Andrew says, is demanding not just money for repair of the building but punitive damages from the UN as well. Yet another potential crisis.

I watch a bat swoop through the air, catching flying insects hovering around the one lamp on the walkway. I don't smoke. Yet I feel the need of a cigarette. I realize that not one of the internationals smokes. I suppose I am grateful they don't—I would start again and I would be a chimney by now.

Chet is saying that he and Brian drove to subclan headquarters on the Jubba earlier in the day to seek security guarantees that I don't become a target of the warring clans shooting across the river at each other. "But it looks like you will have to wait a few days," he says. I accept this news gratefully—I am getting less enthusiastic about the mission with the passage of each hour. It's not that the flooded areas are far distant. Kismayo is eighteen miles down the coast from the mouth of the delta. The Jubba curves back toward Kismayo, and the stranded, the hungry, the homeless, the dying are only a few miles away—not more than twenty minutes by truck. They might as well be on the far side of the continent. The villages that are being swept away by the river are on the other side of the Green Line, the demarcation that separates General Morgan's

Majerteen subclan from the Somali Patriotic Movement forces of the Marehan subclan—historical family enemies. Both subclans are members of the Darood clan.

Upriver, only forty miles to the northwest on the other side of the Green Line, there are sections that are peaceful and secure and are currently served by Wolff's river fleet without incident. The well-equipped Swedes and others are doing their jobs, presumably only worrying about crocodiles and hippos, not incoming artillery. I have yet to help anyone, make a delivery, rescue a fair Somali maiden, or whatever it is I'm supposed to do. A mission from God this is not.

Sierra Sierra says his trip up the road was—his word—difficult, an apparent understatement. General Morgan had guaranteed them safe road passage out of his territory across the Green Line to Goob Weyn, a village perched on the river cliffs overlooking the delta. It had been arranged, Morgan had said. Guaranteed. But someone didn't get the message. At the so-called frontier, they were stopped by the Somali Patriotic Movement. The gunmen claimed the UN had aligned itself with General Morgan. They threatened to shoot them, and Chet says at one point he was convinced they would.

"They were discussing us in Somali. I couldn't catch all of it but it appears our neutrality is compromised—when we accepted Morgan's protection here in town, they think we threw our lot in with him. It is going to take some fast footwork to persuade them otherwise. We were pretty lucky to get out of there. Our driver said that they were planning to kidnap us when we crossed to the other side of the line."

"Were they serious?"

"Well, son, they sure in hell were not arguing about a bingo card. Our driver translated for us later: 'If we don't take them now, it will be too late. It is the one chance we have.' "

8.
A Mother's Gift

ESCAPE from Kismayo is becoming something of a preoccupation. Although Jeri has been able to get some food to the IDP, and Andrew is putting into some order the shambles of an airport, hard as I might I can't think of anything else that has been accomplished, that has required my presence here. There is still no word from the warlords for me to begin delivery runs up the coast and into the river. And the dickering continues over the number of camels a dead pregnant woman is worth. The schoolboy is still alive.

During the morning briefing, Chet suggests another reconnoiter for possible pickup sites, this time along the barrier reef on the ocean side.

"But don't get too close to shore, Juliet Bravo. Stay well out of range."

"What's the range of a Kalashnikov?"

"About four hundred yards."

"Four hundred yards! I was well within that yesterday."

"Guess you were lucky."

"Not much chance I can find a proper landing area from that distance."

"Could be a problem. Well, don't you worry, if it's any consolation, these guys are terrible shots." He chuckles. "Except . . ."

"Except?"

"The gun tends to climb in automatic. That's when they find their range and could peg you. But I wouldn't worry; by the tenth round I suppose you'd be almost as far gone as Kenya."

"Just say the word and I'm *hasta la bye bye*."

"So—give it a try?"

"Sure, glad to get out on the boat. You should come along, see what this place looks like from the sea."

"You can bet on it."

"Don't think I'll do more than one pass. They won't be expecting me, and by the time they decide to use me for target practice I should be well over the horizon. I am sure not going back for a second look."

"Understood. Keep your head down. Now," he continues, including the others, "when—*if*—evacuation is necessary, I'll get on the radio and announce that there's going to be a poker game today. That means we're pulling the plug. I'll ask each of you to acknowledge receipt of the message. At the seaport, Juliet Bravo, you'll be told that the poker game will be at a certain hour. This means that you should take your boat to our predesignated location—you get that worked out on the GPS—and pick up the staff who can't get to the airport.

"Alpha Kilo, you'll have to find out what is flying, what's in the air and nearby. Inform the pilot on your mobile radio—out of earshot of your militia guards—that we need an emergency pickup. Have the plane taxi up to your location, engines running—turn, load, and fly."

"Won't fool the militia," Andrew says quietly. "They'll see us board and they'll know we're getting out. Easy targets."

"You'll have to use some discretion. It's difficult no matter how we cut it. If it looks impossible, then you'll have to stay with those of us who can't escape. Any questions?"

There are none. Except that I feel like asking why he addresses us only by our radio call signs, a habit I seem to be falling into. Of course, none of us knows each other very well and perhaps none can afford the luxury of attachment, as tenuous as it is. With the loner in each of us, who has the inclination to get to know each other? Andrew I know, because we share the same quarters. Maybe Brian and Jeri are close. I haven't seen it. Being so distant out at the port, I am perhaps the least attached, the least connected to the whole operation. When I am with these people, they are either too busy, too stressed, or too exhausted to act very personal. The way things are going, when this is over—years later—I probably will have forgotten their names. I will never, however, forget the faces behind the radio call signs.

"Okay, I realize it is a bit rushed and half-cocked, but it might work," Sierra Sierra continues. "Let us hope we never have to play that game."

"Are the boats operational?" Brian asks.

"Ready to go. I've rewired both and they are stocked with emergency rations and water. I'll put extra fuel in them and break in the second engine during the trip up the coast."

"Good." Beyond the occasional facial tic of his pursing lips, there is something of a smile. "You know, if I ever get a break, I'll take you up on that offer. I'd love to get into one of those boats. Haven't had a day off in weeks."

"*Mi barco, su barco,* Brian. My boat is your boat."

"I could fancy a bit of fishing."

"I haven't been out to the reef yet, but from the shore I saw the birds working, bird-feeds everywhere. Means tuna, marlin, sailfish—well, you know all about that. I'll work up a never-fail lure, try to find some nylon line. Give me a call when the fires are out."

I hope he does get down to the port. He needs a break.

He and Chet are making another trip to Goob Weyn, and without much conviction he says his contacts assure him that this time they'll get through. Sierra Sierra doesn't look too sure. "We should be able to get you security guarantees for the run, hopefully as far up as Hum Hum. Will you be ready to go tomorrow?"

"As ready as I'll ever be." My tone is none too enthusiastic; I have a lump in my throat, a bad feeling about this. They shoot across the river at each other. Why couldn't I have been sent to the "secure" areas upriver like Jamaame or Bardera, where the only worries are about displaced jungle life?

My concern must be evident as I walk to the car.

"Problems, Captain?"

"No problems in Somalia, Harun. Only solutions."

His laugh is genuine. He opens my door and walks around to his.

"Ah, Captain," he says behind the wheel, turning to me with a big grin. "*Diep maleh, diep maleh*—no problem, no problem." His dark eyes glow. "You Captain *Diep Maleh*!" He is delighted with himself. My gun-wielding guards, who are taking on personalities of their own and are no longer mere gangsters, take up the call: "Captain *Diep Maleh*!" They laugh, flashing a thumbs-up sign of approval. Captain No Problem.

* * *

AT the port, the second boat is wheeled out of the warehouse and lowered into the water. The bickering among the longshoremen seems less intense, but I do keep an ear out for the metallic sound of the sliding cocking levers of the assault rifles.

I do my high-five with Isa, who, while still reluctant, indulges me and his supportive mates. He helps move the heavy stuff, even volunteers to siphon fuel from the drums to the boat tanks, an unpleasant process that always involves gagging on the gasoline in the siphon hose. He has appointed himself my personal guard, his automatic rifle slung loosely over his shoulder at the ready, his eyes quickly scanning wherever I go. I am supposed to have at least one Unicef guard with me every minute of the day, but some of the blue pajamas appear so unreliable and sleazy that I prefer to walk alone. Isa, it seems, is always there.

Working with these hair-trigger Somalis—the attendant fear and adrenaline rush, the certainty of violence and the possibility of death—is beginning to fulfill some perverse challenge. I am accepting. I wonder if this adaptation to reality might breed complacency.

Curiously, I find myself frequently happy, almost giddy. Is it the buildup of too much shit? Or is it the result of some recondite satisfaction just now revealing itself? There are moments when some minor success—moving a boat, communicating, merely forcing a smile—brings exhilaration, actual happiness. I suppose it is the unwitting comparison with worse times; in danger and misery, I read somewhere, the pendulum swings.

The men I work with are becoming more understandable and a little more predictable. It doesn't take a genius to learn when not to press a point, when to slink away, when to keep your mouth shut and let someone else do the talking, when to crack a joke or even make like a fool. It is a delicate line easily and mistakenly crossed. I know now that Somalis would rather laugh (but never be laughed at) than pull a trigger. I seem to make them laugh with my crazy antics and my silly appearance. I cannot see myself as they see me when I shake my butt with these men during a high-five. But their reaction to my foolishness is mirror enough, and that is warmly satisfying. I have learned that getting them to laugh at me—the white foreign-aid worker on a mission—seems to level us. It is a damn sight better than a brawl.

So they have come to know me a little, these rifle-toting gunmen with their fascinating brooding faces. I will never get beyond their suspicion, but they have let me in a crack. As violence is their common currency, they do not consider me a threat, because I have shown them I am a poor man.

I sit back against the hard cement wall of the warehouse in the shade of the overhanging tin roof. It is that time of day; the long wall is lined with hot and tired bodies, knees up—it is the midday *miraa* break.

There is a certain style to chewing *miraa*. In Aden, shopkeepers huddle over their paper bags of *qat* behind display cases of feta, pistachio paste, and hummus, ancient tins of Soviet caviar and sardines, and hope no customer will come in during these precious midday hours. Their cheeks bulge like nut-gathering squirrels, and reluctantly they serve customers despite the green slurry that drips down their chins. Chewing *miraa* here appears more refined. Possibly because of the poverty or because of the basic aristocratic nature of these people, a Somali plucks an individual leaf off the stalk, inspects it reflectively as one might a fine Cuban cigar—and chews it with a private look of satisfaction.

Baseball cap shading my face, eyes half-closed, I detect a movement close by. I look up at a bundle of bright color standing before me.

A girl in a chador of cheerful red, yellow, and green looks down at me without expression. She appears no older than her mid-teens. She holds an infant in her arms, wrapped tightly in a cotton shawl. She doesn't seem too maternal about her baby. She is holding the child out almost at arm's length as if she were proffering it as a reward.

I feel lazy, dazed by the heat, the humidity, and the general malaise of the drugged men sitting next to me. I really don't want to be bothered.

Her round childlike face continues to look down at me, waiting, expecting.

"Harun, what does she want?"

Harun speaks harshly in his indecipherable language. Her eyes tighten angrily. She squats down to my level, her little-girl face suddenly too close to mine. I smell her breath, I smell her sweat, I look into her sharp obsidian eyes, inches from mine, challenging. In one easy motion, she places the baby in my lap, gets to her feet, and lords over me, hands on hips, as if assessing my worthiness.

I stifle an urge to toss the baby as if it were a venomous snake. I remain motionless, suddenly aware of the weight of the child.

He is a few months old. Flies swarm around his plump face and puffy eyes. He smells of a musty, pungent wood-smoke odor. Sweat runs in rivulets down the child's face; the bundle of swaddling clothes itself is damp. I feel his body heat through the blanket. The baby does not move.

"What do I do with him?"

"It dies, Captain. It is her baby," meaning, I think, give it back to her, it's her problem.

The child whimpers quietly. The young mother continues to stand over me, waiting.

Getting to my feet is difficult. She doesn't take the baby from me, and I have to sling him under one arm and use the other to push myself up off the wall. I try to return the baby. Her hands remain at her sides. She looks directly into my eyes smugly, confidently, without wavering. She turns and walks away.

"Hey, goddamn it! Come back here. Take your baby!" I shout, but she keeps walking. The men sitting against the warehouse laugh quietly. It must be great theater, and for the first time I am beginning to resent them.

I look down at this Somali infant and know that he is now my responsibility. I feel the infant begin to shake uncontrollably.

"Malaria," Harun says softly at my side.

I radio the Unicef office but no one responds. I suppose they are putting out another fire. What do I do with the one in my arms? The young mother has disappeared. Turned a corner, vanished into the bombed-out port office building, wherever; she is just gone.

"Let's go, Harun. Médecins sans Frontières Hospital. Let's do it fast!"

I cradle the baby in my arms as we speed out of the port, down the dusty road toward town, past the barricades.

The child is shivering so violently my body shakes with it. He opens his big black eyes and I think he is trying to smile. He is a beautiful creature, and I can't help but feel love for this little thing. I take a sweat rag from my back pocket and wipe the child's rheumy eyes and the sputum from around his mouth and the beads of sweat off his face.

The car slows to a crawl. Ahead, a pair of old swayback donkeys stand side by side in the middle of the road, solid and unconcerned.

"Go around them!"

Harun drives up the roadside hill, grazing a palm tree before swerving back onto the road. I clasp the baby tightly, protectively. Before, this was just a job, a duty. Now it is a mission. I want desperately to get this baby to the hospital; I want desperately for this child to live.

The baby's fever has abated apparently, for he is no longer shivering, and I relax. I look down at the infant and smile, talk to him softly.

The child's eyes, heavily lidded, stare back at me. They are glazed and old tears are drying on his cheeks. I wipe his eyes and try to reassure him, soothe him. But now I sense, I suddenly realize, that there is nothing there! A second ago—just a second ago there was life. Now there is nothing, not a living thing, not a soul, not a smile.

A Somali male nurse at the broken-down MSF/Belgium Clinic takes the baby and assures me he "will be taken care of."

I hand the baby over gently, and with the same reverence he takes the little body in his arms, turns, and walks through the hospital doors. I am left stunned. Emptied.

It is written that a child dies from malaria every thirty seconds in Africa. But why do I have to be part of this child's death? Is there a purpose? Am I supposed to get some sort of message? Are we merely statistics?

* * *

IN the driver's seat of the boat, I sit under the sun, staring out at the painful brightness of the water. I am unable to hold on to a thought, a feeling, a reason. I still feel life pour out of the child. I almost remember the physical sensation of the flight of life, as if, had I realized it in time, I could have kept existence from leaving the body. I feel so fragile, so tenuous. And disconnected. I am drifting away from myself. I hope I don't lose it. I've got to get back out to sea, clear my head. I need some company.

I invite gentle Ali, the port manager, and Abduah, the crane owner, out for a run around the point, perhaps along the coast. After all, there is a mission, a reason for my life. Abduah carries the G-3 automatic rifle.

I put the boat through its paces. According to Chet's GPS, we clock forty-seven knots, faster than I have ever been on the water. I need the rush.

What the hell. Ali and Abduah are loving it; it is a vital respite for them. It is vital for me.

So we take the boat outside the barrier reef, eighteen miles up the coast to the mouth of the mysterious Jubba River. There is hardly any wind, but still there are small waves. A small motorboat in the open ocean does not make for a good time; slamming into the foot-high chop is not only dangerous but also hard on the family future. But we are out and away, blessedly free from back there.

The coast, lined with tall stately palms, is stunning. Long, deserted beaches of cream-colored sand, a languid surf, and no signs of people; it may be one of the last unspoiled coastlines on earth.

"No swim," Ali says, reading my thoughts. "Many, many sharks. Many children die from sharks."

Yet a mile or so up the coast, a cluster of thick dark paint strokes moves slowly down the beach toward the water. I slow down and steer toward shore and I sense my passengers stiffen; Abduah casually rests his hand on the muzzle of his rifle. With binoculars, I distinguish a dozen or so women in black chadors, laughing, splashing one another, gamboling along the water's edge, some up to their waists in the sea. Their sense of modesty is impressive and they have my respect. They stop, look up at the approaching speedboat, hurry out of the water, and disappear into the shadows of the trees. I hope I haven't spoiled their afternoon.

A few miles from the Jubba, the azure blue of the Indian Ocean terminates not gradually but distinctly against a flood of muddy coffee-colored water that fans out seaward as far as the eye can see, as if the country is bleeding itself to death. At the mouth of the river, the torrent is re-creating the coast, spilling over the dunes and cutting the peninsula in half. The flow of the raging river breaks as a crushing wall of white water over a sandbar. This is the mighty stream that is creating such hell inland, and with some awe we watch the torrent empty into the sea.

"Want to go up the river a little way?" I ask them half seriously as we circle in front of the mouth. Thick brush and tall trees line the delta. Beyond, forbidding darkness defines enemy country. "I should try to find a way over the bar." I do have a job to do, although the breaking surf in the channel looks nearly impassable. I would not attempt it unless it was absolutely necessary.

Their cheerful faces mask over with a look of horror.

"No, not a good idea," Ali says evenly. "We will be killed. Marehan."

"You're sure? Won't take but a few minutes." I find myself playing with these guys. Perhaps to push my own uncertainty.

Abduah looks up at me with sudden hostility, then to his rifle.

"Okay. You're right." I swing the boat back toward the sea and my passengers relax. I throttle back and enjoy the peace. Ali and Abduah quietly sing. They tell me it is a Somali love song, a tale about a man who loves a woman from another clan.

* * *

THE story of the child's death is met with barely a murmur at the evening staff meeting. In Somalia, nearly a quarter of all children die before their fifth birthday; to everyone but me, it is merely another anonymous death. Their attitude is that—yeah, well, we've all been there, welcome to relief work. The event does not warrant any discussion, and their lack of interest seems to lessen my own—what? Confusion? Guilt? In any case, it becomes easier to ignore the feelings that are trying to define themselves. Like everyone else has learned to do.

Andrew reports that mechanics flew in from Nairobi with nuts, bolts, rivets, strips of aluminum, and speed tape. Four hours later, the Hercules made a practice run, and after a touch-and-go, continued on to Nairobi, about six hundred miles away.

Sierra Sierra says their trip to Goob Weyn was uneventful; the bandits at the checkpoint even welcomed them as if nothing had occurred the day before.

"The good news is that the Marehan will authorize your relief run into their territory. Also, General Morgan now says he will 'consider' permitting a test run of a delivery upriver."

"Well, damn me, that *is* good news." Sierra Sierra does not miss my sarcasm.

"The Marehan are getting desperate—they need the food. They have rising floodwaters at their backs and Morgan with his artillery in their faces. They are trapped. Morgan is being something of a humanitarian to let us take food to his enemy."

"Yeah, I heard what a humanitarian he was." I'm not in a good mood. "How many people did he kill in the bombing of that city up north? Ten, twenty, fifty thousand? And he's permitting us to take food to his enemy? Something's fucked here."

"It is not for us to second-guess the bastard," he snaps. "We should be grateful he will let us—you—cross the line. It is not certain he will permit the run. I said he would 'consider' the deliveries."

"There has got to be a reason."

"No doubt. But if he agrees to the deliveries, then we deliver. That's final."

"What—Marehan and the Majerteen talk to each other? They call each other and say, you don't shoot, we don't shoot? Or is it just you and Brian working this out?"

"There are comms on all sides. Don't worry. We will insist they stop shooting during the relief runs."

"I heard we are expendable. . . ." I know I'm pushing it.

Chet looks up sharply, looks at me as if I'm some subordinate noncom. But then he softens, not quite a smile, but more like an admission of truth; who's shitting whom?

"For whatever it's worth, the general told us that if he can't guarantee your safety, you don't go. And, Juliet Bravo, I won't let you go if there is any danger. Count on it.

"But to be honest," he adds, "your personal safety is less important to him than the boat. He's concerned that if the Marehan get hold of that speedboat of yours he couldn't touch them. With a gun on the bow, they could control most of southern Somalia and as much of the Jubba as they wanted."

He has laid bare a thought, a fear I may have been denying. My little blue boats are considered spoils of war and everybody wants one. The driver is just in the way. "So what is to stop Morgan from trying to take the boat?"

Chet grimaces as if I still don't get it.

"Who is to be my protection—who is riding shotgun with me during the run? The general's men, or the Marehan boys?"

"Well, we're working that out. You can see the difficulty." He hesitates. "You may have to take it up alone."

"Alone?"

I am beginning to feel this is getting out of hand, that I am mere fodder, a pawn in some larger contest with no game plan. Expendable.

"There is another problem that you should be aware of—and it may stop your run," Sierra Sierra says. "I'm not at all sure our good general can control his boys when he goes. They may want to prove something to him or to their own subclans."

"Morgan going? Where?"

"Bossasso, for the 'unity' conference with [Hussein Mohammed] Aideed and [Ali] Mahdi."

"Soon?"

"A couple of days. Or maybe never. You know how it goes. But the last time he left town, he lost control of his forces. Started a clan war."

I shake my head in dismay.

"Look, Juliet Bravo, if your safety is not absolutely assured, I can guarantee you that as chief of security I won't let you go. That's a given. That's my job."

If I was worried before, I'm downright nervous now. None of the combat-toughened militia will venture out of their own territory. I am not going without guards or without guarantees. I'm not in the army. I'm a civilian, for God's sake, a relief worker. I can refuse.

* * *

WHILE Ali, Abduah, and I were puttering up the East African coast checking out Somali bathing beauties, Russ Ulrey, the WFP regional logistics officer in Nairobi, was on a slow boil. The rains were slowly moving southward, and day after day of heavy blinding torrents fell on the Kenyan capital. Like so many others, Russ was sick of it. The problems he was getting from the field did not help his outlook. Following a morning meeting with Matt Wolff, his river operations manager, he had received a report that an Operation Lifeline food-drop zone in Sudan had been bombed by government forces. A Hercules had just dropped sacks of relief supplies near Bahr-el-Ghazal; WFP staff had begun to collect the cargo, and locals were picking up whatever scraps and remains might have spilled when the bags hit the ground. From out of the sun, a lone Soviet-era transport plane swooped low over the drop zone and rolled a single bomb out of its cargo bay. None of his staff was injured, but some Sudanese civilians were killed. Earlier he had received word that one of his relief supply trucks on the road to Lokichoggio in Sudan had been hijacked.

The meeting with Matt had ended some time ago. Never one to lose his temper, this time he came damn close. This kind of crap was exactly what he had hoped just once, just for one crisis, could be avoided; it dragged down relief efforts, turned your hair white from frustration. Yet it was the bureaucracy and it was inevitable.

The UN Country Team (UNCT) report was still on top of other papers where he had tossed it. Compiled by Unicef, it glowingly detailed current relief operations in southern and central Somalia:

> As at 11 December, at least 1,695 people are reported to have died (confirmed deaths) from drowning, accidents, reptile attacks, disease and malnutrition. An estimated 230,000 persons have been displaced while the lives of at least one million Somalis remain at risk as they have lost their livestock, harvest and other supplies. . . . On 9 December, UNHCR reported that torrential rains and flooding of the Tana River in northeastern Kenya adversely affected the refugee camps of Ifo, Dhagaxley, and Hagadera, sheltering 123,000 Somali refugees.
>
> The air-fleet presently available in Garissa consists of one Twin Otter, two Buffalo planes, two Mi-8 helicopters, and two Caravans. Kismayo and Bardera . . . are also operating as bases for the operation. On the ground, 21 boats are operational, distributing relief supplies to distant and cut off villages in need. Boats are

> operating in Bardera, Bualle, Jamam[sic], Sakow, Marere, Belet Weyne and Jowhar. . . . [A]dditional boats in Kismayo are not yet operational. The airdrop operation has now been backed up by two C-130 planes based in—

The innocuous reference to the boats in Kismayo was there for all to see. It did not have to add that the WFP was responsible for the operation of these boats and thus the implied mismanagement was ultimately his. It was hard enough to get the jobs done without a competing agency chortling over the perceived operational failures of his people. Maybe it was because of the dismal weather, but Russ was on a short fuse and he had confronted Matt.

"Explain. Why are those boats in Kismayo not operational?"

"There are some security problems apparently, and I'm having trouble getting the equipment to him. Also the keys to the boats were stolen."

"Who the hell is out there?"

"A yachtie—older guy—you met him."

"A yachtie! You mean he doesn't know how to start an outboard? Jesus, where did you get these guys, Matt?"

"I think he knows what he's doing. One of the security guys brought me this note from him." Russ took the message and read:

> Matt:
>
> I expect to have at least one and perhaps both boats in the water Monday P.M. and tested ready to go by Tuesday midday. Brian of Unicef will probably have a good idea of operational areas once he gets approval from the subclans upriver. There have been a few problems: The keys to both boats were stolen and I have hot-wired one of them, hoping to get the other done soon. The medicine chests were looted. Thus suggest when next transporting any boats, anything that is not screwed down should be sent separately.
>
> DO NOT send any more boat operators or boats

here until cleared with Brian. I think this has caused a problem. There are SERIOUS security problems and we have been in a lockdown off and on since my arrival. Shooting is normal around here. This has delayed launch of our little "fleet."

Matt, can't go to sea without the gear. VERY URGENT: Need two-stroke oil and hydraulic fluid (40 liters), first-aid kits and malaria medicine, more Polypro line (at least 60 meters), the GPS handhelds which I understood were in the customs warehouse, and of course HF communication equipment. I am reluctant to go upriver without HF comms.

Please tell Joe Suits, loadmaster of C-130, that I will return his vise grips and Phillips head screwdrivers when I get back to Nairobi.

Last thing. There is no river in Kismayo. It is an 18-mile offshore trip up the coast so unlikely that we can run deliveries from Kismayo.

Burnett

"Good God!" Russ muttered. "No river, no equipment, and what serious security problems?"

"I looked into that. A C-130 was shot at; there was a killing outside the Unicef compound."

"Didn't you check if there were problems there?"

"I was told there weren't any problems. All of our efforts are upriver."

"We have anyone else in Kismayo?"

"We got someone putting the airport back together, but he's been attached to Unicef. Burnett is the only one. Kismayo is a Unicef operation."

"I know it is! And there is no river in Kismayo? Didn't you know that?"

"Unicef thought it would be a good idea to have the boats

there, and suggested that we should try to run up the river from the sea."

"No doubt." Russ shook his head, knew that Unicef had hoped to control at least that part of the river operation.

"This UNCT report was written yesterday, December twelve. When did *you* get Burnett's message?"

"Only yesterday afternoon. The security man apparently took it home with him when he went on leave. Forgot about it, I guess."

"My God! I want those boats operational—yesterday!"

The discussion rankled him. He liked Matt. It was not his fault, Russ knew. Wolff had to deal with dozens of drivers and boats and their equipment needs, but if he didn't know what was going on in the field, then who the hell did? The Brit was a hard worker, honest and sincere and, in most instances, thorough. Maybe, however, the scope of the remit was just too enormous for him to handle.

The telephone interrupted his dull gaze out into the rain-soaked courtyard.

"What! Jesus, I'll be right there," he said, reaching for his foul-weather gear.

* * *

MATT had returned to the Somalia WFP office in a fury.

He was at the end of his rope. Always the rules, the procedures, the obstructionists, the ego of those who were trying to control. All he wanted was to get the job done. He had boat drivers in the field and they needed backup, they needed equipment, the gear that would keep them out of harm's way. Since the operation began it was never "Can-do, how and when do you need it," instead: "Sorry, can't do it, not possible, sign the forms, maybe tomorrow, maybe never."

Matt jumped out of the UN rig, slammed the door, and stormed through the rain into the old settler's house that was the WFP Somali office. He took a left at the stairs and without knocking burst into the office. The slight, older Ethiopian finance officer looked up and offered an unpleasant patronizing smile.

Before he could speak, Matt leaned across the desk and thrust his face into the stubborn bureaucrat's. The exact conversation is not known, but Matt's booming voice was heard throughout the building. Apparently Matt bawled him out for obstructing at every turn his efforts to get equipment out to the boat drivers in the field. The bureaucrat replied that if Matt only followed the procedures, filed requests in triplicate, and got three quotes for the bidding process when outside material or help was needed, then maybe he would get what he wanted.

The shouting match poured out into the hallway, Russ recalled. Matt started shoving the finance man toward his own office, demanding that he sign the requisition slips on his desk for radios, GPS, and a plane to take the equipment out to the field.

"You are just sitting on your ass, doing bugger-all. I will bloody well make you sign these forms so that I can get this stuff out to those guys." Matt kept pushing the Ethiopian and was apparently close to cold-cocking him when Saskia and other office workers intervened.

When Russ entered the office, the finance minister was on the phone to the police.

* * *

ANDREW and I lie on our bunks in the dark. I can envision the slow run against the current between the shooters. I wonder if I will hear the shots over the sound of the outboard.

"I really don't want to do this."

"I can't blame you."

"I feel like this is getting out of control—like I have no control over my own fate. I always thought I had. I really do not want to go up that fucking river."

"You can refuse."

"I wonder. Well, I hope that I don't have to make the choice. Might not have to go anyway. . . . I've been meaning to ask, what brings you out here?" It has the ring of one prison inmate asking another: What are you in for?

"Money, pure and simple. Money." He laughs quietly. "You can't make this kind of money trying to start a business in Nairobi."

"What kind of business?"

"Party business."

"A what?"

"Blowing up balloons, acting like a clown. I was trying to start a party business. Like they have in London. I suppose in America too. You know, balloons, clowns, party favors—arranging parties."

I can see him in my mind's eye lying on his bunk in the dark. I know his eyes are wide open and he, like me, is looking up in the direction of the fan, recalling the more-ordered life that we left so long ago. There are few men we meet who are immediately kindred, but Andrew is one of them. He is young enough to be my son. Yet we seem ageless together. I was him then; he will be me soon enough. He shows the same awe that I once had for life, we share the same indefatigable curiosity about all things, we ask questions, we need to know why and why not. We think along similar lines but we do not think alike. We can communicate easily, and I suppose that is what makes two persons get along. We have the same cynical attitude about this UN relief mission, and although he has some previous experience, he is as surprised as I am by the fast-moving events and the uncertainty of our future here in Kismayo. I would call him a sidekick, to use a rather dated term, but he's more of a comrade-in-arms and a friend.

"Nairobi is a party town, you know," he says after a while.

"I hadn't heard. I saw a riot the day I was there. I heard people call the place Nai-robbery."

He laughs freely. "Not far from the truth. Nairobi didn't have a party business, so I was trying to put it together. But it was difficult. The people here are the last to come around."

"The white Kenyans?"

"Certainly the white Kenyans. Fifth-generation Rule Britannia, still mired in the colonial days. Some are no more worldly than Welsh coal miners—some have never left Kenya. Never want to. I should have realized that just because something works in England doesn't mean it will work in Africa."

It is quiet. There is only the soft whir of the fan over the report of a single gunshot.

"The rich black Africans first look at how the Europeans do it, whether it is accepted by the Europeans, before doing anything on their own. They are really our market. And they do like to party."

"So why aren't you back partying?"

"*Shifta*. Somali bandits broke into my flat, tied me and my girlfriend, threatened to cut us up, stole all the equipment, the compressors, the helium bottles, even the clown suits."

"You get hurt?"

"No, but Jill was in therapy for a few months. Pretty horrific, actually. We didn't know what they were going to do to us."

"So that's the end of the party business?"

"Absolutely not!" I hear the grin in his voice. "Make some money here and go back and start it right this time. But, bloody oath, if I ever see anyone walking the streets of Nairobi dressed as a clown . . ."

* * *

LATER, when we both might have been sleeping: "You miss your lady?"

Silence. There is no one starting this conversation; either one of us said it first.

"Feeling guilty?"

"Yes. You?"

"Yes. I'm surprised. Haven't had much time to miss her. You?"

"Been too busy."

"And scared."

"Yeah, scared. You hear those last shots? Pretty close."

"Hope they weren't in the compound."

"Outside, I think. I wouldn't have thought about feeling guilty. But I guess I do. We're pretty close. Surprised I don't miss her."

"Same here. I haven't had much time to think about anything but what I'm doing here. And avoiding these stray bullets."

"You wonder if they think about us. And what they're doing. You write yours what it's really like?"

"Some of it."
"Not enough to worry them."
"No, but just enough."
"Yes, just enough. Good night."
"Night."

9.

Suffer the Little Children

MY Somali minders and I sit in a row on the edge of the pier like serried crows on a high wire. It is hot. I have no energy and not much desire to do anything constructive—for what purpose? There is some gunfire from somewhere across the water. Gunfire has become akin to chronic pain—I am not aware of it anymore; I am just too exhausted to be impressed. These events that approach us, slam into us helter-skelter, have a cauterizing effect. I know what is lacking: time to breathe, time for reflection. I can forget about being a journalist—that went out the window not long after our arrival. I have become involved, not the way I expected, but involved. My nerves are raw and at the same time I feel dulled. I play out a role in this Dantesque set piece while constantly staying alert that I don't walk into someone's bullet, yet maybe—maybe not much caring if I do. I wonder if aid workers elsewhere experience this ineluctable ambivalence toward survival. Any one of the events here would make an indelible, possibly traumatic mark in its singularity, but cumulatively, they blend into one continuous and barely manageable bad dream. Perhaps that is healthy.

There was another problem at the airport earlier today, one that might be the final straw. Another Somali/UN misunderstanding. When the UN is in town everyone is supposed to get rich. When they don't, it is a misunderstanding. Baudelaire had it right: The world revolves on misunderstanding. The Somalis live off it.

From their lofty perch in Nairobi and for reasons unknown to us, the brains at Unicef are arranging to use an old American DC-707 to airlift supplies into Kismayo, much of which I, and whoever else is sent to drive the boats, will be delivering upriver. With its four engines and huge wingspan, a landing at our forlorn little international airport seems improbable. Andrew has asked Nairobi to arrange for the use of the less expensive, more compact Russian-built Anotov, which can carry nearly as big a payload. I remember seeing it on the tarmac in Nairobi, large and silent, apparently just awaiting orders.

For motives political or otherwise—the Anotov is the Ukrainian contribution to this alleged flood emergency—Unicef remains firm on its decision. However, before the great white American elephant can land, all the thorn trees and bush have to be cleared away from the sides of the landing strip, because its giant wings will extend well out over the scrub. General Morgan was given the $700 contract, and he ordered his militia to get it done. His militia has "subcontracted" their Bantu slaves to do the work at gunpoint while they sit in the shade of the airport warehouse, chewing *miraa*.

The work started three days ago, yet only ten percent of the bush has been cleared and now Morgan's militia is demanding payment. Bravo Delta and Alpha Kilo won't have any of it and refuse to pay until the job is completed. The militia is mad.

If this is not trouble enough, the *miraa* plane is overdue. Kismayo waits in the noonday heat and it is a dangerous time.

Some garbled voices overriding one another in the one-way traffic roll out of the radio.

"Negative copy, whoever is transmitting," Bravo Delta says.

"This is Sierra Sierra. I repeat, we are being held inside the airport by a Technical." It sounds as if he is taking it in his stride.

"So what's new?"

Another voice announces: "I also got a Technical holding me

outside the terminal." It is Mwalimo. "That gun is pointing through the windscreen at me!"

"Shit," Sierra Sierra says. "Looks like we may have a 'security situation' here," words that indicate that either kidnapping or shooting is possible.

I look down at one boat crammed with emergency rations and water. She's topped up and ready to go, and I wonder if there is anything I've missed. The sleek little craft, which I am grudgingly beginning to accept, dances upon the harbor chop, pulling at its restraining lines like a horse at the post.

The radio, usually busy with requests for transportation, inquiries about rotation schedules, arrangements of meetings, goes unusually quiet. Waiting for the invitation to a poker game, I seek shelter from an unrelenting sun in the shade of the guardhouse with some of the militiamen. I ask one of the young soldiers if I may hold his assault rifle. It is a daring move, but the lad proudly hands it over.

The stock is wood and not plastic, an indication that it is an older model. There are scratchy whittlings of stars, an Islamic crescent, and a few things in Arabic carved crudely into the wood. It is universal; in the West, schoolchildren creatively deface their schoolbooks, desks, school bags, walls, and even subway trains with personal totems, brands, and markings. Here in Somalia they disfigure their guns.

Frustrated, bored, and a bit out of sorts, I tire of waiting for word of a poker game and I decide to return to the Unicef compound.

At the port's main gate, the militia soldiers stoop to window level to inspect those within the UN rig; with *qat*-stained grins, they return my thumbs-up and shout, *"Diep maleh!"* and wave us through.

The last barricade before entering town is more formidable than the others, more solid than the one at the airport; razor wire, steel girders, and a scattering of heavy artillery casings block the laterite road. The roadblock appears unmanned. Anything out of the usual fires the adrenaline, and this unmanned roadblock is unusual.

Harun honks impatiently. I sense my guards tighten.

There is some movement in the shadows of the portal of the cement blockhouse. A little boy not more than ten years old emerges from out of the darkness and marches toward the car, cradling an AK-47. He wears a full-length yellow smock, torn at the shoulder; the rip exposes his brown baby skin. His clean round face and his soft eyes display that precious naïveté of youth—he looks like a nice kid.

With a charming attempt to snarl he orders us out of the car. My guards and Harun look at one another and laugh. A sudden black cloud of anger twists his little-boy face; his small soft eyes narrow with the petulance of a child who is not getting his way. He is not going to be humiliated. And he has a gun.

He steps up closer. He jabs his rifle into Harun's face; the barrel presses the flesh of his cheek. Harun secretly reaches for the door handle. The boy realizes he is vulnerable and backs away. His gun is leveled at the driver's head. He has been trained. The boy squeaks something in Somali, and Harun shuts off the car's engine. Sweat begins to form on my unshaven face.

With measured calm that underscores the danger, Harun tells the boy to stop horsing around and let us pass. He is still not quite sure whether to take this kid seriously.

The child soldier responds: He jerks back the stiff cocking spring of his rifle with his small fist; the final, cold metallic clack defines the moment. Although the proud Somalis have hair-trigger tempers, it often does not get this far; much of the gun-toting is posturing. When a Somali cocks his gun, however, the talking has usually ended—it is the penultimate act.

The boy is staring at Harun with the sort of face seldom seen. This is not the face of a little boy in the throes of a temper tantrum but a face we create in the latter stages of a nightmare when our imagination conjures the unimaginable: the innocent face of a beautiful child that is suddenly masked by the contorted, out-of-control fury of an old man. The frightening combination of the two challenges the senses—he is just a child and I still see a child and I do not want to take all this seriously. Yet his finger is firmly on the trigger and I know there is nothing to stop him from firing the gun. An expression, a noise, something within the boy himself could do it.

My guards in the car are no longer laughing. This armed gamin is more dangerous than any adult. He has no fear of death, doesn't even know what fear or death are. Here in this forgotten land, torn by years of lawlessness and civil war, death is commonplace and of passing little consequence. Except for a tear or two from a loved one, memories of the dead are often discarded.

For a moment I see myself as a child standing tall on a mound of dirt with a make-believe gun, and I wonder if there is any difference between us playing cops and robbers as children and pretending we can kill and this kid with a real gun who knows he can. At his age, there can be little distinction between fantasy and real life, between pretending to die and dying. Because civil war, anarchy, and instant killing are all he has known since he was born, is he not doing something quite natural? For him, childhood is not something he will ever experience. I still feel the baby in my arms. This boy could have been him some years ago, and inside I weep for the futility; this boy should not have a gun in his hands but a future. My compassion for this tough little boy with the gun has no limits and I want to get out, offer my hand, play ball with him, do something normal.

An audience begins to gather under the tin roof of the guardhouse. Dressed in white robes, men and boys drift from out of the shadows, dusty apparitions who watch in silence. This is quite a performance, and the elders, some on canes, with faces toothless and puckered, impassively observe the youngster's moves. The boy feels the audience, and the attention seems to strengthen his resolve.

The fear of my guards is palpable—there is a smell to it. Fingers on triggers, they have lowered their guns toward the mob of indifferent silent ghosts. I share that fear: There is going to be a shooting here. Someone shouts from the side—encouraging the boy to shoot, I presume.

I take my eyes off the boy, hoping that without my interest the situation will somehow defuse itself; this is, after all, between Harun and the boy—not my problem. I am with the United Nations. I have a good humanitarian reason to be here. The boy probably doesn't even see me in the back, squeezed as I am between my two guards. I grind deeper into the seat, a little more behind the fuzzy head on my left. Bloody hell, the guard senses what I've just done and he shifts his position, exposing me even more.

The child straightens. Slowly he swings his gun toward me. I stop breathing. He looks me up and down with a sneer of inexplicable contempt. Small dark eyes blaze with anger, focus, and lock on mine. He ignores the others. Something is getting personal here. He raises his assault rifle to my face. Bile rises in my throat. I am fixed by his eyes, eyes I cannot contact. I sense that if I look away he will fire. My eyes tear; I can no longer see his face. It becomes a blur behind the hole of the barrel of his gun. It is just a small black circle, and it is the most frightening thing I have ever seen. I am transfixed by this cavernous dark hole. I can almost fall through it. Beyond, I am aware of the unfocused image of this boy's hate-filled face. Where could a child learn such hatred? My heart sledges so hard I can't get a breath. Time is frozen, dead, meaningless. The arrogance and the insanity in the child's eyes tell me he is considering shooting. I wonder if it is as easy for him as it looks, just squeeze the trigger. I sense within myself a certain discarnate resignation taking over, controlling my panic, resignation to my death. I am shaking.

Someone bellows orders from the crowd. The child with the big gun frowns in response to the voice. An old man in a dirty white djellaba and a woven Muslim cap, his squinty sun-beaten face deeply creased, raises his cane and barks in Arabic at the boy.

The child momentarily wavers, then straightens. He is not going to back down. He stands firm in a man's role. This is his roadblock.

The old man mutters, spits out a leafy slurry of *qat,* hobbles out to the proud little sentry, grabs him by the ear, and hauls him away. The child drags his big gun behind him.

* * *

IT is this monstrous little creature, obedient, easily brainwashed, malleable, who kills most relief workers.

There are three hundred thousand children under the age of eighteen fighting in thirty armed conflicts around the world. In Afghanistan, as well as in Somalia, thirty to forty-five percent of the soldiers are children. In Ethiopia, Uganda, and El Salvador, almost a third of the child soldiers are reported to be girls. Considered a renewable resource, children have become classic cannon fodder.

Recruitment is simple. A warlord's militia or a marauding rebel force elsewhere enters a village and slaughters wholesale those adults they suspect of sympathizing with the enemy. They are often careful to avoid killing boys and girls. The children, many of whom have seen their parents massacred, are abducted and moved to special training camps. Boys are turned into soldiers and girls frequently are used as sex slaves for the local military commanders.

Children from four to fourteen are the best soldiers. They are easily trained, they don't ask a lot of questions, they are less demanding, their notions of right and wrong are easily manipulated, they obey their elders, who themselves may be veterans of only fourteen or fifteen years old, they don't know the effect of killing, they are inexpensive to maintain because they eat less, and they can easily be turned into killing machines through drugs, alcohol, and sheer fear. In Burma they are told that if they cry during a battle, they will be shot. In Sierra Leone, child soldiers were made to believe in magic; just before an ambush they were assured by their commanders that *juju* would protect them and stop enemy bullets.

Arming them is no problem. The ubiquitous Kalashnikov is so light and simple that it is a perfect child's toy.

At an age when children should be playing games and going to school, they are roaming deserts, city streets, and jungles as humanity's most vicious soldiers. More often than not, they are placed closest to the front. In Guatemala, children have been sent into minefields ahead of advancing older troops. Some children, according to Human Rights Watch, have been used for suicide missions. During the civil war in the Congo, children not quite in their teens were forced into acts of cannibalism. In Sierra Leone, child soldiers of the Revolutionary United Front, under orders from adults, systematically cut off the limbs of villagers suspected of favoring the government. Ibrahim, a child fighting for the RUF rebels since he was eight, admitted during an interview that he drank human blood every morning for breakfast—like coffee:

"When I go to war front, you know, I join a group. Yes, because I was staying with the Zebra Battalion, so our battalion do a lot of things, drinking human blood before going to front. That is my coffee I take in the morning. In the first battle, they gave us blood to drink. . . . It gives us mind to fight more. It tempts us to kill people . . . sometimes for a day, I kill more than five.

"My boys, they are afraid of me because whenever I am with my pistol, sometimes I shoot anything. Like we are sitting down talking, you know, and they want to bring something up. I just shoot and you die. Yeah, maybe sometimes I just see something that is strangeful to me and I say this, I want to kill this person." Proudly, he added he was called General Bloodshed.

There is no dealing with this sort of insanity. I saw in the boy's eyes at the barricade that he could pull the trigger for reasons that I am too old to understand. Age gives us the ability to reason, to communicate, and these children behind the guns, who have no fear, prove to be well beyond our ability to do either.

There is not much the international community can do effectively to prevent use of these cruelest combatants. It did finally create the UN Convention on the Rights of the Child in 2000, which banned the use of soldiers under the age of eighteen in hostilities. It does allow countries to accept voluntary recruits as young as sixteen with certain safeguards, including parental permission.

Britain ratified what is called the Optional Protocol to the Convention, but the Ministry of Defense said it would continue to recruit fifteen-year-olds despite the prohibition against recruiting anyone under the age of eighteen. At present more than a third of the recruits of the UK armed forces are below this age. The deployment of seventeen-year-old soldiers during the 1991 Gulf War and the Kosovo conflict led human-rights groups to compare MoD policy to that of Third World countries. According to one report, an unspecified number of Forty-Five Commando, which joined the U.S.-led attacks on the Taliban in Afghanistan in 2001–2002, were withdrawn because they were under the age of eighteen.

The United States, which has about three thousand seventeen-year-olds serving in the armed forces with their parents' permission, initially opposed the treaty (so did Somalia when it had a government). The U.S. sent seventeen-year-old troops into armed conflict in Somalia, Bosnia, and the first Gulf War. The Pentagon agreed finally to take "all feasible measures" to ensure that seventeen-year-olds do not directly participate in hostilities. It was the first time the United States has ever agreed to change its practices in support of a human-rights standard.

Nations also are required to cooperate in the demobilization, rehabilitation, and reintegration of child soldiers to their communities. Since many of these children were forced to commit atrocities against their own families or neighbors, this is no easy task. Indeed, the crimes of these children are often so heinous that their families and communities refuse to accept them back. Eric Beauchemin, an expert on child soldiers in Sierra Leone and Liberia, who has had his own confrontations with armed children, said many of those he spoke to were forced to watch or take part in the murder, amputation, or rape of their parents, family members, or neighbors.

Sixteen-year-old General Bloodshed wants to go home, go to school, find his lost innocence. He says he wants to repay his debt to his village, where, he admits, he burned all the houses. General Bloodshed says he wants to become a minister "because I want to do God's work." Probably the best the world can hope for is that

General Bloodshed and others like him simply discover an unknown childhood.

As for the tough little boy at the barricade, I can only hope he has put down the gun. But nothing changes in Somalia, and I suspect he may well be dead.

10.

Yo Ho Ho and a Sprig of Qat

THERE was another near miss earlier this morning, not from a bullet but from Nature herself. I was sitting on my bunk after the ritual cold shower and had begun to slip on my work boots. Andrew interrupted my still-unformed thoughts with an announcement that he had asked the pilot of the Cessna Caravan, one of the smaller cargo rotations that occasionally stops here, to drop off a case of beer.

"Well, hot damn!" My boot slipped out of my hands onto the cement floor, and from out of the overturned shoe crawled a three inch scorpion. Its lethal arrowhead tail, curved back over itself, weaved from side to side, looking like it desperately needed to sink its stinger into some warm meat.

I picked up the other boot and began the swing that would conclude its existence. Pausing in midair, I tossed the boot aside, worked a newspaper under the hapless critter, and flicked it out the broken window.

* * *

FOR some reason, I feel that this is going to be a very fine day—a day when nothing extraordinary occurs. I go to work, I get a job done, I return, and if Andrew works miracles, we sink into a few cold beers in the evening. I am in a terrific mood.

After climbing into the rig, Harun pushes a tape into the

dashboard radio, turns, and offers me a fresh *mswaki* stick—is this a message? The squeal from the rusted-metal-coated cassette tape combined with the discordant Arabic melody is difficult at this early hour, and Harun, seeing me wince, turns it down to a lesser pain.

Isa has replaced one of the backseat boys, and he sits in silence next to me with the cataleptic immobility of a palace guard, his hands clutching the barrel of his Kalashnikov between his knees. I wonder what has become of the previous guard—this was good money for him. I don't ask.

We pile out at the warehouses. Isa walks toward the high grass, unzipping his fly, while the others and I head toward the line of rusting shipping containers on the wharf.

My task today is to prepare a jetty at the far end of the port to accommodate my two boats and possibly others that will be flown in. I need wire rope to string tractor tires together for fenders over the pier wall.

At midday, the hard white heat becomes insufferable. Finding shade next to a container, I sit on some cement blocks on the pier and begin to splice the wire. I work alone while Chaco, the silent mobile-crane operator with a round face under an old sweat-stained fedora (I had thought my father, an old "newspaperman," was the last on earth to wear a fedora), uncoils more cable a few yards away. Isa and the other port security men and a lone guard in the blue pajamas sit nearby, finger-eating bowls of rice. The slow-moving Unicef guard is officially assigned as my personal protector, but past experience has shown that the Unicef boys—unless confronted by unarmed demonstrators—are harmless; they collect their money and disappear at the first sound of someone else's gunfire.

A large gray trawler, otter doors hanging brokenly over its rusting deck, lists against the dockside in a state of decay. The name on the bow is covered over by a hasty slash of white paint, but her home port, welded on the transom, is clearly visible: Bergen. Why a Norwegian boat has been fishing off this dangerous pirate-infested coast is anybody's guess.

A coastal tanker, tied up and leaning against the wharf in front of the boat, appears even more derelict. The pier is a buttress, and were it not for its support, the ship would roll over and capsize. It is evident that there has been some effort to change the vessel's identity. The Somali flag, a white star against a baby blue background, has been freshly painted on the funnel, but the paint job on the rust-streaked black hull has been only partially completed. The painters either ran out of paint, out of money, or out of hope.

"Captain!" one of the guards yells at me. "You sit on mosque! Please, Captain!"

I rise quickly. Their makeshift mosque is merely an outline of cement blocks. I was squatting on the apse that faces north by northeast in the general direction of Mecca.

A little embarrassed, I wander over to the fishing boat, swing my legs over the gunnels onto the deck, and climb the ladder to the bridge. The Unicef guard follows. She was once a fine vessel—Furuno radar, joystick controls, forward-looking fish sonar, weather fax, video screen for deck operations, and GPS.

"Pirate," the Unicef guard announces.

"This ship, taken by pirates?"

"Some months past."

The sixteen-hundred-mile shipping route along this coast, the length of the U.S. West Coast, is one of the most active areas in the world for piracy. While the swashbuckling days of Blackbeard, Captain Morgan, and Captain Kidd are legend, piracy is all too real to the hundreds of seafaring men and women who have been injured or have lost their lives in battles with modern-day pirates. Warlords with radar and fast boats lie in wait on the coast and dispatch their militia to ambush passing unsuspecting vessels. Every type of vessel is vulnerable—fishing boats, cargo vessels, even sailboats. Recently a Finnish couple on their sailboat was attacked by gunmen of the Somali Salvation Democratic Front. They were released after ransom was paid, but their proud little boat became the personal yacht of the warlord.

More recently, the International Maritime Bureau of the International Chamber of Commerce, which keeps track of such things, reported one incident in their quarterly assessment of the crime:

> Cyprus registered Bulk Carrier M/V Trader. 12:00N, 051:30E, off Socotra Island, Somalia. While underway, four speedboats with four pirates armed with high-powered guns in each boat chased the ship. Despite taking evasive measures, four pirates managed to board forward and attempted to enter accommodation. Crewmembers using fire hoses, rocket flares and iron bars fought the pirates and prevented the pirates from entering accommodation.

This was one of 297 reported pirate attacks in 1997, an increase of 400 percent over the total ten years before.

It is not hard to imagine the fear of these civilian crew members on this fishing boat, armed only with pipe cheaters, wrenches, and a few fire extinguishers as they fought for their lives and their ship. Standing on the bridge of this luckless trawler, I am struck by the similarities—unarmed crew members, unarmed relief workers just doing their jobs, never expecting that their lives are in the hands of madmen; in Somalia, the thugs are the same.

There are two other vessels here in port, both large Arab dhows, traditional cargo vessels that have for centuries traded between the Arabian Peninsula and East Africa. Sailing ships such as these transported the sub-Saharan slaves to the Persian Gulf from ports in Kenya and Tanzania and ran the spice trade from Zanzibar. These dhows, about ninety feet long, have forsaken their beautiful lateen rigs for large high-capacity diesel engines.

Tied to the far end of the wharf, the boats appear oddly distant and remote. Somnambulant crewmen on one boat, dressed in white djellabas that are darkened with soot, stretch out atop leaking sacks of charcoal. The ship represents Kismayo's primary commerce with the outside world, importing maize meal and flour and returning to Saudi Arabia and other Arab states with charcoal, a fuel vital to Arab cooking. The commerce of Somalia's "black gold" made from hundred-year-old acacia trees has resulted in nearly complete deforestation of once forest-rich areas along the southern and middle Jubba.

The second dhow, its wood sides painted with fancy Arabic scrollwork in green, red, black, and yellow, is tied even further away. This is no charcoal boat and may well represent a commerce of less legitimacy; it looks sleek, its bow less flared and its deck clear of anything but crew busy off-loading wooden crates about six feet long, eighteen inches high. The crewmen of this boat are dressed in shorts and T-shirts, look younger and more fit, almost military. They work efficiently, using the boom as a crane to lift the crates out of the hold onto the wharf. A few guards stand casually off to the side, smoking, their rifles slung over their shoulders, while an older bearded man in a clean white robe who doesn't look Somali at all directs the off-loading. I wonder whose militia this is?

Returning to my cable-splicing on the wharf, I feel a wind of commotion behind us. I turn slowly. You learn never to make any sudden movements. Three young gunmen are running toward us, screaming, waving their assault rifles in the air, like the final charge. The port guards jump to their feet and wait for whatever will happen next.

A couple of rifle lengths away, the boys peel off to the right toward the fishing boat. They look like they are just having fun.

The guards drop their bowls with a clatter and order them to stop.

The gunmen jump onto the deck of the fishing boat and laugh obscenities back. One of the guards grabs his Kalashnikov, slams back the cocking spring, and, in hip-shot Rambo fashion, fires into the air. This damn well changes the mood.

The three on the boat stop in their tracks, swing around, and point their guns at us. The young leader, the tallest boy, with a thin black mustache and a pock-dented face, notices me. He smiles—a big, friendly, *qat*-stained grin, as if he was recognizing an old friend. Stupidly, I find myself smiling back. But there is no friendship in his eyes. His look taunts and it seems now less of a grin than a smirk, a boastful challenge. I try to read his face but I cannot. I do understand his rifle that is pointed in our direction.

I experience an emotional absence, a distance between another gun and me. This is serious but I am not frightened; whether from near burnout from fear past or simply because there are the guards, I stand, watch, wait. I sense more than hear the metallic clacking, a muted sound so far away: Now all the guns are cocked.

A curtain slides in front of me. Instead of the boy's big gun and his vacuous and stupid expression, there is only the back of a floppy palm-frond hat and a long black neck. Isa has edged in front of me, his rifle pointed at the leader.

He mutters something to me in Somali, but I do not move. Isa growls something angrily that jerks me back to the living, and I find myself backing to the rear of a nearby shipping container. The container—my shield—sits alone on the middle of the wharf, so I can get no further away without exposing myself as a target. I crunch down like a beaten old hunchback, waiting for the gunshots, wondering why that boy was smiling at me.

Rifles on both sides are loaded, cocked, safeties off. There are four guns on our side, three on theirs. None has taken cover; the gunmen face each other at point-blank range. There is no apparent thought of cooling down. These men are ready to kill one another. It is a matter of Somali arrogance. My side certainly will not back down. Their job is to guard the port and they are ready to die doing so.

It becomes very still. Minutes pass. The vindictive sun presses its heat down upon us as condemnation of this face-off between egos. Someone mutters some indecipherable words and slowly, grudgingly, in a posture that can define only defeat, the three young gunmen, winding up to speed, storm past my container, laughing a little too loudly—an ill-concealed effort to hide their wounded pride. But they are still armed. Apparently, nobody disarms anyone here, no matter what the offense.

The Unicef blue pajama, who had disappeared during the confrontation, later explains that the boys were members of the subclan militia that had pirated the boat off the coast. They claimed they had heard someone was trying to steal it, so they came down to investigate. Probably they just wanted to chew some *qat* aboard the boat on a peaceful afternoon at the port. Isa turns to me and, with a big dark smile, offers me his open palm—the start of a high-five.

A UN rig pulls up to the warehouse, delivering a short, boxy man in full black beard, dark eyes, and a heavy Scottish accent.

"Juliet Bravo?" he asks. "Mike Dunne. I am going to put an HF radio on one of your boats."

"I'll be damned. Didn't think anybody heard me back there. I didn't think I would ever see the day."

"Well, they're not here yet. I want to see what your setup is on the boats and I'll bring one back from Nairobi in a few days."

Mike Dunne, a former electronics expert on Amoco's North Sea oil rigs and just back from Kosovo, where he and others hooked up communications for the UN peacekeeping forces, is eager to get the job done and just as eager to get out of Somalia. "Not many worse places than this," he says. I shrug, say I wouldn't know, this is my first relief job. Sitting on the boat while he checks the electrical connections and takes measurements, I tell him of the most recent incident.

"Shite!" He looks at me strangely and I look back, puzzled.

"Almost getting used to seeing a gun pointed at me."

"You should never get used to it. Are you crazy?"

I am not sure if he is being critical or sympathetic.

"You know, in Kosovo, the WFP has started training to help people cope."

"Cope? I can cope."

"How do you know? You haven't left it yet. We all think we can handle it. If you are one in a million who is not affected by this shite, then you got something missing. No, you wait until you try to return to normal life. It is the withdrawal, mate, going home, trying to pick up where you left off. That is when you see yourself fucked. They say you are on your own in the field, but believe me, you are on your own when you go back home."

"I've never thought about any aftereffects."

"They get to you."

"What about yourself?"

"Not anymore. There wasn't training when I got in. Had to work it out myself. I'm in for the long haul—don't go home much. Anyway, that training, they call it Re-Entry Syndrome training. Maybe you should see if they got that R-E-S course in Nairobi."

"Yeah, well, I think I can handle it."

* * *

ON the trip back to the Unicef compound for the evening briefing, I cannot help but wonder whether these incidents, each weighted with such horrific portent, are really very unusual. We have not been here before, I have not been here before, these events never took place before, and yet how could they not? There are always standoffs with guns, always fights, always killing, and relief workers are there, living perhaps the most dangerous lives, and so nothing is unique. We could not have been warned what we would face out here. Perhaps a little better idea of the security situation, a briefing that went beyond crocs and hippos, might not have been amiss. However, had we been told, would we have been more prepared? Would it have made any difference?

The evening briefing covers the same ground: logistics, progress, negotiations, threats, camels for the dead, evacuation. Always evacuation. Is evacuation discussed as commonly wherever relief workers are stationed? I arrive after the others and too late for anyone to care how I spent my day. I was wondering what to report anyway. I don't really have anything to say, just another day at the docks—no casualties, only one shot fired.

Sierra Sierra makes several references to closing down the airport at 1400 hours tomorrow, and he instructs Alpha Kilo and Happy One: "I want you two to be on the morning flight to Garissa."

"We don't have to worry about Juliet Bravo," Happy One chirps. "He's got a boat."

"Huh? Sure I have a boat. What's this all about?"

"Oh, I guess he hasn't been briefed," Chet offers.

"Guess not. What's going on? We leaving?"

"Bravo Delta and myself will be at the airport negotiating with General Morgan, Major Yeh Yeh, and the others. I don't think there's much of a chance we can get this resolved—it got pretty heated this afternoon—but we are going to give it another try."

"What happened?"

"It is turning to shit, son. The sultan wants more camels and Morgan wants more money for the airport job. So, I'm sending Happy One and Alpha Kilo out on the Caravan flight to Garissa. That's two less I have to worry about."

"I really can't go, Chet," Happy One complains. "I've got to make sure those trucks make it to the refugee camps."

"Going to pull rank on you this time, Jeri. You do no good to them or to us dead. It was damn close today, and it might be a damn sight worse tomorrow. If we're lucky we'll be right back here in the evening in one piece, arranging for deliveries to the camps for the next day."

Jeri brushes hair off her forehead and sighs. "Yes, I suppose so."

That little sigh—that brief display of, what, femininity?—shakes the previous image. I still see her with hands on her hips, facing down the guns at the airport: her courage, her arrogance, her strength, larger than life—and dehumanized. She made herself then, a little dangerously perhaps, as impersonal as the gun. Yet she is a woman, quite appealing. Her shiny black hair and her firm mouth, her possibly good body and clear blue eyes—away from the stress of the war zone she is probably more than just attractive. But who could really know? Perhaps it is a comment on the febrile nature of our existence that we appear less human. Genderless. Sexless.

She and I have hardly spoken since that first day by the control tower. She looks up and meets my eyes. There is a sudden softness there. Maybe I just imagine it.

Mwalimo suggests the Hercules remain circling overhead during the meeting.

"Won't that be a little obvious?" Jeri asks. She is now hard and businesslike. "I don't know how they'd let us get on an airplane if the talks break down. Probably be held hostage."

"True. They don't want us here but they sure in hell won't let us leave," Chet says. "I am not sure we could sweet-talk our way onto a plane.

"And you," he points at me, "you'll have to ride herd at the port. We'll keep to our previous schedules. We don't want it to look like we're packing. That aerial-survey flight upriver you're planning in the morning? Go ahead and do it. If you get word of evacuation while you are airborne, then haul your ass up to Kenya. Otherwise, try to keep the flight under an hour, and then I want you back at the port, packed, and—if it comes to that—ready to meet whoever can get out to the pickup point. But, hell, that might not be anybody. In which case, just figure on saving your own butt. And don't worry, we'll get an aircraft out there to look for you."

It is a depressing trip back to our compound. Apparently the beer meant for us was mistakenly delivered to our colleagues in Jamaame, a village on the Jubba. There are little more than fumes remaining in my liter bottle of Kenya Cane. There is, however, dinner of a sort. As consultants on contract, Andrew and I each pay thirty dollars a day for our bunks and a staff, and an additional four or five dollars a day for food. None of which is reimbursed. A local Somali woman sweeps the floor, and we have a cook.

Our chef is a short Arab with orange-hennaed hair, who speaks only Italian and Somali. He walks stiffly with the gait of a marionette, proud in his stained and unwashed white apron. I suspect he is the one who tends to the herb plants along the walkways.

We are served the same provender day after day: goat, grease, and starch. Small pieces of lean, tough meat float in liquid fat. Goat has not got an unpleasant taste; in many parts of Africa it is billed as lamb. Ours is accompanied by potatoes, rice, and spaghetti, all mixed together in the same bowl, half submerged in liquid fat. The potatoes actually float. The sauce for the pasta is canned tomato paste with hot fat stirred in. The vegetables are always the same—limp zucchini and raw onions. Every night we pour the fat into the shrubbery. The shrubs are dying.

Permanent employees of the UN are not allowed onto the streets of Kismayo, and consultants are advised against it. Thus we will never be able to go out to buy our own food, much less check what our cook actually spends on the one meal he prepares. But there is little question that our man pockets most of the food money; when the UN is in town, he also gets rich. That, however, is not the problem. He can take what he wants as long as he feeds us decently. We would pay more.

I start to tell Andrew and Chet about the incident at the port but I find I cannot. Something stops me. Something inside is forcing me to ignore it. I make light of it, joke about pirate boys and swashbuckling buccaneers. Chet observes me with a strange clinical look that makes me feel foolish.

There is some movement in the negotiations in the murder of the pregnant woman. Each Unicef guard claims to have fired into the air, one a burp on automatic and the other a single round. Each denies the killing, but Sierra Sierra says there's no question of their guilt.

But he's pleased. The police, appointed lackeys of General Morgan, have discovered that the pregnant woman, interred immediately in the Islamic tradition, had never been autopsied. The documents that alleged she was pregnant were bogus, signed by a member of her family who forged the signature of the attending physician. The doctor says he never saw the papers, never examined the body.

"She wasn't even a little bit pregnant," Chet says. "Just another damn scam. They were looking for a few more camels."

It may not matter that we have discovered the deception. The woman's family and clan cannot lose face. If we reveal that we found out, it could be too late for evacuation. If we do not reveal the scam, the shooter's clan will react. We are again smack in the middle of it.

11.

Who Invited You Here?

ALPHA Kilo is to bring in the C-130 and organize the off-loading until 1400 hours, when the meeting with Morgan and the militia begins and the airport is shut down. I'm to hop on the early-morning delivery flight to the distribution center at the Marerey village airstrip on the Jubba—from what I'm told, just a cluster of tents on a dirt stretch in the middle of the floodwaters. Then, unloaded, we are to follow the river and search for a location for my base near Goob Weyn—ideally, an embankment, flat and wide at the top for tents and relief supplies, above a quiet backwater.

We drive to the airport with thoughts of escape very much on our minds, clutching our garbage bags of personal emergency gear—what those in the aid trade call the Quick Run Bag: passport, money, more beans, Snickers bars, GPS, and Jackie's photo, all that I need and want for escape either by air or by sea. We have accepted the possibility that everything else we brought to Somalia may have to be abandoned.

"It would save a lot of trouble if they just used the Anotov," Andrew says.

"Why don't they?"

"Haven't a clue." He laughs to himself and shakes his head. "Maybe they don't trust the Ukrainians. In '92, the WFP chartered a Russian Anotov to ferry in emergency supplies, but it brought in money and guns to one of the warlords instead. That caused a bit of a flap; the other warlords thought the UN was officially favoring one side over the other. It wasn't the last time. A few weeks later, another Anotov carrying guns for one of the warlords crashed north of Mog—so much for UN neutrality, eh? Somalis don't forget these things."

Beyond the first roadblock of surly riflemen, an old man in djellaba and full white beard is having a tug-of-war with an equally determined unruly camel, which is jerking the Arab back toward the thorn trees on the other side of the road. Barely able to hold on to the reins, the minder swats it angrily with a long reed whip. It looks like a brave act to me—the animal dwarfs him. The camel jerks away; its lofty head held high, its nostrils flared, it high-steps toward the bush with the grace of a Lipizzaner stallion. It appears to change its mind and wanders back toward our car as if curious about its occupants. Harun brakes hard. He dares not hit a camel, dares not get near it in case the animal hits us. Same thing.

The camel stands opposite, looks us over with imperious arrogance, and without warning rears up on its hind legs and aims its forefeet at the windscreen. I am fascinated by the brute power of this beast that rises above us. It is close enough to see the detail of its creamy underbelly—the hairs that are curled and matted in dung. It is a female. Harun backs away just as its hooves glance off the bumper and land where we were only moments ago.

The camel gallops off into the bush, and the Somali shakes his whip at us and shouts Arabic obscenitics. Harun inches forward. The animal bursts out of the tall grass and now dashes across our path to the other side of the road, apparently to where it wanted to go in the first place. The Somali gives chase, his long white skirt and his long white beard in pursuit.

Harun steps on the accelerator and roars away from the area, shaking his head in frustration.

We pull up to a high-wing single-engine cargo plane parked close to the warehouse. It apparently has just arrived; the heat from its engine radiates through the cowling in a shimmer of distorted air. A private near-childish excitement builds, then quickly conflates into unexpected dread. I do not like to fly.

It is the first time I have been back to the airport since picking up the boat. It is evident where the Hercules took a bite out of the warehouse; the hole and buckled wall have not been repaired, nor is there an indication that that will happen anytime soon. Nothing else seems to have changed, however. Except now, from the perspective of what seems a lifetime since, the blown-out cement walls and the broken windows are less curiosities than a depressing statement of the futility of our presence. As well as the efforts of anyone to come in the future. This wreckage of cement, glass, steel, and tin underscores a certainty that five or ten years from now, nothing will be any better for the Somalis than it is today.

A number of boxes are piled atop each other nearby, and I do a double-take when I see a large one with my name on it. I cannot deny that Christmas-like anticipation of what might be inside. Hydraulic fluid? GPS? Radios? I rip open the box, and inside, liter bottles of engine oil and—clothesline. I paw through the rope for more but there is nothing else. How can we do the job if we don't have the equipment? If pilots don't get what they need, they don't fly; if they don't supply me with what I need, why should I be any different?

"Not what you expected?" The pilot has been leaning against a wing strut in the shadows.

"Not exactly. That's all there is?"

"I suppose so. It's the load for Kismayo." I detect a Southern accent. He comes out from under the wing and introduces himself.

"You American?" I ask.

"From Elvis town. Memphis, on the Mississippi. I've seen a few floods before, believe me. You American?"

"Yep. And mail. Did you bring any mail?"

"Yeah, in the cockpit." He reaches in and grabs a few envelopes. "Any of these for you?"

There is nothing. "That's it?"

" 'Fraid so. . . . You know, I don't mind flying the river—these damn rotations bore the crap out of me." I hide my disappointment; I can't imagine the mail from Europe to here in Woop Woop being very reliable.

He looks like he is barely pushing twenty; his cherubic face does not instantly inspire confidence. Apparently anticipating a common thought: "Been flying Somalia ever since UNOSOM. Helped evacuate some of you guys from Mog a few years back. You get airsick?"

"Never have yet."

"Good."

Airborne, we fly northwest, looking for the river. The floodwaters stretch from horizon to horizon, and were it not for a few acacia and mango trees, banana stumps and small hummocks that break the surface, it would be impossible to determine its course. The Jubba has become a vast inland sea.

A narrow slice of land ahead rests upon the waters like a floating log. Marerey airfield, once miles from the river, is now in the middle of it. The floodwaters have claimed the northeastern end of the dirt runway, and it appears they will soon swallow it all. Touching down on the airstrip at the water's edge, the plane taxis to a scattered collection of various-size tents, cots under mosquito nets, mounds of bags of maize meal, flour, and rice, and boxes of high-energy biscuits covered in plastic stacked outside the largest tent. Evidently they are not short on supplies.

Disembarking from the plane in bright sunshine, I look for signs of the disaster, a *M*A*S*H* sort of clinic, some refugees, frantic activity to help the injured, save the dying. Instead, the place is remarkably serene, tranquil, almost sleepy. We are hailed by a voice from under a thick-leaf umbrella tree on a small island that is surrounded by pools of shallow water and mud. The tree provides some shelter for a large wood table, which supports a high-frequency radio connected to a car battery and solar panel propped against the back of a metal chair. Yusuf, a tall thin man with sharp Nilotic features and erect bearing, removes a pair of headphones and wades through the muck, greeting us halfway.

"You bring boats?" Yusuf, who runs the Somali nongovernmental organization that liaises with the local communities, looks over to the small aircraft. He has a cautious, aristocratic air. His dark, grave eyes do not mask his disappointment.

"Not yet, Yusuf. They're on their way. Just tarps, Unimix, emergency rations, and blankets."

"We must have boats," he says quietly. "Please, you look." He sweeps his hands toward the water. "Now we use these."

I don't see any boats. In the water under the spackled shade of the thorn trees, naked boys sit on thick pieces of Styrofoam, makeshift rafts that are strung together by rope and sticks. Their long, straight push-poles lean against the bushes.

"They don't look very stable."

"They are all we have. Insulation from refrigerator containers at the factory." He points to the remains of the once large and profitable sugar mill—bare steel girders that rise out of the haze in the distance and claw the air like the desperate hand of a drowning man.

"Destroyed by the floods?"

"No, by fighting—I have more than a ton to be delivered." He gestures toward the crates and sacks of supplies at the river's edge. "I lost a boy to a crocodile."

"Jesus. I'll see what I can do. My boats in Kismayo aren't doing you any good there."

"When? Tomorrow? After tomorrow?"

"I have no idea, Yusuf. I have been trying to get them going for days."

"We do not have much time left."

"I can see that."

Back in the aircraft, the Memphis cowboy is in his element. With an empty plane he can play.

"Never airsick, right?" he repeats.

"Nope."

"Swell. Then we'll get a real good look at the river."

We fly at five hundred feet, following what we perceive to be the course of the Jubba. Even from this altitude we can smell the stench that rises from the swamp below, the organic bitterness of methane gas. Scores of settlements are submerged, abandoned, left to the mercy of the flood. Other villages on higher ground are surrounded by stagnant brown water, and it is apparent that the river, still rising, is squeezing out the last of the dry land.

Desperate figures camped on fragile thatched roofs of their mud homes wave trousers, shirts, colorful cloths, anything they can get their hands on to attract our attention. Nearby, white humpback cattle huddle tightly on fragile, soggy islands. There will be no saving them. I push the waypoint button of the plane's GPS to record the location of the village. Here, finally, some reason, some purpose. My frustration in Kismayo was once self-centered. Today, redirected, it is even more acute, more aggravating. These are people who must have help now. Some of them probably will not be alive at this time tomorrow.

"Croc!" the pilot shouts above the roar of the engine. He points over the starboard side of the nose, pushes the plane into a shallow dive, and levels off just above the water. Slithering across a marshy area is a gnarled gray beast about twenty feet long, its tail scything the surface.

The guns and the threats and the tension of the past few days are fading into another world. Above the drone of the aircraft there is an unusual, merciful, and soothing silence building in my head, a silence I almost feel. Yet the port's towering container cranes sticking up out of the horizon remind me of what I have to return to.

"I want to check out Goob Weyn and Hum Hum close to the mouth," I shout.

The pilot nods.

"A couple of passes. And low!"

Thumbs up.

We skim over the trees close enough to see fat, ripening mangoes hanging among the branches.

Goob Weyn, atop a cliff near the mouth, is well above the floodwaters. It appears to be a muddy little settlement of dirt-colored wattle-and-thatch homes with an occasional cement building or two with metal roofs. A single tall spire of a mosque rises above the adobe shacks. Further down the river, just over the nose of the plane, is Hum Hum, a nest of small shacks on the river's sloping banks. There's a kink in the river here that forms a bight, a backwater in front of the settlement that looks like a possible delivery base.

A few soldiers look up at us and wave. The pilot dips his wings.

Small popcorn noises crackle over the drone of the engine; they come at once from both outside and inside the plane, like impatient fingers drumming a tabletop.

Off to the right on my side of the river, sparkles of a dozen fireflies light from the wooded banks below.

"They are shooting at us!"

With short jerky movements, I jab in the direction of the muzzle flashes under the mango trees.

The pilot hauls back on the stick with one hand and rams the throttle forward with the other, banks, and heads skyward. His eyes dart from gauge to gauge on the instrument panel.

We've been hit. A row of three clean holes the size of nickels appears on the leading edge of the aluminum wing overhead. The back of a passenger seat next to the window explodes in pieces of foam and shredded cloth.

"Damage! What's the damage!" the pilot yells.

"Shit, I don't know! They hit us back there. And on the wing." The pilot cranes his head and looks up at the wing. The aircraft, screaming for altitude, shudders. The stall buzzer begins an insistent steady warning.

"Fucking hell!"

"We going to make it?" I yell.

He turns to me with a look I hope never to see again from anyone else who is in command, a look of desperation that demands some solution. What do I know? I do feel that the aircraft is not entirely under his control. The sudden accelerated ascent seems to be more than the small plane can take.

"Good!" he shouts a few minutes later, leveling off. "We're out of range. Engine's okay! Fuel's okay! They got an aileron. But, hey, buddy! I got control!"

I hold on to the armrest of my seat with a death grip, willing, praying we get back. I hear the muffled voice of the pilot speaking into his mouthpiece to someone at Garissa. The pilot turns to me and tries to grin, tries to calm his terrified passenger. His reassuring demeanor is belied by the drops of sweat that run into his eyes and down his cheeks.

We bounce to a landing at Kismayo and taxi to the terminal. Mwalimo runs out of the building, followed by armed militiamen. "We heard on the radio," he says, shaking his head in dismay. "What do they say? Any landing you can walk away from . . ."

His good humor is welcome, but I can't respond. We walk around the plane, assessing the damage. There is a random hole or two underneath the fuselage. There is a hole on the passenger's side. I look into the cockpit. I see light through the hole from the outside. An inch or two to the left and the bullet would have gone up my backside.

It's only eight-thirty in the morning.

* * *

HAVING nearly been shot down has not really affected me, I don't think. I was not much fond of flying in the first place, sure in hell even less so after this morning. I am desperate to go to the port. There, for some reason, I feel I can return to some stability, something more ordinary. The port is mine. It has become a refuge.

Chaco, the grinning crane operator with his improbable gray felt hat, tries to tell me proudly in a mixture of Somali, Italian, and English that he has fixed his machine. I didn't know it was broken, but then, it wouldn't surprise me. There haven't been spare parts (except for a fan belt or two cannibalized from something else and resold) for anything around here since probably the beginning of the civil war. The two container cranes on the edge of the wharf that I could see from upriver, indispensable for port operations, have hung motionless and disused and frozen with rust for years. The windows of the cabs broken, the air conditioners looted, and the steel cables dangling from above like tears suspended. I don't see how these good people, dispirited by a generation of war and too much *miraa,* will ever make it. Chaco has a right to be proud, and with those twinkling eyes I think he looks to me for some praise. I have noticed that this kind of pride is not in short supply. The presence of pride is proof of accomplishment. There is hope.

In my little blue aluminum boat under the broiling sun, I move easily with the motion of the swells, awaiting announcement of the poker game over the handheld radio. I've had it—wouldn't be disappointed if it came within the next five minutes.

Odd. My vision is blurred. It is as if I am dreaming awake. I feel cold and clammy, dizzy. I begin to shake. It is a sort of distant feeling, out of body, feverish, and removed. I am not depressed, not feeling in any way emotional, rather detached—almost dead—with images. I sense a building pressure, a frisson of helplessness. I bury my head in my hands and cry. I vomit through my fingers and I don't give a fuck.

A faraway voice. "Captain." One of the militia gunmen is yelling down to me in Somali and asks me, I suppose, if I'm all right. It brings me around. My pride won't permit this public breakdown. The jetty above is lined with silent dark Somali faces. A face, a gun, a face, a gun.

Dipping a plastic bucket into the sea, I dump it over my head, then sluice down the soiled cockpit of the boat. Leaning against the back bench, I pull my soggy baseball cap over my eyes and try to shut out the world. I am not sure what I see: a baby, a gun, a river, a crocodile, a blinding sun that burns through my closed eyes—all unfocused fast-moving images, each superimposed upon the other; I am looking down a barrel of kaleidoscopic horror. The high-pitched scream in my ears is painful. I am in panic, out of control, no hands on the wheel, no feet on the ground, extracted. A panic I've never known.

Somebody takes my hand, holds it tenderly. Harun sits next to me, saying nothing, staring out into the bay. I am furious! I jerk my hand, but he holds on. The sympathy on his craggy pocked face and his broken-tooth smile defeats me. I want to bury my head in his shoulder. I can only offer a weak and embarrassed smile.

"Ah, Captain *Diep Maleh,*" he says soothingly. "Now you have some problems."

I sit up, push my hat back. "Small problems," I manage, withdrawing my hand naturally. He waits for an explanation. "Thank you, Harun. I'm okay." I cannot meet his eyes and I look back at the bay. His sympathy oppresses. I force myself a new face, a new meaning, and I turn to him, belligerence in my voice: "I don't have the problems. This godforsaken land has got the problems. Aren't you tired of all this shit?"

He looks startled, offended, as if I had just displayed appalling bad manners.

"I mean the killing, the dying, the war."

He softens. "Yes, Captain. Somalia has gone to the end. One day we come back."

"Fat fucking chance," I mutter. I look into Harun's soft and sympathetic eyes; it is not his fault. I see he is waiting, either for a further outburst or a breakdown, I'm not sure which. "Such a fucking waste."

"Peace must come, Captain. No land live this way forever."

"I don't know how you live this way at all. Great place to raise a family. By the way," I say, finding another topic, "your mother and father—they live with you?"

"Mother and father killed."

"Oh, shit." It is hard to run into an answer like this, but Harun says it so matter-of-factly, almost dismissively, that any lingering pain is either long gone or well hidden.

"I live with wife—good wife, good rich wife." It is a subject change, and I don't know if it is because the discussion is getting too personal or too complicated but I am grateful for the detour. "Her family has many camels."

"Here? In Kismayo?"

"Wife in Kismayo, camels in Wajir—Kenya."

"Is she Kenyan?"

"Oh, no! She is Somali." I can see that while he speaks he is observing me carefully. I am determined that he should see me as normal. "My wife, she is from Somali land in Kenya." He pauses, catching a random thought.

"Maybe you come to my home. We have *nyama choma*—you like *nyama choma*?"

"Sure."

"Yes, you come to my home one day soon. Eat with me. *Inshah Allah*."

"Yes, I'd like that."

He holds up a stalk of *miraa,* selects a tender young leaf with the eye of a connoisseur, and places it reverently into his mouth.

"I like you, Captain."

I don't know how to respond.

"You are a friend of Somalia." He pauses. "Well, you are my friend. But, Captain? So many problems, so many war. Why you here?"

"To bring food to flood victims, Harun." It's a mechanical response.

"That is good. Yes, that is good. But why? Why the United Nations again in my country?"

"To help the people."

"But who asked UN to come to Somalia? We have government now?"

"No, not yet, Harun. I don't know who asked us to come here. I wonder that myself."

"One day, Captain, I know. I know you go from us. You never come back."

He leans back and stretches his arms on either side of the bench and looks up at the building clouds. We may get rain this afternoon. Maybe that will help. He offers me a couple of choice young leaves. My mouth puckers from the bitter taste.

"We have always floods. We have always war. We have always needed food. I am happy you are here," he says, leaning toward me. "I make money, so I am happy. But I don't understand, Captain. Why are you here?"

"Goddamn it! I told you, to feed the people."

"No, Captain." His tone is now none too friendly. "You—why *you* here? You have wife. You have children. What you doing in my country?" I sense the guards above watching closely.

I look sharply at this guy; what fucking right has he got to be asking? I see my hostility reflected in his eyes. I run my fingers through my hair and take a deep breath and spit the slurry of leaves overboard. His simple coarse face, his dark eyes—I suddenly feel an affection for the man. He doesn't need a psychologist to explain things to him, he only wants a straight answer. I take his hand. This gesture seems to soothe him and I watch the fire in his own eyes diminish.

"Harun, I ask myself that. I guess it is in my history to be here. Considering my own past, it doesn't surprise me."

I see now that I have lost him—it was a straight question that sought a simple answer.

"You make big money?" he asks.

"I make money, yes."

There is a moment of silence. He is considering. "Ah," he says.

"Juliet Bravo! Juliet Bravo! Sierra Sierra." This is it. I hope this is it. I want to get out of here—take this baby and fly! I look the boat over; it is as ready as I can make it. I grab the radio from my belt.

"Juliet Bravo, back."

"Yeah, Juliet Bravo. Problem taken care of at this end. You might as well stand down."

12.
I Will Not Drop Blood

THE meeting at the airport lasted all of a half hour, a hail-fellow-well-met sort of thing. Chet announces at the morning briefing that during an uncharacteristic display of humility and candor, General Morgan admitted that his men hadn't realized what a big job clearing the brush would be; working under the scorching sun, the warlord said, his men were exhausted. Because there is a local Somali liaison man at our briefing, Sierra Sierra offers that statement without comment. Everyone knows who is really doing the work. Morgan wants another hundred dollars to finish the contract. Sloane agreed, but only if the general's men also paint a white line down the middle of the runway.

Brian hands our resident soldier a map of the Jubba River, torn out of a *National Geographic* magazine, and points to where he thinks we could base the riverboats. Apparently my experience at five hundred feet hasn't taken. He still insists on Hum Hum and, as an aside, assures me that when the time comes to set up camp, the warlords will have agreed and peace will reign over the Jubba Valley. I bite my tongue.

With movement that perhaps only I detect, Chet extends the map to arm's length, trying not to squint. I recognize the symptoms. Chet can't quite read the writing and can't find the village we're talking about. I'll be damned, the old soldier needs reading glasses!

I'm reluctant to offer mine; I don't suppose Chet would appreciate my help, and it would reveal to the others that I also wear them.

Brian is saying that he and Chet will have a final meeting with the elders at Goob Weyn later in the morning. He turns to me and, with his tic working overtime, announces that I am definitely going upriver, up to Hum Hum and Goob Weyn—this afternoon. It's the verdict I was hoping never to hear.

"That's where I got shot at," I say quietly. It is time I reminded him.

"Yes, but you were in the air. It was our fault, I suppose. We should have gotten word out that you were doing an overflight," he concedes. "But now you'll be on a boat. They will know you are coming. And why."

"I hear that's enemy territory."

"It is only enemy territory to General Morgan," Chet comments. "Still . . ."

We may take both boats, Brian says, ignoring the remark. He says he is considering taking one up the river himself. That's an improvement. I don't want to go alone.

"What about the guards?"

"Forget them. Pick up Marehan militia when we get there."

"Flak jackets?"

"Sure, we can take 'em. But if you want a flak jacket for the river trip, then you might as well wear one every day here in town. Look, if you don't want to go, I will bloody well find someone else."

If I had expected to steer clear of challenge, then I should not have signed on. The challenge does appeal to a common if not childish weakness. If he goes, then I go. That is my job. That is why I am here. I cannot take a walk. I've got too much pride for that. Organizing the deliveries to the southern Jubba from Kismayo is Brian's job, and he is as frustrated as I that we haven't begun the river operations.

(I mentioned this conversation months later to Matt Wolff. "So you told him to find someone else, right?" he said. No, I didn't. Sometimes I'm a stranger to myself.)

Our trip up the coast, I caution Brian, should be made not in the afternoon but during the early morning, before the sea breeze kicks up a nasty and dangerous chop. A tiny tin can out on the open ocean in fifteen knots of wind can spell a bad day.

"I don't care about the seas. We're going as soon as we get back. We have wasted enough time."

I suspect he knows nothing about small boats; I am my own captain, and if the ocean passage appears too risky, my boat doesn't go. Full stop. In acceptable conditions, however, I can't refuse: I am just the captain, not the organizer. On the other hand, I owe no obedience to heroism.

Back at the port, I tell my Somali mates that I'm going upriver to Hum Hum this afternoon. Everyone talks at once, to me, to one another. The Marehan, their sworn enemy, they warn me, are bloodthirsty, cruel, and crazy. They think this *gal* is just stupid.

There's an intellectual exercise here, one that I am sure confronts many others out in the field: At what point does one's life become more important than the mission and the paycheck? Andrew remained in Mogadishu after most of the military forces had withdrawn "to keep an eye on" the millions of dollars of equipment left behind at the airport. That lasted only a few days before he was evacuated and the equipment became the booty of the warlords.

"I wouldn't know when my life becomes more important," he says later. "By the time I find out, it will probably be too late." That says it. We paint ourselves into that corner. We might realize it only when it is too late. What is it that interferes with good judgment? Pride? Face? Ego?

I don't fear death. Just, like most, the inability to control it. But then, had we the choice of time and place, would we accept it?

Years back, I once had an opportunity to find out. I was living alone in a small cabin well north of Fairbanks, just below the

Arctic Circle. I was totally isolated and often snowbound; I did not open my mouth except to feed it for months at a time. Upon completing the last draft of a little dime novel and with a treasured publisher's contract in hand, I had reached the conclusion that life had been fully digested. Life could hold no more joys, no more loves, no more secrets. I could hope for no better. I had lived it to the fullest, had met senators and presidents and dined with ambassadors and rock stars, had worked oil rigs and fished commercially. Hell, what was there left to do? I concluded, perversely, that as much as I loved life, it was a good time to end it. Armed with the euphoria of well-being, I considered that this point was as good a time as any—a time of my own choosing.

I look back on that night and realize clearly the utter absurdity of that decision. I also think that my self-imposed solitude, combined with my eremitic tendencies, caused me to see existence from another level. Or, as they say up there, perhaps I had simply gone "bushy."

Going bushy is more than just a precarious mental state. The physical manifestations are also strange. During the isolation there was no noise, no sounds other than those I created: the crackling of burning wood in the jerry-built fireplace, bustle and movement. I heard nothing. The only constant sounds were those inside my head (I am not one to talk to myself), and they were ancient melodies, tunes, music I had heard as a child: "Take Me Out to the Ball Game," "Round and Round," "Love Letters in the Sand," "Heartbreak Hotel," but mostly "Take Me Out to the Ball Game"; I repeated this over and over until I thought I would go nuts. The music died finally and was replaced with unidentified male speakers, voices all heavily accented—Southerners, Germans, Jews, Frenchmen. Each babbled unrecognizable words. Those voices lasted for no more than a week, and I was abandoned to merciful silence. Then I heard the engine. A plane flying down the valley, I thought. But the sound of the motor never varied. A new settler, I thought, I hoped, I feared. But in February? I strapped on my snowshoes and scuffed up the frozen creek to higher country, and yet I could get no closer to the sound. I returned to the cabin disappointed and pleased—disappointed that I couldn't solve the mystery, and pleased that whoever was out there was far enough away that I would not have to see them or meet them. (I discovered years later that this is the affliction of single-handed sailors who cross oceans: If after a long solo passage at sea you have concluded that you are just as happy being alone and keeping your own company without the need of others, the approach to land is fraught with fear and dread. There will be the communicating, the relating, the returning to the world of people. Misanthropy starts here. As well as in the Alaskan wilderness.)

It was not until a year later that the source of the mysterious motor was revealed. A psychologist from Johns Hopkins University who had specialized in the effects of isolation (she had studied POWs after they were released from Vietnam) told me she was quite convinced that I had been so long without real sound, without real input, that the motor I heard was the sound of blood rushing through my head. Apparently, there is no such thing as total silence.

So I suspect I had gone a little bushy when I concluded that this night was a good time to end life. It was minus forty Fahrenheit and blue dark outside the log walls of the cabin. It was so cold that if you were foolish enough to piss outdoors, your pee would turn into ice before it hit the ground. Dressed in no more than my union suit and felt-lined boots, I dragged an old wooden chair behind me, pushed the door open against the freshly fallen snow, sat back, and gazed contentedly at the confusion of stars above. I felt I was sane and I knew I was committed. My fate, my death, was in my hands, my hands alone. The conclusion was a luxury I was thankful to reach.

The Alaskan night sky is perhaps one of the most brilliant on earth—little moisture, pollution from afar thinned by distance. This night, the Northern Lights covered the frozen land as a veil with threads of iridescent shades of blue, green, pink, and lavender, sinewy ribbons of variegated color that wove seductively along the ecliptic. They straightened and curled, rose and fell in the form of a wave that rolled gracefully toward the horizon in a ballet of color. The performance was accompanied by sharp cracking, like the snaps from a fire of freshly felled wood.

I didn't feel the cold, although I should have already begun to turn to ice. I was in awe of that which I could not explain, of this display, of this message, of this gift. I returned inside, stood before the fired-up drum stove, and, beating some heat into my body with one hand, took a swig of rum with the other. I dressed properly and returned to the chair outside to watch the light show.

* * *

AT the port, sitting on a flat rock of the seaward breakwater, I finger-eat some rice and beans and stare hard at the sea. A ship moves slowly along the horizon. In any man's marina language, the local conditions—an onshore breeze from the north against a southeast current—would be considered a notch or two above "small-craft warnings." My sixteen-foot tinny doesn't even qualify for that moniker. I sure in hell am not going out today, whatever the orders.

This existence is one of contradictions and unexpected change. After these days in this place, I wonder if I will ever take seriously events over which I have no control. I used to plan, scheme, prepare, anticipate my life. Now I know better; it just doesn't matter anymore. I am now sure that I have less confidence, less certainty about my own place on this earth than Euclid, led across the Pons Asinorum by his blind ass.

By the time Bravo Delta and Sierra Sierra return, it is too late to discuss the issue. More negotiations tomorrow. Postponed for a day or two. Thank God.

I am securing the boat for the night when Chet's voice barks over the radio: "Juliet Bravo, if there is still time, I thought we might come down to the port and take a look at your operations."

"Good copy. But you should get down here ASAP. The sun will be setting soon."

"Be there in about twenty mikes."

The high-speed ride around the bay is cathartic. I push the boat to its screaming limits, carving dangerous snap turns, bouncing over our wake with a ball-breaking thump. Brian and Chet hold on with white knuckles. I notice our battle-tested security officer observing me with a mixture of curiosity and anxiety, but he withholds comment.

The radio barks as we get back into the Land Rover:

"Good news, Juliet Bravo," Andrew says cheerfully. "Our CARE package has arrived. See you back at the ranch. Out." The first shipment of South African beer has been delivered. Sloane flashes a grin and a thumbs-up. I don't know whether to laugh or be embarrassed. How do you expect to give a thumbs-up when you don't have a thumb?

"It got in the way," Chet had said enigmatically, turning his hand this way and that as if looking for the missing part.

"How did it happen?"

"Shot off."

What did I expect?

"I notice you haven't exactly got the hands of a concert pianist."

I look at my own damaged forefingers on my right hand, which I jokingly refer to as my claw. These are perhaps one of the first things most strangers notice. I watch their eyes drift down to my mangled fingers that look like stunted chicken legs.

"Fishing accident."

Funny thing—once, a long time before, I did take piano lessons.

* * *

THERE is no evening briefing; there is not much to say apparently, and I pick up Andrew at Unicef and we return to our compound with the precious taped cardboard box at our feet—labeled as Mombasa bottled water. Warm or cold, the beer will be ambrosia. I salivate at the thought.

Two Somalis talking quietly between themselves are waiting in the open-air dining area of the HCR compound. One is Omar, a paid translator for Unicef; the other is Major Yeh Yeh, with his trademark Palestinian headdress and pointy goatee and dark evasive eyes. He wears loose-fitting gray trousers and blue blouse and a pistol jammed into his belt.

In our imagination, Andrew and I have drunk that first cold beer a half dozen times these past few days, but we don't in front of this imposing stranger. We are not supposed to have alcohol here, and if they knew, they probably would want a few. We drink tea and make light talk with Omar. Major Yeh Yeh says nothing but occasionally offers a vague smile. I'm not sure he speaks English. But Omar, with his squeaky voice and inflated ego, keeps up a steady meaningless chatter. Andrew shoots me an angry look when I excuse myself. He knows. I do feel guilty but, hell, he is the Empire man. He can drink tea at this time of day. Me, I need that medicinal ale.

Chet arrives, hot, tired, a bit cranky, and ready to sink into a beer, whatever its temperature. He draws up short when he sees the two Somalis.

"Good evening, Major Yeh Yeh. Omar. What brings you here?" Barely concealed dread clouds his face.

"There are small matters the major would like to discuss," Omar begins. "The major is aware that this is the end of your day, and he is concerned that this may not be a good time to discuss problems of some minor importance to him and his people."

"As good a time as any," Chet says tiredly, taking a seat. "What's on his mind?"

The major, in steady emotionless tones, describes the good work the UN is doing for Somalia and for the region and on and on. Chet sits impassively across the table with one hand atop the other, staring at nothing in particular, during the droning translation. His eyes seem glazed but he holds on. Major Yeh Yeh doesn't see Chet's reaction, because he, too, is speaking to some distant point before him.

Major Yeh Yeh is both military leader of the Somali Patriotic Movement and our guarantor of security. I wonder if he isn't the one playing us like a cornered mouse. His is a curiously unctuous statement. A thousand polite words convey the meaning of about ten.

I can imagine I am sitting in a Bedouin tent with T. E. Lawrence, listening to negotiations with a white-robed Arab sheik; this kind of communication, this double-talk, is a traditional art form.

"I have been responsible for the protection of the United Nations for the past fourteen months," Yeh Yeh says. "I have lost many of my friends, lost much of my influence, and have been too long away from my village and family."

He comes to the point: additional payment for himself and for his men.

"As you know, Major," Chet responds, "all compensation for security is paid to General Morgan, who pays you."

"General Morgan does not pay me."

"We pay General Morgan for security for our personnel here, and I was under the impression he pays you. That is my understanding."

"General Morgan does not pay me."

"That is between you and the general."

The handheld radio interrupts the discussions: "Sierra Sierra, this is Bravo Delta. There is an emergency at Jamaame town. Will you call them on 7756 Upper Side Band?"

"Roger, Bravo Delta," Chet says, rising. Major Yeh Yeh, reluctant to lose the flow, presses ahead. In his only demonstrative act, the militia leader jabs a finger hard into his own chest. "When I am wronged and if I am shot, I will not bleed. I will not drop blood."

"Major, this is between you and the general—"

"No, it is not." He glares at the big American. "I represent the Somali Patriotic Movement. I do not represent General Morgan."

"Major, if you'll excuse me. I have an emergency to take care of. I'll be right back." He pushes his chair from the table and heads off into the darkness across the compound to the radio room. Andrew and I follow.

"Jesus," Chet mutters, rubbing the back of his thick neck.

Through a crackly radio connection to the Jubba River village of Jamaame, a woman's shaky voice tries to communicate.

"We have a problem here. Can you hear me? Our situation is deteriorating!"

Earlier in the day, one of the lorries carrying relief supplies to Jamaame had broken down. It had taken less than an hour for word to get out and for gunmen to loot the vehicle. Tons of relief supplies disappeared into the bush.

The UN project officer in Jamaame is demanding from the village elders seventy percent of the value of the stolen cargo, payable in cash, labor, or equipment or, better still, all the food returned. Otherwise Unicef and WFP will pull out of town.

"The district officer is telling us to get back to work or get out," the woman says.

"Okay," Sloane says. "So get out. Let's close it down. The hell with them."

"We can't get out."

"You can't get out? Why can't you get out?"

No answer.

"I say again, why can't you get out?"

"I have visitors," the woman's voice says. "I cannot communicate."

"I copy that, Jamaame. I'll get onto Nairobi Security they will handle it from that end. There is nothing I can do from here. I've got a little crisis of my own at the moment. Hang in there. Kismayo out."

Our situation is more important than hers? Her desperation, urgent and pleading, is heartbreakingly evident. I can see the guns at her back and hear her fear. But she is on the other side of the Green Line and there is nothing we can do. I've never met her, but I do worry about her.

Chet returns to the meeting with Major Yeh Yeh with new energy. His gray eyes are alive and determined; while the other crisis was unfolding, he was giving some thought to the one at hand.

"Major," he explains, looking directly at the Somali, "I want you to understand that my hands are tied. There is nothing I can do."

"Mister Chet, I and my people have worked very hard. Now they are waiting to hear from me. I don't know what to say to my people. I do not want to return with such an answer from my good friend. You must know that they are not pleased with the present arrangements."

"I am sorry about that, but, like I say, there is nothing I can do."

"Mister Chet, I cannot be responsible for my people. I cannot predict what their actions will be," he says, barely above a whisper. Omar's translation takes on the somber, almost threatening tones of his master.

Chet looks sharply at the Somali gunman. "If you mean that something could happen to our personnel here in Kismayo," he says finally, his eyes narrow and his voice hard, "then we will have no choice but to leave, and if we do, General Morgan and the community will hold you, Major Yeh Yeh, personally responsible. I will personally see to it."

The major studies his hands, which are clenched tightly in his lap. His dark angular face sinks deeper into the nighttime shadows.

He looks up at Sloane. His black eyes glitter with anger. He says in unexpected smooth English: "This is very wrong, my friend. We have shared some bad times. Here. Mogadishu. I am very disappointed. Now, it is better at times like this that there is no more talk. I will go back to my people and will give you my answer in the morning." Standing, he glares down at Chet: "I am sorry to tell you that I cannot be responsible for your safety." There is an ugliness in the voice, a tone full of menace.

The two Somalis vanish into the night.

"Not very happy," Andrew says.

"No, not very."

"Serious?"

"It always is. Let's just say I'm concerned. But then, I'm paid to be."

"It could blow?"

"Maybe," Chet says, rising. He walks outside into the darkness. Minutes later he returns, zipping up his fly. He continues: "Yeah, well, when they don't show their anger, when there's no screaming, then you know it's usually time to think about packing."

"Like now?" Andrew asks.

He shrugs. "Maybe. But at least he didn't put his pistol on the table. That happened to me in Mog. When that happens, there is no maybe."

13.

Nobody Knows Where the Bullets Go

WE have armed guards of unknown effectiveness inside and outside the compound, but as far as we know they sleep most of the night, rising only at dawn for prayers, their holy murmurs our wakeup call that drifts through the quarters. We think they serve as weathermen; we think they will let us know, unwittingly perhaps, which way the wind is blowing. If we were going to be attacked, the guards would be forewarned and they'd slink away into the night. If the confrontation were less than violent, merely another siege, the guards would be permitted to tell us directly and to play out their role as protectors. If we were to be removed and held hostage, they would presumably turn on us and for the real money join forces with the kidnappers.

We had locked the door and propped a hardback chair against the knob. But it was a puny barrier that anyone with a good foot and hard boot could kick in. How serious was Major Yeh Yeh? Was it a threat? What did he intend?

I awaken from a fitful sleep in the early hours, suddenly alert and laved in sweat.

"You turn off the fan?" I ask quietly.

"Listen!"

The night is filled with a liquid emptiness, hollow, without even the sensation of sound.

"Doesn't sound like anybody's out there."

"You think the guards are gone?"

"I don't know. It feels bad."

"I'll go check." Swinging my feet off the bunk, I duck out from under the mosquito net and creep barefoot down the hallway, feeling my way in the dark. I make not a sound. Outside, around the corner, I can look out onto the dirt lot and the small open shed where the staff usually gathers.

In the shadows under a single lightbulb, our trusty guardians lay snoring, sprawled out on their robes in the dirt, their guns propped nearby against a wall. It is unlikely anything is going to happen this night.

Here in Kismayo, none of us really expects to get shot. In spite of my ill-fated plane ride over the Jubba—and there is a burning sensation deep in my gut when I think of it—we believe that at least here and now, no bullets will be targeted specifically toward us. Down here on the ground the bullets that will kill us probably would be meant for someone else. We are of no value dead. While we have been under siege, held hostage, threatened, and shot at, we are alive; some of my colleagues somewhere on the river are in fact doing the jobs to which they were assigned.

There is, however, an underlying certainty of kidnapping.

Two Italian relief workers in the north were kidnapped only a few days ago, and our fear now of being held for ransom is acute. Somalia is known for its copycat events; a clan kidnaps an aid worker in the north, then a clan in the south realizes that this is a splendid idea and attempts the same.

A conversation with Chet in the morning in the open dining area is one more attempt to put into focus this tooth-and-claw existence. It rattles me, and I later regret the near-personal rancor. It is fortunate the man has more control of his emotions than I.

"The security of our personnel is extremely important," Chet says.

"I heard we were expendable."

"I don't know—more like cannon fodder, I would have said."

"I don't get it. We plan for evacuation, but it always seems that we have to be dragged one step further before we really do evacuate. What will it take?"

"A hell of a lot. In '93 when one of the staff was killed outside the compound, we made a little protest, packed up, and left for a few days."

"What happened?"

"The Unicef project coordinator here—Murphy, I think that was his name—was ambushed on the way to the market."

"Ambushed. Not a mistake, a stray bullet?"

"No, they were apparently gunning for him. Got on the wrong side of one of the subclans. The times were different then. Thank God. But, yeah, we were back before the blood dried."

"So you are saying that even if someone gets shot—not just shot at, but shot—the show goes on?"

"I'm afraid so. Pulling out would be seen as a provocation—sometimes more dangerous than staying put. Operations is the word around here." He pushes himself away from the table and walks over to the electric kettle and instant coffee. His cup is already half full. "Doesn't make my job any easier, I'll say that," he says quietly over his shoulder.

"I guess not." It takes a moment for this to sink in. Up to this point I have always felt at least partially sheltered from the storm. "Operations, you say. Not security? What operations, Chet? Dodging bullets, trying to stay alive? I mean, honestly, what are we really doing out here?" The big aging soldier with his short white hair and square jaw sits back and waits to hear me out. I wonder how far I can go with these thoughts.

"Jeri sends her trucks out and they get hijacked," I say. "Food gets distributed and that causes riots and people get killed. Morgan and the others jerk you and Brian from here to Sunday, stringing you along, never saying no, never saying yes. I go to the port day after day, tinkering and diddling, waiting to hear whether I'm going to offer myself as a moving target in a turkey shoot. Operations? You do have a full-time job making sure we don't get killed. Those are your operations. But the rest of us? We are just catnip! Because we are here, there is a new game in town called 'Let's fucking terrorize the UN people!' A game anyone with a gun can play. A game they play every few years when the do-gooders from the West come to Kismayo. It sounds like fourteen-karat bullshit to me, Chet. Jobs for the boys, I heard. At our expense."

Sloane leans back in his chair; I have no idea what he's thinking, but his eyes convey the ominous patience I saw with Yeh Yeh last night. Venting a little steam was not meant to be personal, but it is turning out that way.

"All I've seen is death and near death, Chet. Without purpose. I am not saying that I'm out here to save the world, but, shit, at least something along those lines would give this useless existence some meaning. I don't know, maybe I shouldn't give a damn," I continue, a little embarrassed. "It doesn't seem anyone else does, at least not outside Kismayo. You know, I just wish I felt good about being here—like I'm doing something worthwhile, some good for someone. But 'operations'—what operations?"

Sloane grimaces and shakes his head slowly. "Son, you're not out here to help anyone," he says evenly. "That's not why you are here. You are here to help yourself."

"How the fuck am I helping myself?"

"Don't you think I've heard this self-serving crap before?" His gray eyes bore into mine. "You, like the other part-timers, are here only for your own reasons." He jabs a finger at me. "You're here only for Number One. You ever spend a lot of your life helping others? I doubt it. You suddenly feel put upon because you are not following some calling? You didn't join a relief organization to help anybody. That is the lie you give to your kids. You got lucky and hopped on the UN gravy train just like the locals. Your reward is your paycheck and whatever else it is you need to keep going. Not some satisfaction that you are helping someone, for Christ's sake. You really want to do something for these people? Go join the MSF or some other NGO and get paid squat. What're you making a month? Five thousand? Six thousand?"

He has a point. Maybe when I actually do begin to help someone, then I'll know that that was at least part of the reason why I came here. But without the experience, I can only admit that I came to earn some spare change. Money has a certain value, a different value from one person to the next. I may not have known quite what I was getting into when I signed on, but then, I wasn't blind either.

"You're not here to serve anyone but your own master, whoever, whatever that is—money, ego, adventure—who the hell knows?" he continues. "So you got shot at. It's probably your whiny nature to need that kind of thing anyway. Otherwise why the hell would you be here? You feel a little righteous? Great feeling. And you feed yourself and your own private needs. But you are no damn hero.

"I've seen you before. Guys like you. You work here for a month or so, fill your pockets, then run off. Not satisfied with television anymore? Got too many toys? Son, for you and many of the part-timers, this is the ultimate entertainment."

I want to protest. I have no toys. I have got a clapped-out leaky old boat that, after working my ass off in the States, I coaxed from one port to another. Sometimes I feel as much a refugee as those we're trying to help. "You are a professional soldier, Chet. Getting shot at is maybe nothing new to you, but I am a civilian. We are civilians in the UN. We're not paid soldiers. Whatever I get paid is not worth my life."

"Nope, nothing is worth your life. I'm here to make sure of it. But no one forced you to come here. Here is a statistic or two that you should know: A third of all deaths among relief workers occur within the first three months of arriving in the field. And the average age of those who die is about forty, not some starry-eyed young people. So the odds are not in your favor—you got it all going against you. Now, if it is all too much for you, you can take the next rotation back to Nairobi. Nobody is going to fault you for that. But I gotta say, I didn't figure you to be another candy-ass civilian who got in too far over his head."

"Yeah, well, I'm not such a wuss. I had some asshole kid point a loaded gun in my face and tell me I was going to die. I nearly got shot down over Bum Fuck Somalia. I am about to be a practice drone for the guns of the warlords so the UN boys at the top can tell the world they have 'operations.' I'm just trying to make some sense of this. And, shit, Chet—maybe I'm just a little nervous."

I am relieved when the mobile radio interrupts and he's asked to get over to Unicef for a meeting with the sultan.

He pushes his chair back and gets up slowly, strapping on his radio: "My old man used to tell me: Keep your pecker up. Good advice." He cuffs me lightly on the shoulder and leaves.

* * *

HIS judgment is correct. If there are any heroes in this world, we are not among them. Who of us is in it for altruism? Maybe Jeri, but then, who can get close enough to her to know why some hard case from the Main Line is out here? We each have our reasons. But I don't think compassion is what drives most relief workers. At least not here in Kismayo. Those who are actually delivering food, rescuing people—I would presume they feel some inner satisfaction. I wouldn't know. I haven't saved a life or handed a moldy biscuit to a starving child. I know there are people dying out there—I practically saw it happen. I remember the desperate pleas for rescue when we flew over the makeshift shanties on the dikes, families on their rooftops. In Kismayo, we are satisfied to know that we are hanging on, that we have survived another day. We are being paid, and that for now is one reason we are here, to buy that dream machine to vanish into the heavens—money for a yacht to sail around the world, for a party business in Nairobi. I need it because I have sailed the world and I am broke. The job offered money. It did not guarantee satisfaction. It did not guarantee survival.

I return to that truth Chet so well defined. The inner master in all of us does not usually need to be identified. Out here, the question is forced upon us. Yet who wants or needs this knowledge? Even out here, many do not want to know. Others do. This is a defining opportunity few ever get.

In the eyes of the mainstream, I suspect we all could be considered a bit mad, loonies pursuing some mythic quest. We have become too antsy and too deterred for a life of spiritless routine, too selfish for much compassion, and too human for heroism. All this for a lousy paycheck.

The thought of dying here is never far from the surface, but I am also conscious of a less well-defined, building pressure, terrifying and irremediable, that I cannot seem to control: complacency. I have wondered whether the near misses, the constant fear, the taut nerves, our adrenaline rushes, as exhausting and exhilarating as they are, won't inevitably result in carelessness. It is one thing to learn to take matters here less seriously, for the maintenance of sanity to adapt, but it is quite another to become complacent with its obvious risks. Does not complacency lead to indifference? I do find some comfort in realizing that—at least at this point—my will to survive is stronger than complacency, for while I no longer duck at the sound of gunfire (and if I duck, there's a chance I duck into the bullet anyway), a sudden report close by, a gunshot, or the backfire of a car stops me in my tracks, turns my legs to pasta and my guts to water.

* * *

HUNKERED against the outside of the warehouse in the shade, with Isa, Harun, and the laborers on either side, I gaze proudly over at my handiwork. I have done something quite childish, satisfyingly childish, something that I have always wanted to do since I first had the opportunity as a kid on a city street. Earlier, I had chipped off a section of the jetty and poured cement for a couple of cleats that I made out of half-inch rebar. I had screeded the wet cement to a smooth finish, not a blemish—a professional job. When I was certain that no one was looking—the boys had been drinking *cha* in the Land Rover—I knelt down and with my finger scrawled in the wet cement: ***JSB 1998***. Had I the time and space, I would have added a postscript, a line from that paperback I had borrowed from the Unicef lounge: . . . *to make thee a native in thy perverted land*. I have left my mark upon Somalia.

Harun, clutching a fresh bundle of *miraa* in his fist, squats in front of me. I decline his offer of a little pick-me-up, although what is the harm in sitting back in hundred-plus-degree heat in a drugged stupor, watching life pass by?

"You want a Somali wife, Captain?" he asks.

"Already have a good wife, Harun. One is enough for me." I wonder if he has someone in mind. Maybe a sister?

"But it is better to have two. Three."

"So you said. But you only have one."

"Yes, Captain, but, *Inshah Allah,* one day I will have two. Three. Wives cost much money. For rich man like you."

"In my world, Harun, I can't afford more than one wife." I chuckle at the irony: In Somalia you buy a wife and pay forever; in the West you buy a divorce and pay forever. "You told me you have a wife, a cow, and a gun. You really have a cow?"

"Yes, my friend, I have a cow." He gets to his feet, reaches down for my hand, and helps me up. "Come, Captain." Reluctantly I rise and follow him to the other side of the car.

He seems a bit shy and his usual brashness is missing.

"You come to my home."

"Yes, okay, Harun. I'd like that."

"Good." He beams. "I find you at seven." He starts walking back to the warehouse.

"Hang on, Harun. Seven when? Not tonight!"

"Yes, Captain. Tonight. You eat in my home. *Nyama choma.* You like *nyama choma.* Good Somali food."

"Oh, no. Look, Harun, I can't." A shadow moves over his cheerful brown face. It's a mix of disappointment and insult. "We're not allowed out of the compound after dark."

"Is that truth, Captain? Mister Brian has been out. . . ."

Now I feel trapped. If the Unicef chief can get out at night for whatever purpose, then I can't use that as an excuse.

"You don't trust?" A sharp look of challenge.

"I do. I do. I have trusted you with my life, Harun. Right?" The Somali darkens in thought. "Yes, of course I trust you. Believe me."

His is a remarkable offer, an evident reward of friendship. But I remember the warnings, the report of the killing of the international five years earlier. Looking into his hurt and possibly angry eyes, my own sensitivity writes the script: You too good to visit my home? "Okay, yes, Harun, seven o'clock."

He smiles with gratitude. Back at the warehouse, he laughs and jokes more exuberantly than usual with my militia guards. I wonder if I should bring anything and laugh privately. A bottle of Chianti? A potato salad? I'm not going to a barbecue.

I pull out a photo of Jacqueline. Her smiling, open face seems so distant and so remote. It's odd to look back and think we had a problem or two; we may have needed space, but this is carrying it a bit far: She is in Holland and I am on another planet. I haven't had much time to miss her, to think about her. I know the future, our future, is uncertain. For how will it be when we are together again? How will I be, how will I have changed? What of my patience? Will I have more? Or less? Probably less, I fear. How can I explain all this? And not just the events. Maybe I should look into that RES training.

My thoughts are broken by the crackling of the radio. Alpha Kilo reports more shooting at the airport. Every gunshot is serious, and everyone wonders whether there is a name on the bullet. This time it could have been anybody.

Later Andrew relates that an old man guarding a Technical, zonked out on *miraa,* fell asleep with his finger on the trigger of his rifle. In a spasm of sleep, he pulled the trigger and the weapon, cocked and on automatic, went off; he awoke to his own gunfire. In panic, he tried to shake the gun off his finger and it fired even more erratically. The Somalis around him dove into the bushes. Still half asleep, the old man extracted his finger and leapt for safety, still convinced that someone was shooting at him. Nobody knows where the bullets go.

14.

One of the Local Girls

IT is not without some nervousness that I wait inside the big swinging steel doors of the Unicef compound. I had been advised against this sortie with heaping specifics of the Murphy assassination. Each additional minute of discussion with Brian revealed more of the frightening details of his ambush. I am somewhat comforted that it was an apparent assassination of one who was well-known to the local people; one subclan thought Murphy was favoring another in the distribution of relief supplies.

"I can't stop you from going, of course," Brian had warned me. "You are not a permanent, only a contract worker, so it's your call. But it is not something I would do anytime soon."

"But you have been out at night, I heard."

"Who told you that?"

"My driver."

"Well, he must be thinking of someone else. I would definitely not go out in this town after dark. And no one on my watch ever has, to my knowledge."

He runs his hands through his shaggy blond hair and shrugs. "Tomorrow you go up the river. It's your last night in Kismayo. You might as well have a night on the town—although, again, I strongly suggest that you don't."

"A night on the town isn't exactly what I have in mind."

"Well, if you're not back in the morning, we'll assume you ran off with one of the local girls."

A Unicef guard beckons me into the guardhouse and points through the peephole. Harun waits outside, standing a little uneasily. Instead of the outfit that he wears daily to the port—baseball cap, ragged aloha shirt—he is clad in a clean white shirt over clean trousers and a traditional round flat-top Moslem cap. He has dressed for the occasion. Even his assault rifle looks like it has taken a little polish. For some reason this gives me some comfort.

I don't see his dented UN rig with the smoky incense burner and scratchy music tapes. Perhaps it is off to the side, beyond view. It is getting dark and I can't imagine walking the shadowy streets of Kismayo at night.

"Ah, Captain *Diep Maleh*! We go?" he greets me as I come out of the high-walled compound. He shakes my hand and grins, still apparently unsure I'm really coming.

"No car?"

"No car, Captain. UN car not my car. I'm just driver. Car in shop."

I hesitate, look down the street. "Come," Harun says. Looking up at our dun-colored compound and the security it represents, I realize I have never actually stood on the ground outside, only whisked through the heavy reinforced gates in the UN rigs. It is imposing. Our redoubt could be a lonely undermanned French Foreign Legion outpost of seventy-five years ago on the edge of the Tunisian desert. I suppose there is little difference—this citadel of turrets, sandbags stacked around the gun emplacements (that have no guns), even the pockmarks from bullets that have chipped away at the massive walls. The suspicions, the guns, the hot Arab tempers, and the dusty Islamic town itself provide the same tangy ingredients. As a youth, I enjoyed watching the adventurous movies of the Foreign Legion. I never wanted to appear in one.

"You come now, Captain."

"Okay, Harun, let's go."

Harun takes my hand and we begin walking down the pitted

dirt road under the compound. I don't like this hand-holding business, as common as it may be, and I walk stiffly, my arm rigid and unable to relax. Harun doesn't seem to notice, or mind. As we walk away from the security of the UN, I feel like a kid who has met a dare and is following an older boy to the highest diving board, knowing he will have to jump. I am protected only by my faith and trust in this young Somali whom I've known for little more than a few weeks.

The little children who once might have been so friendly when I was in the car see us approach and run away. The youngest flee in tears at the rare sight of a white man walking in their midst.

There are no telephone or electric poles; they've been cut off at the ground and used as building material or firewood. There's a railroad line through town but there are no tracks; the rails have been welded into antitank traps and the heavy cross ties used to build fortifications. There is no city sewerage, and the oppressive sweet stench of ordure mingled with the smells of frying goat for the evening meals assails the senses. Cholera is common here.

Hand in hand, we pass in front of the Somalia National Bank, a stately Italianate whitewashed building in the throes of destruction. Round tents of stick and animal hide, reminiscent of those of Native Americans, litter what may have been a well-groomed lawn. On the balcony of the building, colorful sarongs, cotton shawls, a few frayed men's and boys' trousers, and other indefinable clothing—squatter flags—flutter in the evening breeze. The top floors probably house the more powerful and wealthy of this seedy commune, perhaps even our salaried day workers—the cooks, the radio operators, the cleaners—those who keep our operation going.

Away from the compound and out of a car, there is noise. The din of Somali and Arabic, the crowing of roosters, the laughter of naked children, the tinny competing sounds of faraway radios. The eerie call to prayer in no melody any Westerner could compose drifts through the streets from a nearby mosque.

We turn another corner, onto a deeply potholed road lined on both sides with tall leafy trees. Complemented by the dusk, it is possible with some imagination to see that Kismayo was once a well-laid-out colonial city.

We pause by the Catholic church that stands enisled among the acacia. The dusty area in front of the building, blemished with random sprigs of dead grass, is oddly free of the shanties that clutter most of this despairing city's free spaces. The building's black stone facade of Gothic symmetry weeps with the stains of weather. It is a sharp contrast to the whitewashed flat Arab buildings and the mud-colored shanties that surround it.

"Church," Harun says. It is as if he is proud to be able to identify, to acknowledge the symbol.

The poetic brutality of the building, standing defiantly among the shabby surroundings, is singularly disturbing. Why does it still stand when so many other buildings of more local importance are mere shells? Curiously, the church's heavy wooden portal is secured by a large rusting padlock. Who would care to lock a church in this nearly entirely Muslim town so long ago abandoned by Christians? Who is preserving it? Is it part of someone's dream—a hope that one day the West will return?

Carved in the black stone above the archway is a sculptured relief of Mary holding a swaddled Jesus. A bearded Joseph stands proudly next to his family. All wear tarnished halos. The paint on the relief is faded. Mary and Joseph look happily down at the baby. The face of the infant Jesus is little more than an empty cement hole, gouged out by hundreds of well-aimed bullets.

Chet tells of the days following the UN's ill-conceived occupation of Mogadishu. Children emptied their recoilless rifles and grenade launchers at the modern Western-style buildings, smashing offices and apartments into rubble just for the hell of it. The youths were not shooting at one another or at anyone inside but at a world they could not see or reach, a world that had abandoned them to their fate. It is not an idle wish that the UN presence in the form of seven internationals might restore a faith in an outside world. Yet I know now that few here or on the outside really give a damn.

I notice more frequently men walking the streets holding hands, and I begin to relax. Unconsciously I begin to appreciate our display of friendship; it is something of a security guarantee and it makes me feel invisible. As long as Harun is holding my hand, I feel safe.

Night comes quickly here, just a few miles south of the equator. There are no street lamps, and in the gathering darkness, the soft lights of the kerosene lanterns dance mysteriously in front of small makeshift stalls along the road. There is still light enough to make out the wares on the tables: detergents, cigarettes sold individually, soft drinks, sesame biscuits, and some rusty tools.

We are walking toward the end of town and it is nearly dark. The weak glow of the lanterns and the charcoal braziers lights the way, casting surreal designs before us. Shadowy Brueghelesque figures, bent and secret, drift across our path in a *danse macabre*. We have become one with these ghostly apparitions, and our own movement seems to drift over the surface unnoticed. Something moves under my foot. A snake? A rat? I stumble, and Harun tightens his grip and keeps me from falling.

There is a timeless indifference here. Despite war, no war, UN, no UN, Kismayo will probably go on this way forever, as it did before and during the days of the Italian and British administrations, as it does now with us, the benevolent troops crusading under the banner of the White Man's Burden. Here, the hard fight for survival continues as it always has, whether the colonialists are European exploiters or relief workers.

"My home!" Harun says proudly.

He motions ahead to a collection of silhouetted adobe shacks randomly huddled at the end of the road. Tiny dancing flames from stoves and burners form a narrow corridor to the cluster. Flickering lights briefly illuminate dark, quiet figures. A donkey brays nearby.

Harun's hand tightens. I feel his tension.

Harun is acknowledged by his shadowy neighbors with a few cursory words and muffled grunts as we pass the small cooking fires toward a single mud shack in the back. An old gray cow, with ribs exposed like the dusty exhibit in a museum, stands patiently next to Harun's home. A rope around her scrawny neck is anchored to one of the protruding sticks of the hut.

Light glimmers through the sides of the animal-hide door. Harun lifts the heavy skin and motions me inside.

My eyes take a moment to get used to the brightness within. The low walls of rough red clay slapped onto the interwoven wattle reach to a roof of *makuti*—woven palm fronds. Many of the village homes in Somalia are roofed with grass, and a house of *makuti* is one that is considered well-constructed. Harun's home is a single large room, bedroom and living quarters as one. In the dark corner on the ground away from the lamp is a thin American-made Sealy Posturepedic mattress with the tag still on. The bottom of the mattress is spattered red from the mud. A couple of shawls are thrown over the bed.

The dirt floor is spotless, swept clean of everything but dirt.

A current calendar with a photograph of New York Harbor hangs on a peg on the wall.

Harun barks something in Somali, and the animal-hide door is slowly swept aside by a tall woman clad in a red sarong with a green leafy border. Another *kanga* of strange desert-colored logos is carelessly wrapped as a shawl over her head and around her shoulders; wisps of long silky black hair peek out from under her scarf.

Her contented air vanishes at the sight of my presence. She pulls up in sudden fright, black startled eyes defensive and fearful. Harun speaks and she appears to relax a little. There is something of a faint smile forming. With slow purposeful movement, she lifts an edge of her *kanga* to cover all but her eyes, yet her eyes, dark and warm, never leave mine. The look through that narrow window appears tantalizingly daring.

She has nearly taken my breath away. No older than her late teens or early twenties, she is a stunning classic Somali beauty, every bit as beautiful as those Somali models all the rage on a Western catwalk. Her light brown skin is smooth and flawless and velvet; her high cheekbones, a gentle nose, and a rather challenging mouth with a bit of an overbite accent non-African features. Her high forehead boasts a proud Nilotic heritage.

As she leaves, he turns to me and smiles proudly: "My wife."

"She is very pretty, Harun. You are a lucky man."

The girl reappears moments later with an earthenware vessel with a long graceful spout and long neck, its rounded bottom charred where over the years it has been set in the coals. She pours thick sweet tea with camel's milk into two glasses and then withdraws into the shadows.

Harun does not introduce us. He ignores her as if she had ceased to exist. Dragging my stubborn Western ways along with me, I feel I must say something innocuously polite: Lovely home you have here. Or anything. It is not clear if that would be out of place.

I am so far out of my element. Harun is my driver. But now I am in his home as a guest. A role reversal. I don't know small talk anymore. I haven't anything to say. I cannot identify nor relate to anything here, and Harun and I sit across from each other in silence, smiling and drinking the lukewarm tea.

A movement in the shadows enters my periphery, and now accustomed to the fluttering half-light, I watch a rat poke his nose and forefeet into the top of an open white bag labeled in blue: **Maize Meal, 50 kg, Unicef.**

I begin to notice a few other items. Hanging near the bed is a framed mirror. Below, under an American flag, is a fresh cardboard box of yellow HDRs—Humanitarian Daily Rations—marked **Food Gift of the People of the United States of America,** RIGHT AWAY FOODS, MCALLEN TEXAS. On a peg on the opposite wall is a new UN-blue flak jacket. It is the lighter Kevlar type, a damn sight lighter than the ones I have seen lying around the Unicef offices. Maybe he has also got the lighter-style blue combat helmet I could borrow. Then I realize he probably never was issued this gear.

Harun sees me scanning the room and, rising from the table, retrieves a thick book from inside a small locked trunk in the corner.

"The Koran," he announces. It is a richly inlaid leather volume with red marker ribbons and pages yellowed by age. "It is the book of my father and of my father's father and his father's father." He stands over me as I leaf blindly through the pages of Arabic scrawl.

"It's very beautiful," I say, looking up. "They say every Somali man can trace his family back twenty generations. Is that true?"

"I believe it is so. For me, I know my family from long ago. We once had many camels in Ogadĕn, but they were taken by Ethiopians and Russians. But now I have a cow." He smiles ruefully. "My father and my wife's father were enemies. Now they are both dead. I have the woman."

Harun issues another quiet instruction and his wife, waiting in the shadows, slips out the door.

Harun replaces the Holy Book and returns to the table.

He raises his eyes to mine. "You are my brother." His voice is gentle. If he had said I was his lover, it probably would have sounded the same.

"Thank you, Harun," I say quietly. I don't know what more to say. The import of this statement is evident. "I will be leaving Kismayo tomorrow."

"Tomorrow," he repeats. He does not hide his disappointment. He looks down into his glass.

"I'm taking the boats to Hum Hum. I'm setting up a base on the river."

"Marehan clan, Captain." He looks up, proclaims, "You will be killed."

"No, my friend. Don't you know? I've got nine lives." He looks confused. "I have many lives left on this earth. We will have the permission of the Marehan and General Morgan. They will guarantee my safety. It will be all right. It will be safe."

Harun stares at his tea and shakes his head. "You will get permission and they will kill you just the same. After you bring them food. Tomorrow," he repeats.

I shrug. But the fears I have been trying to deny are again demanding attention. I shouldn't have mentioned it. "What is your wife's name?"

"Holaan."

"Like the country?"

"No, Captain. Ho-laan."

"Does she speak English?"

"No, no," he laughs. "She is only a stupid cow, Captain. She does not speak English. She only speaks Somali, Arabic, Kiswahili, and maybe little Italian, I think."

In spite of his words, he leans back on the heel of his chair and grins proudly.

"She is a *shifta,* from a family of thieves. You know *shifta,* Captain? In Kenya, everyone from Somalia is called a thief. But only she is true *shifta*. Her father was rich, had many camels because he steal so many from the Bantu. You are American?"

"Yes."

"Her father was camelboy. Like American cowboy. He was camelboy with many camel."

Holaan appears in the room and places an enameled bowl of *ugali,* a mush of maize meal in coconut milk, in the center of the table. She sets before us small tins of boiled black beans and a saucer of green chili peppers fried in salt. She returns with enameled cups filled with camel milk, yellow and thick. She withdraws silently to the shadows.

There are no utensils and I don't expect any. Forks and spoons are not common in this city. Those left behind by colonialists and once used in hotels most likely have been collected and sold as scrap. I finger the first of the beans and mix it with the mush. Although it is bland and unappetizing, I'm hungry. I've eaten far worse. But I look forward to the *nyama choma*.

I look up at this mysterious woman whose languid eyes regard me through the veil. I try to imagine her beautiful face. I am compelled by those eyes. I catch myself gawking.

"We have baby," Harun says quietly, as if it is a secret.

"You have a baby?"

"Yes. Soon."

Despite the loose robes, it does appear that his wife is pregnant. I can't help but feel—a sensation from memory—the body of the dying infant that I held in my arms outside the MSF compound. I pray theirs will survive.

Pushing the *ugali* away, Harun looks up at Holaan and speaks, mentions something about the *nyama choma*. I hear only the whisper of her reply. He appears surprised. He repeats the same thing and she answers, it seems, somewhat defiantly.

He backhands the bowl of porridge onto the floor, jumps up from the table, knocking over his chair. Standing before her, he slaps her full across the face.

I jump up, my fists clenched, but I really don't know what to do. She cowers back against the mud wall and whimpers. He lords over her, his fist poised within inches of her face. Her eyes, large, malevolent, and frightened, glare back at him.

I would have never thought Harun capable of such demented violence.

She mutters something, deep and guttural, unmistakably challenging.

He explodes. Wrenching her head back by her hair and scarf, he begins to haul her out of the shack. Her veil has slipped off and her pretty face is contorted by fear. "Harun!" I shout. I must stop this. I want to grab him, pull him off, slam him against the wall. I reach for his shoulder. But never touch. He ignores me.

Outside in the night, pressed in by other shanties and silent figures standing, sitting around their cooking fires, he throws her to her knees and stands over her, shouting abuse. I look around for help. Suddenly, he reaches down for her hair with one hand and, wrenching her face upward, slaps her again with the other. She screams, tries to twist away, then she stops resisting. Her mewling seems to inflame him more. Without warning, he slams her face into a still-steaming pile of wet cow dung at our feet.

Grabbing Harun's arm, I try to pull him away from the sobbing, sputtering girl. He rounds on me with uncomprehending disbelief. And blind personal hatred. His furious dark eyes drill into mine.

Softly I plead: "Please, brother."

The fires of fury in his eyes begin to ebb. He releases his grip on his wife. She is gagging from a mouthful of dung and begins to vomit. Dark shapes have risen and are gathering around us. Their attention seems to be on me, their toneless muttering a frightful incantation. I sense they are not shocked at the display of domestic violence but at my interference with it. I am surrounded, trapped by their ghostly indecipherable enmity.

On her hands and knees, Holaan stumbles forward into her home. Harun slaps the cow shit off his pants and looks contemptuously over at me. Without a word he disappears into the shack, jerking shut the animal-hide door behind him.

* * *

DURING the long walk back to the compound, I relive, over and over, those frightening moments. I hurt with guilt, I hurt for her.

It is later now and the street activity has diminished by half. It is darker, and I wonder whether it is obvious I don't belong here. I seriously question whether I will make it back alive. I try to force myself into anonymity. I take some comfort that no one expects a crazy *gal* to be walking the night streets of this lawless town alone. It hasn't been done in years. Still, I walk tall, purposefully, afraid that I might show that I am scared to death, a figure sneaking, squeezing past shadows.

Like most children, I was once afraid of the dark. That was before I realized as an adult there is sanctuary in darkness. But this darkness is different; this weighted blackness seems to shift and flow, black against black, and I'm certain death awaits behind each tree. I pray that I can find the way back to the compound. I have been praying a lot recently, and it is not without some justifiable need that I start believing again. I suppose foxhole religion is as valid as any other, assuming all things are equal. At least we don't have to specifically address our appeals. I wouldn't know who to pray to.

The girl's beautiful young face smeared in dung is seared into my mind. Again, I relive it and I try to see me doing something. Anything. I had heard that brutality toward one's wife in many parts of the Arab world is accepted and expected. There is a Somali proverb that says: *A man who can control his temper is not a passionate man.* But such cruelty against a woman hardly seems to warrant the honor of passion. Harun's violence remains with such awful clarity that I feel, I taste the cow shit as if it had happened to me. Unconsciously I run my hand over my own face. Many times.

As I step carefully through the night, an equally terrifying fear begins to course through my veins. Tomorrow I will take a boat up the river and I will run the gauntlet between warring subclans.

15.
Saved by the Bush

ANDREW and I mush through bowls of soggy Weetabix and UHT milk in silence. My mind is a rat's nest of tangled thread knotted with recollected viscera and the fear of the moment: Faces and ghosts—and the imagined smell of dung, as if I had stepped in it and carried it back—combine with an almost sickening nervousness about going upriver. I am wired to the past, wired to the future. To save myself, I must force myself to concentrate on the job ahead. Just get in the boat and drive. My tin lockbox and backpack together with some supplies and emergency rations are to be "airlifted" to me at Hum Hum. I am not sure what "airlift" means—dropped by parachute, lowered from a helicopter, hurled by catapult; from what I understand there is no landing field in the area, otherwise I would have been delivered.

I have been so preoccupied with the run up the river that I have never spent more than a glancing minute wondering what it is I am supposed to do when I get there. Establish a base for the distribution of the relief supplies, which is to presume that I know how to set up a distribution base. What is a distribution base? Something like Marerey, I would imagine. The idea, it appears, is first to get someone out there and figure it out on the spot. My presence on this part of the river apparently will establish a bridgehead, and back at the office the bureaucrats will tack a colored pin on a map on the wall and tell the donors: "We also have a base here at Hum Hum, very effective, very effective, indeed. We are well covered. Yes, spending donor money wisely . . ." Am I to be met by village elders, or warlords? Have they arranged for locals to help me? What do I do with the emergency supplies? Are they going to helicopter others out there to join me—some of Wolff's river people? Has anybody thought of these things?

"I've been thinking," Andrew says cheerfully. He fishes out a large greenhead fly from his bowl, examines it, and flicks it away. "Think it came from the milk?" He reads the label on the paper carton. "I don't think they have tsetse flies in Italy."

"You've been thinking . . ." I am in a resentful mood.

"We could defect."

"Defect!"

"Sure, why not?" He grins. He's got me. I am taking things too seriously. "You go to General Morgan and offer your boats and your services. You offer to run the port until the tourists come. I'll bring the radios and offer to run the airport. He would pay better than the UN."

"You have been working too fucking long in the sun, my friend."

Whether it is the fragility of the moment or the absurdity of the notion, I wonder if I do not actually begin to consider it. I mean, what do I owe these people—the UN? "Yeah, I'll help the good general market Kismayo as a new ecotourism paradise where things are as they always have been, as they always will be, guaranteed by the city fathers never to change. I'll run his water-sports operations."

"I'll start a gliding school—there are good thermals in this area."

This nutty conversation reminds me of the one with the Swedes in that fancy Nairobi hotel. That was so long ago that I remember more the nervousness that triggered the humor, less the discussion itself.

"Too late for me. I'm supposed to visit the competition today."

"Well, when you get to the other side, you could defect to them. They might pay better anyway. When do you go upriver?"

"Before the wind gets up."

His is a good attempt, an appreciated effort to steer my thoughts away from what lies ahead. I know about today, about running the gauntlet, about ducking the bullets with anything but full clarity. It is as if I am looking through a ground lens, an unfocused view of an event of absolute certainty. I suppose I am as prepared as I ever will be, although that is not saying much—like taking meager comfort because I am wearing my fast running shoes through the bad part of town. A bitter taste of bile rises, burns, subsides. I am starving, and I feel nauseous and overfull.

One of our compound guards with deferential bow and scrape begs to interrupt us. "Sirs, big problem at Unicef. No UN move today." With some difficulty he tells us the guns are out and aimed at our colleagues' headquarters. A deep breath—another delay. I expect to rouse Chet with the news but find him sitting in a straight-back chair against a wall reading a paperback.

"Thought you were still asleep."

"Nope. Just doing a little reading. *The Unbearable Lightness of Being.*" He turns the book around and looks at the cover as if appraising its value. "Have you read it?"

"No, not yet." How he finds the time or the presence to read a book I will never know.

"Interesting."

"It's the militia again. They got the guns on the Unicef compound—maybe no river trip." It is more of a statement than a question, as if the way I present the suggestion might influence the outcome.

"I wouldn't worry about that—I suspect we'll be able to work this one out. You packed and ready to go?" Chet doesn't seem to give a damn one way or the other. It is the only thing I think about. I nod glumly.

"I wonder if they know? They are probably still asleep over there—it was a long night last night. Might as well wake them with the news."

Chet radios Happy One and tells her to wake up, look outside, see the guns—you are under siege. The sleep is still in her voice. "Yeah? Okay. So what's new?"

An unidentified Somali voice snaps over the radio: "All expatriates are to remain in their compounds! Out."

"Who was that?" I ask.

"Anybody with a handheld. We're not the only ones with comms." A number of locals wear the small black portable VHF radios—"gifts," Chet says, from the UNOSOM forces that wisely got out of town in a hurry.

"What's the problem?"

"Same thing. The shootings, the blood money. We were dealing with them well into the night. They got us by the *cojones*."

The poor kid hangs on but he is as good as dead. It apparently makes no difference that the woman was not pregnant and that the schoolboy is not yet dead—the demand is still one hundred fifty-six camels. While Brian and Chet have agreed to the number of animals, there is some dispute about their value. The families don't really want us to deliver a herd of camels to their wattle shacks, just the money they would fetch on an open market, a market that exists only in their imagination. Payment, they are insisting, must be in U.S. dollars.

Two hours later Bravo Delta announces over the radio the guns have been withdrawn and negotiations have resumed. Always guns first, then negotiations, and during negotiations we are allowed to continue to try to help these people. Somalis, it appears, need to cock their guns, point, and then talk. A Somali would not a good next-door neighbor make.

During the morning briefing the siege is shrugged off matter-of-factly. As the others file out to start their days, Bravo Delta asks me to wait. He wants to discuss the logistics of the turkey shoot. He drums his fingers on the surface of a small writing pad, a sign he's impatient to get this over with, as if his taxi is waiting.

"Rather plan an outing on the lake in Central Park on a lazy Sunday afternoon," I say glibly.

"You could be there. And we would be here," Brian says. That puts an end to any nervous reverie. "We are going to be leaving in a few minutes for Goob Weyn to get final approval for your trip. They've told us there shouldn't be a problem, but Sierra Sierra and I want to have guarantees that we can get up there without incident."

"Real fine idea!" My sarcasm does not go unnoticed. Chet furrows and Brian's eyes flare.

"Look, there is no trip if we get no guarantees. You can trust me on that." No longer is he offering to get someone else if I am too much of a pussy to make the trip. "In that case we'll probably take the boats up to Marerey."

It does not make any difference to me, I'm thinking—a short gauntlet, a long gauntlet. "Also up the coast and up the river?"

"If it looks dodgy, we can use a helicopter to take the boats up to Marerey."

"A helicopter! Why the hell haven't we done this before? I have had two boats ready for days."

"Because, goddamn it, we will bloody well deliver our supplies from Kismayo. That's what you are here for!"

I suddenly understand. If the boats are based any further than Hum Hum or Goob Weyn, Brian and his agency no longer have any control and he loses my boats and his flotilla. Other than trucks—and most of the roads are washed out—there is no other way to distribute. Could this determination to send me upriver be simply a matter of losing power, of ego?

"Well, I hope to hell we go by chopper."

"Chet and I will radio you after our meeting with the elders. In the meantime, prepare the best boat for both events. And suss out a landing area for a helicopter at the port—I think there's one marked on the wharf. It needs about three hundred meters for an approach."

"What do you mean, best boat? You and I going together in one boat?"

"No, I'm not going. You're going to Hum Hum when we give you the signal from Goob Weyn. Don't worry, we will be waiting for you there and—"

"You're not coming!"

"Can't. By the time we get back, as you rightly point out, the wind will be too strong to go. We have to get a boat upriver today. If we don't, we'll lose the one chance we have. We will wait for you there."

I shake my head and repress a smoldering anger. I suppose I had always thought I would be going alone. I look at Chet for some support. His hands clasped behind his back, he stands next to Brian without expression.

* * *

I am a little anxious about seeing Harun this morning but the drive to the port is almost routine. Other than a noncommittal "*Subah wanaqsan,* Captain," Harun says nothing to me and only a few words to the guards. It is impossible to know what he is thinking or if he is thinking at all. Just as well. He sings along to the whiny Arabic tune on the cassette, which seems to be a little louder today than usual, and that precludes any conversation. I am now cautious of the man; at least by the end of the day I will be elsewhere.

We pull up to that one formidable barricade across the road. I still get the jitters each time we drive through it. The guards peer in, flip thumbs-up, and smile and pull away the coiled razor wire. The little sentry with his big gun stands proudly by the cross ties of the antitank traps. The little bugger who may have earned his bars at our expense motions us through with solemn authority. As we rumble past, the kid breaks into a friendly grin of recognition and waves. I could never hope to understand these people.

At the port, fat little Chaco is lowering boat number one into the bay, ignoring the differing instructions from the surrounding workers. I look around for Ali, but only Abduah, the crane owner, is present.

"What's going on?"

"Boat in the water!" Abduah says proudly.

"Yes, but who told you to put it in the water?"

"Boss."

"What boss? Ali?"

"Bigger boss."

"Which bigger boss?"

He nods toward the port office building. "Many bigger boss today," he says ruefully.

A white UN Land Rover speeds into the port in a plume of dust and drives up to the wharf's edge. Mwalimo, the pleasant Tanzanian procurement officer, emerges without greeting.

"Glad you are still here. I thought maybe you would have left."

"Waiting for the word, Mwalimo. Here to see me off?"

"No, no. I brought you these."

He opens the rear door. A couple of baby blue UN combat helmets, **Unicef** stenciled on the brow, lie on a heap of flak jackets on the seat.

"Bravo Delta thought you should carry them. Just in case."

I had given up asking. Their delivery now is not a particularly good omen—like the boat in the water, another nail in the coffin.

I put on the helmet, adjust the chin strap, and grin stupidly at Mwalimo, then at the crowd of dockworkers who have gathered around.

"They are very good," he assures me. "That one is new."

I would expect the Somali workmen to laugh, but a shadow of suspicion falls over the men. One voice, dark and murmurous, rolls over the mob. I don't much like the change in mood. So I ham it up, bang a fist against the helmet, and make silly faces. Still there is no laughter. I unbuckle the chin strap, wondering if I haven't abruptly become someone other to these with whom I have worked so long. Maybe they see me now as a peacekeeper, maybe as an interventionist; maybe they think I have betrayed them.

"Will it take a bullet, Mwalimo?" I say, taking it off.

"Not directly. Not supposed to."

"Last time I had a helmet like this was in high school. American football."

Mwalimo, a Dinka from central Tanzania, looks at me blankly.

The flak jacket that he hands me must be about twenty to thirty pounds. It is not like the one I saw in Harun's home. Not baby blue, not Kevlar or whatever it is supposed to be; this is Vietnam or World War II vintage, olive drab and dusty and stained with old mud or old blood. It is not easy to put on. How the hell is anyone expected to wear this thing when driving a speedboat at forty knots down some winding river? One bad turn and, if you fall in, it will take you straight down to the bottom like diver's weights. "This is supposed to stop a bullet, right?"

Harun approaches, grinning. What does that smirk mean?

"Captain. You go now?"

"Soon, Harun."

He looks below at the lone boat bobbing on the water.

"You must not go," he says quietly. His tone is gentle, his eyes sympathetic; I cannot imagine him capable of such anger.

"It's a job, Harun."

I give the flak jacket and helmet to a Unicef guard who shoulders them down the metal ladder. The boat is ready to go, loaded with a few bags of maize meal, blankets, a couple of tarps, and jerry cans of water and extra petrol. With all the gear stowed, the small boat lies heavily in the water. There is precious little freeboard for any kind of seaway. If I leave soon, I should be able to make the entrance to the mouth of the Jubba in less than forty-five minutes, just before the sea breeze gets up. That is my professional view, thoughts I now concentrate on to avoid defining the real feelings that churn through my system.

I feel deceived, cheated. Brian had said he was going and if he was going, I was going. Yet here I stand looking down at this puny toy boat, waiting for the phone to ring, for word that the governor has refused to commute my sentence.

"We've got a shooting at the airport," Alpha Kilo announces over the radio.

"Anybody we know?" I ask.

"Don't think so. A couple of gunshots just under the tower. There were some people running around down there yelling like fools, but it's quiet now. No one has come up the stairs yet."

Sierra squawks back from some obvious distance: "Sounds like another Somali conversation."

"Roger that. The same one we hear every day."

"Sierra Sierra, this is Juliet Bravo."

"Sierra Sierra back."

"Sierra Sierra, I got a boat in the water and we are ready to go." Unwittingly, my trepidation is succumbing to excitement.

"Good copy. Alpha Kilo, you on station?"

"Alpha Kilo," Andrew answers.

"Where is the chopper? Nearby?"

"Just left for Bardera."

"Better tell 'em they may be needed in Kismayo. We'll confirm in about twenty mikes or so. Copy?"

"Good copy."

"You copy, John?"

"Juliet Bravo back. Roger the helicopter and fingers crossed! Juliet Bravo is standing by."

I dare not think it, dare not hope it. It is possible, though. I pray for the reprieve.

It is an endless, mindless wait. Some people yawn constantly when they get nervous. Others yammer on about nothing in particular, tell jokes. Some pace, walk around. Some scratch their heads, their balls. Right now, I need a cup of coffee and a good laugh.

I realize these are my last moments in this place. I don't really think I will ever see Kismayo again, and that is a comforting thought. Yet I find it extraordinary that I came to know the place with such frightful intimacy. Amid the days of *Sturm und Drang,* there was relative peace, a sort of security, an equanimous routine. I had a bunk that I was calling my own, colleagues I was getting to know, local people I could work with. I was even able to recognize their guns. Now I fear leaving this for an even greater unknown.

I wander over to the warehouse and peer inside for anything overlooked. Another UN rig pulls up. Jeri McGuinness, Happy One, steps out; long white dress, radio packed like a pistol, short black hair luminous in the sun, she seems uncertain, lost. A few workmen in the area begin to gather round. Jeri may be a powerful fixture in the IDP camps and at the airport, but my men have never before seen anything like her. They hold back, out of respect, awe, even fear.

"Thought I'd come down. I've never been to the port." She looks around the warehouse and at the remaining boat. She seems stiff, possibly critical.

"My office." I can think of nothing clever to say. "Show you around?"

She walks with me out to the pier. Her UN rig follows behind. She gazes down at the two sunken patrol boats clearly visible beneath the water, their missile tubes straining to break through the surface.

"Russian, I'm told. Bombed. Don't know when." We continue walking along the wharf.

"Is that what you're taking up the river?" she says, squinting in the sun toward my small blue boat tied to the pier.

"That's the one."

"Doesn't look so ugly in the water. You could ski behind it."

"It has been suggested."

I am finding this difficult. I don't feel like being a tour guide or being conversational. Or even pleasant. She is offering no personality, nothing to go with, nothing to react to. I have my own problems: My stomach is in knots with something like the first-night jitters before the curtain is raised. I don't want to talk, I just want to hop in that boat and hit the road.

"Well, I just wanted to see the port," she says abruptly. She shakes my hand stiffly. "Good luck." I expect her to turn on her heels, but she hesitates. Her eyes are remarkably clear, suddenly soft, that impenetrable patina removed. She leans forward and kisses me lightly on the cheek. She turns, ducks back into the car, and is driven quickly away.

My cheek is afire from that whispered touch. It has the same impact as everything else—extreme and frightening—and without a history for me to know how to react.

"Juliet Bravo, Sierra Sierra.

"Juliet Bravo, Sierra Sierra—you copy? Juliet Bravo?"

Chet has to call twice before I realize the call is for me. Here I go. My bladder flutters.

"Juliet Bravo, stand down on Hum Hum. I repeat, stand down on Hum Hum. Having a little trouble with the elders. They can't—or won't—guarantee your safety. Have Alpha Kilo get that chopper to the port. You're flying to Marerey or Bardera or Sakow—your call."

"God damn! Great news, Chet!" I respond, forgetting all radio etiquette. "Fucking great news! You all right up there?"

"Yeah, we're okay. We should be back at the port in about thirty. Don't forget, three hundred meters for the chopper's approach."

Leaning back against the cold cement warehouse wall, I regard Brian and Chet in a fresh light—did I not give them enough credit? Did I exaggerate the dangers of the trip, building my own fears without warrant? Such thoughts are a luxury I can afford to have now that it will never happen.

Part II
Death Be Not Proud

16.
Gentle Sleeps the Night

Marerey Base

IT is natural to feel a little out of context when arriving at a strange place that will have to become home. Strange place, indeed: This dusty airstrip that appeared too short a few days ago is considerably shorter today, nothing more than an elevated two-track. The wide area at the northeast end of the runway where the tents are located is being swallowed by the encroaching floodwater; in the opposite direction the strip vanishes into a vibrating heat that hovers above the last of the dry land. Conical red-dirt termite mounds rise out of the scrub. Shoulder-high grass on the embankment waves gently in a slight breeze and disappears down into the deeper water beyond. A row of steel ribs, remains of the bombed-out sugar factory, reaches out of the horizon. This is one hell of a lonely place.

It was reported that the rains were particularly heavy in this area, but you would never know it by the parched land yet unclaimed by the rising water. It had been raining as we landed, but minutes after the passage of the shower, the moisture steamed out of the ground and the earth caked dry and hard. While part of Somalia is hemorrhaging into the Indian Ocean from the torrents in the high country, the serious rains here have let up for a time, although evidently they are not far away: A dark squall line lies ominously to the north; sweeping gray brushstrokes from the distant downpour drag obliquely over the earth.

I stand as a solitary figure on the airstrip with my tin lockbox and my old backpack at my feet. I am no longer certain I want to be here. I have an odd sensation of being exiled, banished from a place that I was beginning to accept as home; to some degree Kismayo had become livable, endurable. Looking over this desolation, I feel very alone.

* * *

LESS than an hour before, the Mi-8, preceded by the thumping of its rotors, had sped out of the west, skimmed across Kismayo Bay, and settled onto the helicopter-landing zone on the wharf. The Russian-built helicopter, with World Food Program initials stenciled roughly on its fat belly, appeared big enough to carry the boat and then some. The blades had hardly stopped spinning before three crewmen, loud, good-natured South Africans, alighted.

"Well, now, who is Juliet Bravo?" one of them bawled. This was a big man, with giant calves, huge hands, cheerful blue eyes, and a bushy cavalry mustache.

"You Juliet Bravo?" the pilot asked the gawking relief worker.

"Yes, and you're the angels of mercy come to take me out of here."

"Yah, okay. We have another stop after this—what are we taking?"

"That." I nod toward the still dripping boat lying on its side on the pier. "And my gear, and that stack of relief supplies over by the warehouse. Will it all fit?"

"Yah, we can take up to three tons. Let's get the boat loaded first."

"You guys look like football players—or rugby. You ever play for the Springboks?"

"He's the one," the man said, pointing to a smaller blond companion who leaned against the aluminum fuselage, drinking out of a plastic water bottle. "He once played for them—fly half." He grins, apparently pleased with the question. "I was too bloody slow. You a Springboks fan?"

"Absolutely. Great team."

"We think so. Where are we taking you?"

"They haven't told you?"

"They said it was up to you. Heard Bardera, Sakow, or Marerey."

I jerked my thumb upward. "Anywhere that is up and out. Marerey will do."

It was not important where I went; it would be out of Kismayo and I would be able to start work: delivering, rescuing, feeding, whatever it was I was hired to do. Although I was not certain that in Marerey I would do anything more than I did in Kismayo: sit on my ass, duck the Somali tempers, find make-work, collect the time and the money. Possibly that is what UN relief workers were supposed to do. In the many weeks in Kismayo I had not seen any humanitarian efforts. Jeri was apparently trying to feed the IDP, but I didn't see it and so it meant nothing to me.

Sakow was a consideration, a town on the middle Jubba where Wolff's flotilla had been working for weeks. The bridges were washed out and the boats were being used to ferry villagers across the river. There was ample reason to choose to go to Sakow: Andrew had said he heard that there was plenty of cold beer, and the sociable Swedes were there. But could I handle communal tents, sitting around a campfire, and someone with a guitar kicking off a singalong? Perhaps it was because of my reclusive tendencies but after Kismayo and the strange intimacy shared with the others, I didn't think I was prepared to adapt to some marshmallow camaraderie, some Adirondack bonding. There was Marerey, on the other hand, a small base next to an airstrip, no more than a few tarps draped over some stakes chopped out of the bush—that was good enough for me.

Loading the boat onto the helicopter's ramp went remarkably smoothly—no shouting, no pushing, no punches thrown, and no clacking of rifles cocked. There was no tense selection of men to heave the thing up the helicopter's gaping backside. Without so much as an angry word, the Somalis positioned themselves behind, beside, and under, and for the last time we good-naturedly *koh, laba, sader, hoek* the boat into the aircraft. One of the men with whom I had worked caught my eye, grinned, and flipped me a private little thumbs-up.

A UN rig sped onto the wharf. A change in plans? Sierra Sierra popped out, serious and dour as usual, announced he was joining the flight to . . . "Where did you decide to go?"

"Marerey."

"You've been there before?" He apparently didn't remember.

"Brian not joining us?"

"No." No explanation.

"I would have thought he could use a break from this place." Chet simply shrugged. I sensed there might have been some conflict between the two.

The loaded boat and a few extra bags of maize meal and other relief supplies filled the bird. Turbos on, the eight-bladed chopper began its windup with an ear-piercing whine. Sitting on bags of relief supplies, I stared off into the middle distance, curiously deadened. I knew with some certainty that I had gone to the edge and I dared to be pushed over. I felt I had seen into that window of my fate. I knew absolutely that the chances of surviving a run between the warring sides were not good, no better than those of someone walking between German and Allied trenches in WWI. My reprieve was a divine gift. I am hardly a religious person, but it has since become a conviction of faith: Someone or something decided to rework the future. And, too, I suppose I should have expected that if the United Nations was not able to guarantee my safety, it would not send me into the lion's den. Or would it? At what point do the decisions in the field conflict with official policy and the need to please the donors? There comes a time, but more often in the military, I suspect, when the requirement for victory, success, advancement, ego—call it what you will—overrides common sense and soldiers are sent marching foolishly to their deaths—the last soldier to die in a war that was a mistake. Are relief workers really fodder, expendable? Here in Somalia, despite the talk, I don't think I will ever have an answer. I will never know who made the final decision to cancel the run, but I feel certain it was Chet. He is the security man. His is the last word.

As we lifted off the landing zone, I peered out the porthole for one last look at the wharf. Harun was there among the dockworkers. He held on to his baseball cap against the rotor wash and looked up. His thin dark face grew smaller. He offered a blind uncertain wave, then walked slowly back to the car.

Skirring over the bay to the mainland—a little higher than roof level to avoid drug-induced potshots—we reached the murky floodwaters, a blurred brown canvas underneath, and later hovered, then landed on the single strip of burnt earth that was Marerey Base.

The dry land at the site appeared to have been halved since my visit. The camp balanced on the very edge of a watery grave, about to tip over and drown in it. Open living quarters and storage areas of poles and gray tarp flapped and shook in the prop wash of the helicopter's blades. A blinding rain shower pelted us and quickly passed on as we piled out and ducked instinctively under the slowing blades. The Somalis at the camp wandered over to the chopper and waited for the rear ramp to lower.

"Not much of a place." The bushy Afrikaner wiped the back of his neck with a kerchief and stared at the collection of small tents.

"Hell of a lot better than Kismayo."

"Yah, I've heard. I'd say these would come in handy." He reached through the door and pulled out a six-pack of beer in a black plastic bag. I'm not one to demonstrate affection for other men, but I came close to kissing the guy. Not just because it was beer but because of the unexpected friendship. "From the Springboks."

"I owe you a few in Nairobi."

"Sure. Keep your head down out here."

Within minutes the boat was off-loaded, and with the encouragement of the Somali chant it was eased down the embankment and into the water next to a row of small Styrofoam rafts. The helicopter lifted off and away and disappeared with its noisy thumping chasing not far behind.

My boat attracted a crowd. Some glided their fingers reverently over its smooth metallic-blue hull. Others reached over and cautiously turned the steering wheel.

* * *

ALONE on the dusty strip with my gear at my feet, the chaos that surrounds me should provide the makings of a fine new adventure. This, however, has become less an adventure than something more personal. It has become an emotional and mental testing ground. Whether because of the events in Kismayo or because of some unknown or smothered fragility that I have always had, I find myself now overwhelmed by dislocation and dissociation. I don't know where I've been, where I'm going, and in the private scheme of things, to what purpose. I don't know whether I am happy, sad, or fearful. By God, I think that for one of the few times in my recent adult life I am experiencing real emptiness, a hollowness.

I drag my tin trunk toward what looks like the largest tented structure. Yusuf Hersi, the soft-speaking NGO representative in charge of organizing the deliveries in the area, appears from behind the largest of the tents at the end of the runway and shouts a greeting and approaches. He cuts quite a figure walking down the airstrip; erect bearing, long narrow black face, long legs, tall as a Masai warrior, he might have carried a spear but he carries a notebook, his finger still in the pages where he had been interrupted. His saintly eyes confer gratitude undeserved. Tucking his papers under his arm, he takes my hand with both of his and thanks me for bringing my boat here. He makes me feel needed, a savior. Lifting one end of my lockbox, he leads the way through ankle-deep water to a large open tarpaulin-covered shelter on dry land at the other side of the compound.

Turning the corner, I jerk back at the sight of a white man inside, reclining against stacked bags of maize and reading a newspaper. He is a big man, more brawn than fat, balding at the crown. His insouciant pose and his loosely wrapped sarong immediately suggest Charles Laughton acting the part of some jowly Roman emperor, popping grapes into his mouth as Nubian concubines dance naked before him.

"Hello, who have we here?" he says, peering over his glasses. "A new arrival, is it? Well, very good, very good indeed. The more the merrier."

I did not expect another international. I think I'm pleased. However, privately and immediately I wonder what this guy is doing sitting on his ass while all around people are supposed to be dying. Is this relief work?

The man leans forward a little and offers a limp hand of welcome. "Robin Pierpoint-Twitchell. At your service." His voice is softly resonant, and his diction imprecise, the loose and lazy marbles-in-the-mouth speech that hints of some refinement.

"Cup of tea?" he offers.

"Thanks."

"And what brings you to our little gathering? I heard the helicopter. Brought some supplies, I hope."

"Some. And my boat."

"Another intrepid mariner. Excellent. I'm afraid there is no milk. We do have sugar. Where did you come in from?"

"Kismayo."

"Ah, the port. A lovely spot for a resort, I understand."

"Not anytime soon—fifty years, perhaps. A hard place to call home."

"Yes, I've heard. You won't find the security situation here as bad as Kismayo. Still, we have our own troubles, hippos and pythons, that sort of thing. Fortunately—"

"You're also a boat driver?" I ask.

"Six trips today. Quite a challenge, as you no doubt will discover." Frowning, he adds, "As I was saying—the security situation is a little different here than in Kismayo. Fortunately, the children with the guns are more interested in the helping than in the killing. I rather suspect it is because they are getting paid to do so. Not sure how long that will last, however."

"I have noticed a lot less guns." The few assault rifles I have seen are carried casually across the top of the bony shoulders of the young soldiers. Not a posture that lent their weapons to immediate use. "How long have you been here?"

"This is our third day. Still getting our feet wet, you might say."

"We?"

"My partner, David, is on a run at the moment. He should be back soon."

"Some palace you have here," I say, looking around.

"Yes, we do quite well considering our circumstances—something like a home. Our storeroom, vegetables and the like, is in that corner. Our kitchen is here where the kettle is. We take turns cooking for each other. Our library, such as it is, is next to the veggies. You're welcome to what we have: some old *Spectator*s if you are of the conservative bent, an outdated *Guardian Weekly* or two if you lean a little left of center, and a few *Granta* if you have some literary interests."

"Quite a library."

"David tends toward the literary. I, on the other hand, tend toward the political. I wonder which are you?"

"Somewhere in the middle, I guess."

Robin Pierpoint-Twitchell, who drops that he is a Cambridge graduate, strikes me as the sort who should be wearing a bowler and carrying an umbrella to his nine-to-five in the City, London's financial district. He says he and his partner own a camp on the Tana River in Kenya. Because of tribal battles on the coast and preelection riots in Nairobi, tourism in Kenya has taken a hit and their safari business is temporarily closed. "Nothing like a little local disaster to keep the coffers full in times of need," he says.

"You've done this sort of thing before?"

"Two years ago in Loki."

"Loki?"

"Lokichoggio—the Sudan. Before that, Mogadishu. You can usually count on a humanitarian crisis somewhere in the area. Usually comes around Christmastime. Good for the finances, you see. You?"

"First time."

"Well, I suspect you will become another disaster junkie like the rest of us. Are you a Yank?"

"You mean American? Yes. Are you English?"

"No, Kenyan. You know, I quite like the Americans. I am going to marry one." I am not sure whether this is a boast—I've bagged an American—or condescension to marrying one. It might be that communications between us will be difficult. "Yes," he continues, "the money from this job should get us off on the right foot."

"Is the river still rising?" I ask, nodding toward the floodwater that nibbles away at the dry earth a few yards from the shelter.

"Actually, I don't believe so. It has peaked."

"Looks like it has risen just since I arrived. Looks like it might drown this place."

"Rubbish. Don't you know? It simply must go down. Because we are here."

"I brought some beer."

"I could tell straightaway you were a gentleman."

The tinny sound of a small outboard grows out of the distance. "Ah, that would be David. Another cuppa?" A few minutes later a bright red motorboat, one of those I had seen in front of the hangar in Nairobi, putters through the tall grass up to the edge of the airstrip. A wiry figure in short-sleeve shirt, multipocketed shorts, and a faded baseball cap on a ponytail of white hair unlatches the outboard and tilts it upward. Two young gunmen jump out into the ankle-deep water.

Robin's partner sloshes toward us, lugging two jerry cans. "That's it for the day, Robbie," David announces in a scratchy voice. A singsong quality accents a slight brogue. He places the jerry cans neatly in a corner. "How many trips today, Robbie?"

"Six—three up, three down. You?"

"Five." Turning to me he offers his hand. "That your ski boat, is it?"

"In a manner of speaking. I brought it in from Kismayo. Doesn't look like it's the right boat for the job."

"No, it doesn't really." His boxy red runabout tethered to a bush seems ideal: higher freeboard and lying not as deep in the water. The draft of my go-fast with a planing V-hull may not permit me to get too close to the supply tents. I hope I can get help lugging full jerry cans of fuel and the fifty-kilo bags of supplies, more than a hundred pounds each, through the mud.

"Tea, Robbie?" David asks.

"Well, of course, old chap. It is usually your job, you know, but I forced myself since you were on another perilous mission. Did it go well?"

"No problems. Managed to avoid a small crocodile." David withdraws a red bandanna from his back pocket, wipes his brow, and gazes hard at the edge of creeping water. "You know, Robbie, I believe the river is still rising."

"Oh, no, it just can't, David. I was just telling our new American friend that it couldn't possibly. We do live here."

"I don't think that matters very much, Robbie."

"Well, it certainly matters to me, David."

This sententious banter is the form through which these two, evidently very close friends, communicate. The antiquated style of stereotypical English, I am to discover later, is also the manner of speech of many of those white Kenyans whose ancestors, sons of the English aristocracy, colonized the nation at the turn of the century. Robbie natters like a woman of the landed gentry playing whist, and David responds like a quiet husband who never takes his wife very seriously. He is the straight man. It is a routine that apparently has been well practiced over the years, a competitive and playful verbosity that keeps matters from becoming too serious.

In the course of introduction and small talk, David reveals that he is a fourth-generation Kenyan of Irish descent. When Kenya was still British territory, he started a survey business charting frontiers as well as boundaries for wildlife parks and game reserves. He makes it quite clear that he is not Irish and certainly not British: He is a white Kenyan. Robin interrupts that despite these depravities, his partner has somehow managed to learn the difference between a rutting hippo and a love-struck rhino. David's darkened leathery skin, a victim of years under the tropic sun, attests to his lifetime in the bush.

Both David and Robbie appear to be the quintessential "Kenya cowboys," those frontier types who feel just as comfortable in the bush as on the streets of Nairobi. Fluent in Kiswahili, they are not long-standing expatriates but in fact are Kenyans, regarded as just another tribe, one with its own strange codes and rituals but African nonetheless. While many are sent to England for their education, most return to the family business or to the interior, where through the generations their families owned or managed huge coffee, tea, and sisal plantations.

The younger Robin, the self-appointed grand seigneur of our estate here on this part of the Jubba, keeps the records and reports to the office in Nairobi the daily tally of the supplies delivered. I cannot help but wonder if he has not already tried to organize a cricket team among the Somalis.

"I've suggested to J-B that he put his tent next to yours, David. Improve the neighborhood, I should imagine."

"Yes, I think the neighborhood could use some improvement, Robbie."

Robin sleeps on the same ratty mattress he says he carries with him on safari. It looks moth-eaten but it is clean enough for him. Like a child's tattered security blanket. Whatever critters reside therein, at least they are his own. He sleeps in public view under a large mosquito net strung from pole to pole.

I set up my tent nearby on a small patch of dry ground next to David's. His old dirt-brown tent, stained, frayed, and repaired with duct tape, looks like it has seen a thousand bush camps. It is about the same size as mine, a little two-man affair. My tent still boasts the store-bought sheen of a greenhorn. It is not mine; carrying a tent across oceans in a boat is unusual—the boat is tent enough. The German owner of a fishing club in Kilifi loaned it on the condition that I ask the UN people in Nairobi if there was work for him during his off-season. I asked. They laughed. You want the job, you come get it. We don't call you.

The humorous tweaking between the two old friends is a blessed relief; they seem to find humor in most of what they discuss. I take long healthy sighs, breathe the air that is free of tension, fear, and the threat of violence. We sit around the gas camp-stove cooker. David chops onions into some packages of Chinese noodle soup.

I step out into the dark for a pee. The soft glow from the many cooking fires illumines a strange night scene: The fires line the edge of the strip like a row of landing lights; their smoke floats low over the camp like a gentle blanket. The hundred or so locals who off-loaded the aircraft sleep under mosquito nets on army-issue-type cots on the side of the runway. Their murmuring voices create a gentle current under the din of strange night sounds from outside the base. Stars and a thin slice of moon reflect on the still water at my feet as motes of dancing light: Orion, the constellation, sprawls across the sky overhead, and down to the northwest, the Pleiades, the cluster of seven sisters. The Southern Cross leans on its side just above the horizon. Fresh out of Kismayo, it is as close to the heavens as this earthbound mortal can ever hope to get.

I can't walk far; there is not much land left. At the rate the water is rising, it might reach us sometime tonight. The last dry land then will be the edges of the strip and the strip itself. Landing a cargo flight here on this shrinking airfield should test the best of them.

The mosquitoes in Kismayo were a nuisance, but here they are pestilential. At dusk they arrived at the camp as clouds and attacked as a swarm. I have no Somali *kikoi,* that light cotton sarong that the workers and Robin wear during their off-hours, but I did bring a pair of Thai fisherman's trousers, baggy loose-fitting pants held up by cinching the waistband and folding it back upon itself. Despite the bug dope and long-sleeve shirts, the mosquitoes still manage to needle through. I have seen what malaria can do and I don't fancy a case of it.

"Now, do tell David and me everything you can about Kismayo," Robin says. "Our little outing is quite a change, I should imagine."

I am eager to talk. I begin with the pirates on the wharf and intend to tell about the child at the roadblock, the dying baby, and the shooting of the airplane, and I begin to lose my audience. They are not much interested, and although both make pretenses of being fascinated, David's eyes grow heavy and he wants to sleep. Robbie's attention is wandering, I suspect more from some solipsistic affliction than from the telling. Maybe it cannot be told. Maybe it shouldn't be.

Sitting in a lotus position inside my tent, sipping a warm beer, I listen, revel in the peace. This is not a Kismayo silence, a silence of suspension, nerves open, alert, tense, ready to spring, ready to dive for cover, broken by the rattle of automatics. This is a sound of nature, a tender scherzo of frog croaks and cicada scratches.

A sudden unexpected grunt, loud and impatient from within the grass next to us, makes my back hairs stand. "What the hell was that?" David's tent is so close that I can hear him rustling inside.

"Warthogs."

"Dangerous?"

"Sometimes."

The ratchetlike chatter from the cicadas comes in waves, softly at first, then reaching a volume that briefly overwhelms all conversation. They fall abruptly silent, then tentatively begin again, reaching a drawn-out crescendo; the wave collapses upon itself and the silence is sudden, total. During the intermission a slough of a breeze and the delicate piddling of the water as it laps the shore only a foot or so from the tent create a soothing berceuse. I lie in relative peace, feeling safer inside this flimsy shelter than I did behind the walled fortress of the UN quarters in Kismayo. Yet I am mindful of those who remain. What will become of them? In my mind's eye I see them going about their jobs, bouncing like pinballs from crisis to crisis. Blood money and the number of camels now seem so absurd, so otherworldly. I must not forget them, I should be concerned for them, and for a fleeting moment I am and then I sleep.

17.
The Tribe of the Damned

THE peace I felt as I knocked back that can of beer, absorbing the gentleness of the moment, was not the peace I experienced in my sleep. Inside my dream, I relived the events at Harun's home. The buildup to the final insult is painfully slow, fleshed out, filled with portent. For I sensed, knew what was coming. Harun slapped her. And slapped her again and that frightful sound woke me. I sat bolt upright in the darkness.

A frog jumps onto my tent: *Slap!* It loses its grip and slides off with a splash. The tent is one of the few dry spots; the frogs regard it as an island, and clinging tenaciously, they are taking refuge on it. The roof sags under their weight and I punch it from beneath, sending them flying into the water.

The stars dance on the sparkling surface of sea that is at my door. The four-inch rubberized strip above the floor holds back the flood, but it won't be long before the water pours in over the top. The river is here. Surrounded, it is a sensation of being adrift on a life raft. Across the compound, the breeze ruffles the water under the canopied cots upon which the Somalis sleep.

"Good God!" Sounds like Robbie.

I crawl out naked and barefoot and stand surveying the rising water. Robbie is sitting up under his net, a bit dazed, looking puzzled. Water is lapping at his mattress, soaking it through.

"Morning, J-B. I say, David," Robbie calls over quietly. His tone is now one of mild interest. "Do you feel like you're living in an aquarium?"

A clear voice responds from within the old tent. "Should I, Robbie?"

"I should say so. Take a look outside."

The tent flap opens and David's stubbled face pokes through the opening, his white hair splayed in every direction. "I thought it was something of a wet dream, Robbie."

"This is no time for levity, David. For God's sakes, man, we're sinking!"

"Shall we bail?"

"I shouldn't think it would do much good. Perhaps it's time to shift our homes elsewhere. Then perhaps a predawn cup of tea."

Do people really talk like this? Why weren't these jokers in Kismayo where we really needed the relief?

The process of moving is surreal. Through dark tones and tenebrous colors, ghostly figures rise from their sleep and look around in dismay at the shimmering water that ripples under them. In the dim light of the partial moon, with voices deep and hushed, shadowy Somalis with the movement of sleepwalkers carry armfuls of personal gear through the gloom, a dark-time shuffle accompanied by the laughter of frogs and cicadas.

The three of us sit together on the dirt alongside the runway, looking out upon the destruction. A few workmen sit beside us, finger-eating bowls of cold *ugali*. The sun is not quite up and lightning flashes to the northwest. David's blackened kettle steams atop the small gas canister stove at our feet. We are surrounded by water; rubbish floats upon it like flotsam from a sunken ship. Something is skewed here—we are becoming those we are here to help.

The Somalis start removing the old warehouse shelter and recreating it on the berm alongside the strip. After tea we will have to set up a new home for ourselves. It will be close quarters, bundled together on the end of the strip.

"Our backs are to the shag, gents," Robbie says quietly.

"Shag?"

He sweeps his hand over the endless miles of uninhabitable scrubland behind us. "British administrative term."

Staring at the water that eats away at our feet proffers a curious sensation: The almighty power of man is impotent here. The Somalis with all their weaponry are powerless to stop the work of nature; they cannot shoot guns at the rising floodwater that drives them from their homes and expect it to obey. Watching the river chase us onto the runway is comparable to the sensation of the helplessness when the ground begins to vibrate with the first movement of an earthquake or when finding oneself at the mercy of a cyclone at sea. Nature does what it does. Sometimes it is healthy to be so reminded.

* * *

THOSE red flat-bottom eighteen-foot motorboats that Robbie and David drive are nearly perfect for the job. Each is powered by a Yamaha 40; they scoot right along. Comparing mine to theirs is like comparing a Maserati to a Datsun; with its sleek lines and shiny metallic blue hull—the cartoon faces long ago removed—I feel I have come to the party overdressed.

Driving my little go-fast loaded with supplies on fast-moving floodwater is not like tooling around Kismayo Bay. All our boats were designed for waterskiing and are tender and unstable when loaded, but mine, with its V-hull, is the least steady, as I discover during my first delivery.

My passengers are two village elders, dignified older men dressed in clean but threadbare shirts and trousers. In the absence of a formal government authority, it is the elder who administers the day-to-day affairs of the community. Joining the trip are two small children belonging to one of them and a couple of boy soldiers with their AK-47s, and they are all quick to get in. The children lend an air of excitement, as if we are going on an outing. We have been loaded with twelve fifty-kilo bags of maize, an assortment of blankets, and cartons of the Humanitarian Daily Rations. With only a few inches of the sides of the boat above the surface, I am worried. Yet David's was similarly packed and looked as fragile, so I say nothing. I am the last one to board and I can't move it—it sits solidly in the mud. We could just wait it out; the rising waters will float it eventually. However, some of the nearby workmen push it through the razor grass until it is free and pointed in the right direction, down what is known as the airport road.

Mounting the boat without spilling passengers and goods is difficult. As I crawl aboard, a strong current begins to sweep the boat downstream toward a half-submerged thorn tree. The groping fingers of the thorny branches beckon us closer into their clutches—we are about to be made a pincushion. Frantic, I try to start the engine. The startled eyes of my passengers turn to me with one common question: How are you going to stop us from getting hurt? One of the boys, holding his assault rifle by the barrel, tries to fend off the tree. The engine finally kicks in just in time for the thorns to miss the children and the elders sitting atop the supplies in the front. The guards move quickly out of the way, but I am at the wheel and cannot move and drive at the same time. The spiky tree claws at my exposed skin. I don't feel the sting; I feel stupid. I know now the engine should have been running before we pushed the boat into the stream. I'd considered that, but I didn't like the idea of starting it while I was still in the water. This was the way I saw David do it.

We were to follow David on this first trip, but he has disappeared—not an auspicious beginning. David is used to these little boats, apparently, having one or two of them at their river safari camp. I have never driven a wobbly overloaded boat with nervous, shifting passengers down a narrow winding road, through conflicting currents, lifting overfalls, and surrounded on each side by the gnarly fingers of twisted and broken trees. To maintain steerageway I have to keep us powered up to at least fifteen knots, dangerously fast considering our low freeboard (the distance between the water's surface and the top of the sides). We are too loaded to rise to a plane, so we plow through the water, pushing out a large rolling wake. I am driving by the seat of my pants.

There is no chart to follow, not even a road map. But I was told how to get to the village: Drive down the airport road, then through the fourth break of the partially submerged hedgerow on the left (the breaks all look the same), past the big neem tree across from some protruding steel fence posts, across a field, which is about six feet underwater, but careful to avoid some sunken irrigation pipes that are near the two banana trees—those pipes will tear the bottom out if struck—through a copse of mango trees, diagonally across another field, under the long broken overhead line of irrigation pipes, then—careful again—a quick sharp left turn up the fast-moving waters of the canal, and then right at the white water that pours over a submerged bridge. Now you will be in the main irrigation canal. However, some of the landmarks may no longer be there, either washed away or submerged during the night. "Take care in the backwaters," David had warned as his parting words. "Hippos like the quiet water."

With David out of sight, I expect to be able to rely on the young gunmen and the elders for directions, all of whom assume I know where I'm going and how to get there. I try to ask for some directions in my kitchen Somali but am ignored. After a wrong turn, one of the puckered elders—he has no teeth—turns angrily and begins jabbering and pointing this way and that. His tirade is interrupted by a sudden jarring crunch that kicks the engine out of the water. The spinning propeller screams. We have hit the roof of a house. The current grabs us and sends us backward, spinning us in a vortex. I throw the transmission into neutral, then turn to the big engine behind me and bear-hug the thing back into the water. We are under way again, but I am shaking.

"Diep maleh! Diep maleh!" I say lightly. I am the pilot reassuring my passengers. They look up with suspicion. In the distance, the thumping of the rotors of the Mi-8 grows louder, apparently on the way to the base with another delivery.

The villagers on the dike about a hundred yards to the left, alerted by the sound of the outboard, begin massing before their temporary homes of plastic and poles and sticks and random cloth. These are the people I am here to help, those without potable water, food, or much adequate shelter. Spotting the boat, they begin yelling, waving pieces of rags, trying to attract my attention. Small children run excitedly up and down the dike. That, I think, is where we are headed, but we cannot get there directly; if we could go in a straight line we would be there in minutes. It will take another twenty minutes of this exhausting wrestle with an unresponsive overloaded boat in a current that attempts to spill us.

We never make it to the village. Two figures on the far side of the submerged field appear to be sitting on the water, perhaps on an island, and one is hailing us. I throttle down the engine and approach very slowly. A boy on a disintegrating polystyrene raft struggles to hold on to a bush to keep from being swept downstream. His passenger is a frail old man in a mud-covered djellaba who sits cross-legged at his feet, his possessions in a plaited basket in his lap. His silvery goatee is stained with drying blood and he is bleeding from the nose and ears. As the boy squawks a greeting and appeal, the old man slowly raises his canceled eyes.

Despite the muffled protests of the elders—I wonder if they would have me leave these two and continue the delivery?—I tie a rope to a nearby upstream bush and pay out the line until we are next to the raft. I order my passengers not to move; a little imbalance could overturn us. I reach over and lift the old man. He is merely a bundle of bones and loose skin. His fingers clamp on to my arms and dig into my skin like talons on a field snake. He communicates briefly through frightened clouded eyes, seeking less my physical help than some reassurance. As I haul him up and over the side of the boat, his body begins to convulse and he vomits blood—over himself, onto the white foam raft below, and over my hands. I am paralyzed. I freeze. There is an explosive movement of bowels and a terrible smell. My passengers are all shouting at once, angrily, but I jerk him onto the one unoccupied space available, atop some thick woolen blankets. My guards have scurried away to the front of the boat.

I scrub my hands desperately in the floodwater, put the boat in gear, and return to Marerey Base. The old man lies brokenly, his white robe soiled with color. Back at camp, the Mi-8 has landed by the water's edge on the airstrip and is being off-loaded. I am almost able to run the boat up to the helicopter's ramp.

Interesting, the expressions of disgust on the faces of the Somalis as they lift the stained and nearly lifeless human off the boat into the interior of the chopper—as if they haven't gotten used to spilled blood by now. With some luck he will be alive by the time he arrives at the MSF hospital in Kismayo. But not likely.

"What do we have here?" Robbie stands by the chopper, his arms crossed like an inspecting sergeant major. "Rather messy business."

"Bleeding from everywhere. Don't suppose he has AIDS, do you?"

"At his age? Probably not. Though you might get yourself checked, old fellow. I'd say Rift Valley Fever, by the look of it. Or Ebola. Some sort of hemorrhagic fever, certainly. Surprised it is here in Somalia, though."

"Infectious?"

"Don't think anyone knows. Get it from flies or mosquitoes, I hear."

Africa is the breeding ground of a number of mysterious infectious viruses, and new unidentified strains crop up with frightening regularity. (HIV/AIDS, which kills three million people each year worldwide, is thought to have originated in west-central Africa when an isolated tribe ate infected chimpanzee meat.)

Viral Hemorrhagic Fevers (VHF), and this is probably one of them, are some of the least understood diseases and the most difficult to control. According to the Centers for Disease Control in Atlanta, Georgia, they affect the body's organs and vascular system. While some types of hemorrhagic fever viruses can cause relatively mild illnesses, many trigger diseases that are contagious and particularly deadly.

It is not surprising that out here, where cholera, malaria, dengue fever, typhus, and other diseases are widespread, especially during the floods, locals pick up the virus. There are enough transmitters. According to the CDC, humans get hemorrhagic fevers by coming in contact with urine, fecal matter, saliva, or other body excretions from infected rodents as well as from bites of mosquitoes and ticks. Initial symptoms include fever, fatigue, dizziness, muscle aches, loss of strength, and exhaustion, and those with severe cases bleed under the skin and from the mouth, eyes, or ears. It is not the loss of blood that causes death but shock, nervous-system malfunction, coma, delirium, kidney failure, and seizures.

"Very little one can do, you know," Robbie says. Noticing the thorn slashes on my arm: "Missed the turnoff?"

"You might say. Shouldn't we have gloves when we handle people like that?"

"Probably. Oh, Yusuf has other plans for you now. Needs a boat with the bigger engine—he wants you to go downriver. Your supplies are being loaded onto mine. I think he wants you to take him to Gadudey. Cheers," he says, and returns to his own boat.

A torrential downpour rolls across the camp and my instinct is to seek shelter, but no one else seems to notice. Within less than a minute, the few clothes I wear are soaked. I raise my face to the rain and I feel at least partially cleansed. Still, I cannot wash out a feeling of revulsion.

If there is a headman at Marerey Base, it is Yusuf, the link to the elders of the nearby villages. Dressed almost always in a long-sleeve black shirt, black trousers, and muddy running shoes, Yusuf is sophisticated and well mannered. A member of the feared Marehan clan, he is one of those I was warned about in Kismayo, but he seems anything but cruel, murderous, bloodthirsty, or crazy. I would have thought there would be some noticeable cultural difference between the Somalis in Kismayo and those of this area. Yet these people, the sworn enemy, speak the same language and worship the same god, look the same, act pretty much the same. Before the factional divisions of the grubbing warlords, when there was a government, Somalis traveled from village to village, from clan to clan, visiting kin without shooting or being shot at. It would not be unusual for many on both sides of what is now the Green Line to be related by blood. More than a simple two-sided civil war, it is a conflict of subclan against sub-subclan, village against village, family against family, brother against brother—between hundreds of factions with little cause and limited purpose. Adding to the confusion of alliances, yesterday's enemy often becomes today's ally. Subclan militias will switch allegiances for as little as an insult or for the proceeds from a *qat* delivery. It is often difficult to know who the enemy is at any given time. Anarchy seems to be the result.

Yusuf approaches the boat, seems to have been reading my thoughts.

"You were very lucky to get out of Kismayo alive, my American friend."

"I know, Yusuf."

"General Morgan is a very crazy man—the Majerteen are all crazy. They kill for sport."

"I think they feel the same way about you, the Marehan."

"But we have the history. Kismayo was once our home. General Morgan wants to control all of Somalia. He is not to be trusted."

"But you are both Darood clan. You are brothers."

"Once we were brothers. Never again."

* * *

MY boat has been loaded with a few sacks of maize meal and flour and boxes of BP-5—dried, unappetizing compressed biscuits that the WFP distributes during the first days of an acute emergency where cooking is difficult. Each BP-5 tablet contains 458 kilocalories (a unit used by nutritionists to characterize the energy-producing potential in food) and is fortified with protein, fat, and carbohydrate, vitamins and minerals. Six of these unpalatable tablets, according to the WFP, will provide one starving person enough for the "short-term maintenance of a healthy body." All the moisture has been removed from the biscuit, and the bars look like cardboard and taste like cardboard. According to the manufacturer, CompactAS of Norway, these things must be eaten slowly and chewed well, and for children they can be turned into porridge by dissolving in boiling water. Basically a survival ration, the biscuit is packed in foil that is moisture-proof and resistant to germs, insects, and rodents; a ton of them costs about $3,000.

This voyage has its own particular nasty stretches. We travel fully loaded with different supplies and different village officials, and at the end of the airport road I am directed south on the wide irrigation canal. As the flood pours down the Jubba on its last twenty miles to the ocean, the current is so strong that I must travel much faster just to maintain control, and at times we reach a thrilling but incautious fifty knots. I feel I have about as much control as I would have trying to control a raft with a broken paddle down the white water of a Rocky Mountain river in the spring. We wind our way over an invisible route that Yusuf seems to know intimately. I am not unused to trailblazing or sailing through uncharted waters, but to me every towering mango tree, every torn and rusty pipe poking out of the water, every isolated island looks pretty much like all the others. I have a small compass but it is useless; the river winds, turns, doubles back, and then disappears. The only certain direction is with the current.

A large earthen dike materializes out of the haze. It appears more solid than any of the others, and at least for now, it holds. Still, the flood has picked away at it, ripping great chunks off the embankment; portions of the dike crumble away like a calving glacier, and in places where it has been breached, torrents of muddy water pour through the breaks. There is a wide opening ahead and Yusuf signals me to drive through it. This is like driving down the Ventura Freeway at top speed and being told to turn into the exit that we are about to pass. It will be tricky. This overloaded, any attempt to steer and turn the boat into the current will set us broadside to the flow, and that could swamp us. We cannot go directly into the opening while flying at this speed, so I steer high and slow and try to make a wide swing. I misjudge it and nearly lose control. Aborting the turn, we are set downstream well beyond the entrance. There is no other way: I make a fast, sharp U-turn, and as we lie briefly broadside to the fast-moving current, water starts to pour in over the side. My passengers hold on with a death grip. I steady her just before we would have swamped. Nose finally into the stream, we barely move, but we are stable. Eventually we motor through the break in the dike into still water, toward the remains of a village on a slowly disappearing island.

"Whew!"

"There is much water now," Yusuf says. "More difficult every time. You do well, my friend." I am cheered by his confidence.

"A strong current, Yusuf. Next time I'll know the entrance."

He smiles genuinely, turns, and raises his face to the villagers waiting above us. This is a village that was originally some miles from the river but now is in the middle of it. We motor around the island to a small half-moon backwater. A crowd watches silently as I ease the bow onto the embankment. These are a different people, not like Yusuf or other Somalis but darker, smaller, less prognathous. They stand above in tiered ranks, ascending rows according to social position. Excitable little children in threadbare clothes, with bones that look as fragile as bird wings, splash in and out of the water's edge at the bottom, pushing and shoving, daring but afraid to get too close to the strange craft and the strange-looking foreigner. It is evident by their curious eyes they are keen to touch the boat. Older boys and sullen teens stand behind and above them, arms crossed, saying nothing, watching; their eyes are on mine, sizing me up. The village women, clad in T-shirts and torn blouses and colorful *kangas* that wrap their particularly steatopygous bottoms, stand above them. Several hold rheumy-eyed infants in their arms, others breast-feed their little bundles. Only a few of the women wear chadors. The men rank them all and stand on the highest ground, looking down in a pose of communal authority.

"These are the Bantu," Yusuf says. "Not Somalis." I would find the matter-of-fact comment odd; was not everyone a Somali? Not to the indigenous Somalis, many of whom proudly trace their ancestry to the nomadic tribes of eastern Cushites who collected incense and myrrh for the pharaohs in the southern Ethiopian highlands. Somalis do not consider themselves African, not like the sub-Saharan Bantu, whom they treat little better than animals. The majority of Bantu are relative newcomers to Somalia, stolen in the nineteenth century from the shores of Mozambique and

Tanzania and from the depths of Malawi and brought here on Arab slave ships. The Bantu are an animistic people, who still today tell time by the rising of the sun (their midnight coincides with six in the morning, local Western time). The Somalis, who have always derided the Bantu for their darker African color and wide features, often call them *Jareer,* meaning "thick hair." (Naturalist and explorer Peter Matthiessen wrote that Bantu simply meant "people" and was used by scholars to describe a language family rather than an ethnic group.) Small-scale farmers or laborers of the Somali heartland, they have been persecuted and marginalized and kept outside the system of clan alliances and protection. More commonly, indigenous Somalis call the people of the Bantu *Adoon*—slave.

In 1999, the United States officially recognized the Bantu as a persecuted people, and in the largest resettlement program since the Vietnam War, the U.S. offered asylum to about thirteen thousand who had fled the civil war to refugee camps in Kenya. Life in the squalid camps where they lived for more than a decade was not much better. Even there, indigenous Somalis, waiting for peace to return to Somalia, treated them as second-class citizens and many Bantu were victims of violence, starvation, disease, and death of newborns.

The refugees were flown to fifty cities throughout the U.S. Many suffered from the traumas of readjustment, isolation, and the startling change in culture. For most, their voyage of thousands of miles had less impact than their passage through time. Denied access to education and jobs in Somalia, most Bantu were illiterate; they had never turned on a light switch or ever seen a telephone. They had to be taught how to tell time the Western way, how to be punctual, how to flush a toilet. Before their flight to the U.S., many had never seen an airplane except for the mysterious white streaks that sliced across the sky above them.

Ten Christian relief organizations had been charged with helping the Bantu integrate into American society. Churches throughout the U.S. sponsored families at a cost of about $5,000 per family of four to help cover rent, medical care, and start-up costs like dishes and diapers. Local community volunteers took the new immigrants to grocery stores, doctors, and on field trips, easing them into modern American life. After one year in the U.S. the Somali Bantu were to be granted permanent residency, and after five years they were to be eligible for U.S. citizenship.

State Department officials responsible for refugees reported that the resettled Bantu assimilated well and were generally regarded as hard workers; many took part in community affairs and their children often excelled at their studies. More than half found some form of work within six months.

While thousands of Bantu had been accepted into the Promised Land, more than a million Bantu (and another million of other minorities) remain in Somalia. Today many of those continue to be held as slaves. According to the State Department, they are part of the estimated four million people bought or otherwise treated as slaves globally each year. Human-rights advocates say that there are more slaves in the world today than there were during the entire four hundred years of the transatlantic trade.

"These people have no more place to go," Yusuf says. He lowers his eyes to the rising flood. "*Inshah Allah,* the water will come no further."

The crowd parts, and he and my passengers disappear over the ridge. The villagers close up quickly, swallowing any traces of those I ferried, and now I feel eerily alone under their critical silent stare.

This is my first village, and it is momentarily disconcerting. My instant reaction is to confront the challenging looks. I am not so stupid.

"*Subah wanaqsan! Subah wanaqsan!*" My attempt is greeted by giggles, mostly from the older girls and women. Some children respond with delighted squeals. They grow bolder and approach the boat.

The villagers are beginning to prattle among themselves, pointing down in my direction, a sign I would like to think indicates that they are accepting my presence. Is it my machine that attracts their fascination? I rather suspect it is the older long-haired white man with the cutoffs, sleeveless T-shirt, and baseball cap that is such an oddity. Some of the younger men timidly ask me questions in Somali, and I only shrug. Yusuf returns and works his way back through the crowd and shouts from above to join him in the village. After climbing the slippery hillside, I find myself pressed in by the villagers. The older girls—some toothless, some with perfect white teeth, some with curly Bantu hair, others with long black hair and Somali faces—smile and, if I didn't know any better, flirt. The men stand off and speak among themselves appraising me—with wonder, with compliments, with derision. It is all babble. A scruffy little boy with crossed almond-shaped eyes and shredded clothes stands before me and with a stern little face demands something. I shrug and continue onward, and the crowd parts. Some children dart in and dart out of my walking circle, like children chasing sprinkler water on a suburban lawn. Yusuf takes my hand and leads me through the crowd.

The little boy tries to imitate my strange gait, my poor posture, the swing of my arms. He is mocking me and the villagers laugh. I stop, turn suddenly, and make some silly face, and he scrabbles away with a shriek. There is plenty of laughter and it appears to be good-natured. Yet some of the older eyes in the crowd watch me carefully.

Our procession leads to a square encircled by mud-daub and brick buildings of thatch and metal roofs. Village life, it appears, continues apace, and those who were not curious enough to see our arrival go about their business: Women balance on their heads bundles of wood, buckets of water, sacks of charcoal; some sweep the packed red dirt in front of their buildings with brooms of twigs; men and boys who once tended the fields and livestock squat on their haunches or lean lazily against the building corners, waiting for the water to go away. A few open stalls serve as community shops; other than some mangoes and stringy roots, the shelves are bare. The village boasts a hotel. At least the faded sign above the open-fronted whitewashed building proclaims in English it is one: THE SANGA HOTEL. A few thin mattresses lie scattered across the dirt floor inside. Under a palm tree, four large black ravenlike birds with white necks squabble over some meager pickings. A scrawny, almost featherless chicken pecks at the dirt.

Yusuf suggests the shade under one of the two large mango trees near the building of his meeting, and I sit back against one, looking up at the surrounding villagers looking down at me. Yusuf's business with the local officials does not concern me. Here I am only a boat driver, and it is wonderful to have so little responsibility.

"You!" I beckon to the little boy who has been dogging me since the boat. He appears to be the town clown or its mascot. "Come!"

He turns to the crowd for support, which offers none, then back to me. Leaving the protection of the others, he cautiously starts to advance. Slowly, in the crouch of the stealthy, he comes closer, poised to bolt. The villagers go quiet. One of the older children runs up to the boy and cruelly pushes him toward me, and the boy screams in fright and disappears into the safety of the crowd and I laugh. The villagers laugh. Emerging from between two very wide women, he looks up with those queer, crossed but beautiful dark eyes and comes forward. Getting slowly to my feet lest I spook this skittish little mustang, I hold out my hand and he darts sideways like a crab on a hot beach. With a mixture of fear, caution, and bravado and urged on by the other boys, he starts to return. Like a clown, he exaggerates every move, every sneaking step. This seems like a lot of work, but we have the time. Rising from a slouch, then more confidently, chest out, chin high, and proud, he stands before me.

I take his hand. "Give me five!" and go through the routine. He is quick to learn, and after only two attempts we are slapping hands and shaking our butts in front of the dumbfounded villagers. They are delighted and cheer at the final bump/grind. Some of the mothers push their reluctant children toward me for a lesson. Soon a mob of children gathers round, all wanting to give me five.

Yusuf comes quietly through the crowd and stands unnoticed while I teach some of the youngsters.

"Chanti kan." He smiles. "I have seen that on television from America. *Chanti kan*—how you Americans say, high five."

I offer to slap hands and shake butts, but he declines. Yusuf is a regional leader with responsibility and stature. He would never be seen making a fool of himself. When Somalia gets a government, I suspect he will run for office.

18.
Python in the Bath

THE chatter of frogs, the twitter from early birds, the muffled voices of men rising, and the tinny sounds of David's little shortwave radio confer within the darkness of my tent a peace that I still cannot accept. Despite the trips yesterday upriver, downriver, and a growing knowledge that I may be doing something worthwhile finally, I cannot unload Kismayo; it is baggage I cannot abandon simply because I am elsewhere.

"Excellent, David! Excellent," Robbie calls out. "Let's have some news, shall we?"

The BBC Africa Service is telling its listeners about the devastation in Somalia. Some official interviewed is predicting hundreds of thousands will die unless Unicef and the WFP receive more contributions for the flood emergency efforts. I suppose we should be pleased to know that someone realizes there is a crisis and that relief workers are out here. It is a small feeling; we know that few are really interested, and I am too corroded to care. But Robbie, ever offering his insight, opines from under his net: "Yes, right. Quite right."

I have to take a shit. I had held back yesterday because I did not know the routine, but I cannot wait around to be told. It is a fast hands-on lesson. During nonworking hours many of the men wear cotton *kikoi* around their waists instead of trousers or short pants. Clad like this, it is quite simple. They wade off into the current until nearly knee deep, hoist up their skirts, and squat. There are no thoughts of privacy and apparently no need for it. It will take me a little time to feel comfortable enough to join them at the communal toilet, so at the boat, which is further away, I mount the boarding ladder, hold on to the rail, and hunker down.

David has put the kettle on for tea and my instant coffee when I return.

"Pour some more water in the kettle, John, there's a good chap," Robbie says.

"This stuff?" I say, indicating a nearby plastic bottle filled with murky water.

"Yes. It's perfectly all right to drink even though it is the local brew."

"Floodwater?"

"Certainly. As long as the water is moving, there is no risk at all. Quite pure, you see."

"Don't you sterilize it or put chlorine in it?"

"No need to. We let it sit, wait for the dirt to settle, and then drink it. We've never gotten sick from it, have we, David?"

"No, Robbie."

I shrug.

"We *are* experienced bush wallahs, you know. Or certainly David is. I am merely a wallah."

Not quite sure what a wallah is, but I doubt Robbie is precisely that. He is, however, someone who might have been at home a hundred years ago as the educated adventurer with pith helmet, swagger stick, and a line of natives carrying boxes of Geographic Society equipment on their heads through dense unexplored jungle.

"Looking steamy, guys," he says. "God, the miseries of hell. So let us have tea before we disappear into this watery wilderness."

My trip upriver to Hargeisa (not to be confused with the city of the same name in the northwest bombed by General Morgan), the village I never got to yesterday, is less eventful than the first attempt.

Apparently it is not uncommon to clip a submerged roof, a tree, or an irrigation pipe on these delivery runs. It was in one of these fields that Robbie claims he made hamburger of a floating corpse on his very first trip. How long can these boats last? Without equipment and spares, our part of the operation will come to an undignified halt if, when peeling the top off a submerged roof, we lose a propeller. The engines tilt forward and this gives us a chance to inspect the props; already the prop on my boat is well nicked, chewed, and a little bent. David's metal file and a pair of pliers seem to keep her spinning smoothly enough.

Some of Hargeisa remains above water, at least enough to see that it was once a large settlement. On the riverside where the water is deeper, the houses are submerged, and as we approach—*thunk!*—the engine kicks out of the water. I have struck something metallic, a car or a farm implement or irrigation pipe; who the hell knows? Once the engine is back in the water, the vibration from the bent prop is irritatingly obvious.

Toward higher ground, the buildings rise out of the water in progression, and it is now possible to drive down the clearly defined streets toward dry ground. At the edge of the shoreline, a family is removing the last of their mean possessions from their partially submerged mud-brick home, handing what is left down a line of neighbors who stack it on the bank. The river is pinching this town on all sides, a disappearing island of mud; the roads that once connected it to other villages in the region disappeared long ago under the flood. Hargeisa is a write-off. Soon it will be submerged. Most of the residents have evacuated, forming crowded makeshift communities on crumbling patches of nearby dike.

My arrival here sparks the same reaction that it did in Gadudey: giggles, comments, curiosity. I pull up to the village like Santa Claus on his metal steed. I am guaranteed to amuse. Instead of a "ho ho ho" with a bag of goodies over my shoulder, I shout, *Subah wanaqsan! Diep maleh! Diep maleh!* and toss down boxes and sacks of emergency supplies to village youths helping to unload. I spend every Somali word I know. While the adults stand on the higher bank, silent and watchful, the children below are eager to interact, to talk, even to teach me Somali. They want to learn English in return. They are starved for knowledge. Like children.

"Setih?" How are you? I shout.

"Ficaan! Ficaan!" Good! Good! the children respond.

A little girl with tangled hair and a torn mud-stained dress wades boldly up to the boat and with doleful eyes says quietly, *"Bia mehisa? Bia?"* A teenager standing nearby at the edge of the flood offers, "Water—to drink—no water to drink." I will try to find a jerry can back at the base and fill it. It is the water we drink, almost the same sludge water they stand in.

It is not clear how much my deliveries help these people. Before these low-yield efforts, they subsisted only on mangoes and water-lily roots. We have heard the WFP is delivering eleven hundred tons of emergency food—biscuits, Humanitarian Daily Rations, flour, maize—enough food to feed a hundred thousand people for a month. I see no evidence of that. Perhaps those Herculean efforts occur upstream. In this area alone, there are an estimated fifty-six thousand people to feed. My boat is so small that a dozen trips a day may help, but only three or four seem to do no more than boost their morale and let them know that outside their world, their sunken villages, someone gives a damn. We should be airlifting supplies with that big Russian helicopter, but when I ask Yusuf why this isn't being done, he just looks at me with his soft sad eyes and says he has asked. Can't do more than that. Our success seems so insignificant.

* * *

DAVID and I arrive back at the base camp at about the same time, he from upriver and I from the river south. While we are being loaded for another run, I remark that it is gratifying to feel like I might be doing something worthwhile instead of ducking bullets and worrying about my own skin. "Although I am still not sure that we are making much of a difference."

"You make more of a difference than you realize. These people won't forget what we are doing." I am too much of a cynic and find that hard to believe.

We carry the conversation toward the fuel drums, where Robbie is pumping gasoline into a jerry can.

On the way, we pass a figure in a dark chador who sits cross-legged on a wool blanket under a tree near the supply tent, a round woven basket at her side. With just her eyes showing through the crack in her veil, she stares out into the scrub beyond, immobile, like a stone. She may have always been there, but I had never noticed her. She must have arrived in the night.

David is saying that he always signs up whenever there is a humanitarian crisis. "It is for the money certainly, but it is also because of a debt. All of this is my country, from here to Zaire. I have lived here all my life, know no other land. No, there is nothing wrong about wanting to serve your fellow man and save a few lives in the bargain. It is not just for our own satisfaction that we might be saving a life or two. There's something more profound. You could feel it one day."

"Yeah, I suppose."

" 'Save one life and you are saving the life of all mankind'—the Koran."

"You Muslim?"

Robbie overhears the discussion and remarks, "Right, boys—that's it! Enough of that altruistic poppycock. We are all here to fill the war chests, and let's not deny it. It is also written: 'Scratch an altruist and watch a hypocrite bleed.' More to the point, I should imagine."

It is a valid point. For the time I had spent in the field, it was still no clearer to me why anyone would want to become a relief worker. Back in the other world, I had heard of one humanitarian disaster and then another, heard appeals for aid, rock concerts for the starving, but I never really considered going out in the field and doing anything about it. Nor do I suspect many others are so inclined. Sitting comfortably away from the action and hearing about a remote humanitarian crisis, I doubt many perk up and say: By golly, I am going to go help someone. Yet there are thousands of relief workers risking their lives. They are out here for some reason.

I had a chat in 2003 with James T. Morris, the Executive Director of the WFP, and I asked him if he knew what motivated his people to go into the field. This soft-spoken Midwest industrialist was quite convinced that most of those entered aid work solely for the pleasure of helping others, serving mankind. I suggested that money, adventure, even sometimes the inability to survive in the mainstream could be primary motivating factors, but he demurred and, with the enthusiasm of a cheerleader, spoke of the "sacrifice and the commitment" of his employees. "You never feel better about yourself than when you are helping others," he said. "They are remarkable people." I wondered if I had felt any better about myself.

* * *

A small cargo plane makes a flyby, skims over the tented roofs, then touches down. We had been radioed to expect guests, and Robbie, who usually doesn't move very fast, is up like a shot when the aircraft lands. With stiff gait he struts out to the airplane and waits for the doors to open, like a welcoming potentate with chest out and hands clasped behind his back. I once tried to keep up with him when the chopper landed, but it was no use. I would have had to run.

Robbie's safari business makes it important for him to be at the forefront, where he might snare a client or two. I have nothing to gain from anyone here, and it is a relief to put a lid on the ego.

I have developed an attitude from Kismayo. I cannot think of anything worth competing for. I hope I take this away with me, an attitude of indifference, non-interest in anything other than what I am paid to do. Since I have always been too enthusiastic, childishly so to the point of occasionally irritating people (Andrew, not unkindly, told me I had the enthusiasm of a fifteen-year-old), I think this new look might be rather becoming.

Our visitors are from Nairobi: an agronomist, a marketing man, and a nutritionist from Unicef's Food Security Assessment Unit armed with scales and height sticks. Our loquacious colleague who has undertaken the role of base spokesman proudly describes our operations and the area around us with the zeal of a real estate salesman describing the grounds of a château in Provence. Our guests wear dark sunglasses as they talk. I would presume they know enough to take them off when dealing with the village elders; communicating in this part of the world while wearing shades is very bad form.

David and I chauffeur the visitors to the emergency settlement of Marerey. The original village, located at the confluence of the main irrigation canal and the river not far from the airstrip, was one of the agricultural centers of the Jubbada Hoose region on the southern Jubba. Once, before the war, before the floods, time, money, and energy had been spent to make this village and its surrounding fields important to the region's economy. That was before 1975. Under the Marxist regime of President Siad Barre, the lands were expropriated and the Bantu farmers forced to abandon their holdings—hundreds of mango trees, large fields of maize and underground crops—without compensation. Much of the area's assets were distributed among the president's cronies from the Marehan clan. With the overthrow of Barre, the rich agricultural region became just another territorial spoil for feuding warlords. The lines of broken aerial-irrigation pipes, vast cultivated fields, the shell-damaged cement walls of the fertilizer-storage buildings, the half-submerged ancient John Deere tractor lying on its side, the neatly planted lines of mango trees, the torn banana stalks poking out of the shallow sea, and even the twisted spires of the sugar factory are proud but pathetic indications of the importance of the area.

The entire town is underwater. The protecting system of dikes along the canal and river collapsed, submerging homes, mosques, and shops. Like Gadudey to the south, the villagers have sought refuge on top of a small section of dike that could go at any minute. We bring them tarpaulins, which they stretch over poles to keep the rain and sun off, but it is not much. We deliver bags of maize, their main staple, but who wants to live on gruel alone? They hunger for the small things—matches for a fire, a clean used T-shirt without holes, a piece of candy.

A few half-naked youngsters begin to unload the sacks of flour, Unimix, and maize meal. Many of the bags are gaily colored with the American flag, the clasped hands of friendship of the U.S. Agency for International Development, and, like the HDRs, the message: **Gift of the People of the United States of America.** I wonder if these illiterate villagers, so isolated from the affairs of the outside world, recognize the flag or can identify the origin of these rations—writing that is possibly no more decipherable to them than hieroglyphics. I wonder, too, if they might believe that the food is a gift from us, the relief workers.

I mentioned to Director Morris that in the field I had questioned whether those who received American aid knew or really cared where it came from. The United States donates more than half of the world's total to feed the starving, $1.4 billion in 2003.

"It is important to see who cares about them, to know of the genuine goodness of the United States," he said.

It is natural to accept that this brightly labeled foodstuff, the HDRs, and the tarp that covered the boat that I had delivered to the port in Kismayo should boast the national origin of these donations. On the other hand, was not such an obvious display of the national goodness a two-edged sword?

The global community marches into disaster areas with an international duty to intervene: to feed, to house, to heal. Bernard Kouchner, founder of Médecins sans Frontières and former UN administrator of postwar Kosovo, was one of the first to outline the doctrine of *devoir d'ingérence*. He also noted that such intervention comes with a price: "I believe in the right to intervene and people must recognize that humanitarian aid is political. A boat sent to rescue people is making an inherently political act."

Were not those bags of lifesaving supplies with the colorful Stars and Stripes a political tool, a weapon in the battle of influence in the war of winning hearts and minds? I put the question to Director Morris.

"I know the President personally. I have spoken to him about this," Morris said. "He told me that the U.S. will never use food as a political weapon."

As we delivered those relief supplies decorated by the clasped hands of Uncle Sam, I had wondered vaguely if we could be identified with the donor. If, in Kouchner's view, our work was a political act, then by extension were we not associating with a donor nation's foreign policy? Thus, was not the professed neutrality of the UN and the neutrality of its humanitarian workers compromised?

Russ Ulrey, who had worked on the ill-fated 1992 famine relief mission in Mogadishu, echoed this apprehension:

"At the end of the day, Somalis know that aid agencies are funded by the U.S. We carry bags that have *USA* written all over them, but we say we are the UN, we are neutral, not the military. Yet we were funded by those with the guns. How do we separate ourselves from them? Damn good question."

The answer to the question was offered years later by the administration of George W. Bush. The new canon of humanitarian assistance post 9/11 was clear: Aid workers should *not* separate themselves from United States policy. Addressing NGOs during Operation Enduring Freedom, the attack on the Taliban in Afghanistan in 2001, Secretary of State Colin Powell put paid to the notion that humanitarian work could ever be considered anything but a political act.

> . . . just as surely as our diplomats and military, American NGOs are out there serving and sacrificing on the front lines of freedom. . . . NGOs are such a force multiplier for us, such an important part of our combat team. [We are] all committed to the same, singular purpose: to help every man and woman in the world who is in need, who is hungry, who is without hope, to help every one of them fill a belly, get a roof over their heads, educate their children, have hope.

To equate humanitarian organizations with an American combat team sent shivers through the international relief community. Had "combat team" not been uttered by a former general and one of the President's good soldiers, one might have interpreted his intention to create not an alliance in a war but a force to combat the humanitarian ills that affected an oppressed people.

Andrew S. Natsios, administrator of USAID, the world's most generous food aid donor, left no doubt how the administration felt when he told international humanitarian leaders that by receiving U.S. government money for their activities—and most of them do—they were in effect "an arm of the U.S. government." At a speech at the InterAction Forum, the umbrella group for American humanitarian and development organizations, Natsios challenged relief workers to do a better job of promoting connections to the U.S. government or else he was going to personally "tear up their contracts" and find new partners.

Most humanitarian workers do not consider themselves arms of the U.S. government, nor, while on the job, do they associate themselves with any nation's political or military policies. To be perceived in the eyes of locals as aligned with the donor nation often results in tragic consequences.

Such occurred in June 2004 when five relief workers of the unquestionably neutral Médecins sans Frontières were assassinated by the Taliban in Afghanistan. Three of those slain were doctors. A Taliban spokesman said they were killed for "working and espionage" for the U.S. After twenty-four years in the country, after saving countless lives during what had been the worst of times—Soviet oppression and Taliban restrictions—the MSF, which won the Nobel Peace Prize in 1999, pulled out. Kenny Gluck, Director of Operations for MSF/Holland, said the withdrawal was due in part to the American military's use of humanitarian aid for "political and military motives."

"Independent humanitarian action, which involves unarmed aid workers going into areas of conflict to provide aid, has become impossible," Gluck said at the time. "The Americans are pretending that NGOs are with them fighting the war against terror, and they are not. That puts us in danger. We want to be relevant medically and irrelevant militarily and politically." Gluck, an American, was himself held hostage for twenty-two days in a moldy root cellar in Chechnya because, in part, his unidentified kidnappers questioned MSF's neutrality.

Some aid workers have suggested that all national labels and identifying origins be removed completely. As I deliver the bags of USAID-donated flour and maize, it is natural to wonder whether these people, wretched and desperate, pause to ask who is giving them this food. And why.

* * *

WE off-load our visitors from Nairobi and wait under the broiling sun for them to take care of whatever it is they came for. David remarks that he suspects that the visitors—here for only a few hours—are sightseers on holiday wanting to see what suffering is all about.

I have been clowning with the children, yet despite my antics, I still feel privately a little uncomfortable. The adults, men mostly, stare directly at us without a word uttered. Each face seems to bear a message, a question, an answer. I look up at any one man and there he is, eyes drilling into me. Not with hostility but not without. I wouldn't know. These people are unreadable.

"Half-devil and half-child," David mutters.

"What was that?"

"Half-devil and half-child." He looks up and grins:

> "Take up the White Man's burden—
> Send forth the best ye breed—
> Go, bind your sons to exile
> To serve your captives' need;
> To wait in heavy harness,
> On fluttered folk and wild—
> Your new-caught, sullen peoples,
> Half-devil and half-child. . . .
>
> "Take up the White Man's burden—
> The savage wars of peace—
> Fill full the mouth of Famine
> And bid the sickness cease;

And when your goal is nearest
The end for others sought,
Watch sloth and heathen Folly
Bring all your hope to nought."

As David recites the Kipling poem, his long ropy hands, with personalities of their own, dance with the verse, writhe, twist, probe the air as if palsied, reminding me of an old rocker's finger gyrations during Woodstock. I am captivated and listen and watch in fascination every illustrated word. It is evident to the villagers that this is a performance, and they observe in silence.

An old man atop the embankment yells down to David and me and beckons. Because of the children hanging on to the gunnels, we are reluctant to leave the boat, but through sign language and gesture, some of the nearby adults who have been staring at us from above yell at the children to move away and indicate the boats should be safe.

At the top of the hill, we follow this silent ancient fellow into an open shack walled by a sheet of plastic. Turning to us, his shriveled face and tiny eyes constrict as he begins to scold us, gesticulating toward his open mouth. There is nothing I can do; I do not even have a BP-5 in my pocket. But a teenage boy interprets in surprisingly good English: "He says you stupid men. You do not bring water to drink." The old man nods and breaks into a *miraa*-stained grin. He picks up a plastic bottle filled with off-colored water and hands it to David. "Can't insult the gentleman," David says. He takes a swig and passes the bottle to me. I expect a case of cholera in the morning.

Two other weathered men, nearly as old, sit upon a board laid across some cinder blocks nearby, observing us. A small, ornately carved meranti wood box rests, almost as a secret, between them. Leaning forward on their walking canes, they call us over.

"Shikamoo, Mzee," one of them greets David. It is the traditional Kiswahili greeting to a man your senior and presumably the wiser. Does he really think David is older?

"Marehaba," David returns.

They speak briefly in Swahili. One of the men affectionately pats the wood box. David's eyes focus on the reliquary and he breaks into a wrinkled smile.

The other old man taps the ground in front of them, an order for us to squat on our haunches. Reverently, he lifts the lid of the little box and passes it before our noses. A strong odor, pungent and sweet, makes my eyes water. He pinches a black leafy powder and places it between his cheek and gums, nods to us to do the same.

The tobacco, initially puckeringly bitter then sweet, kicks the salivary glands into full gear. This is not like Skoal or Copenhagen—certainly less refined than store-bought—but, after the first taste, instantly sweeter. I had done some PR work for the Mountain States Circuit of the Professional Rodeo Cowboys Association in Cheyenne in the seventies, and to be a good old boy I had pinched snoose with the best of them; I always carried a round tin of Cope in my pearl-button shirt pocket. As hard as I tried, including once riding a bull out of the chute, I never could be a cowboy, always would be a "damn Easterner." But it never stopped me from trying real hard.

* * *

OUR deliveries concluded and the day-trippers now on their way back to Nairobi, Robbie announces that it is time for a bath.

With towels, soap, and shampoo, we pile into David's red boat and motor slowly down the airport road into the field and tie up to a fence post. The sun is not far above the horizon and it will be dark soon. Clothes off, soap in hand, we dive in, just three little boys at the local swimming hole. As I lather my armpits, something big, rough, and slippery wraps itself around my stomach, then slithers off.

"Jesus wept!" I jump out of the water, claw back up onto the boat. A thick sheen of slime around my belly marks the creature's embrace.

"Fish nibbling at your toes?" Robbie asks.

"Fucking bigger than that!" The slime shines in the sun. It is not easy to wipe off.

"Yes, well . . . Possibly a python. Time to get out, David."

Later, cooking over the gas burner, I think about whatever it was that tried to seduce me. I toss some chopped tomatoes and onions in with some beans, stir it up, and stare at the slop. I can't eat. I still feel that slimy creature moving across my belly.

Yusuf emerges from the shadows. Clad in his black shirt, Somali sarong, and rubber sandals, he sits cross-legged in front of the fire in silence. He is a mystery. Despite his easy empathetic nature, he holds himself regally, somewhat aloof. It is hard to know which is the dominant personality. His private and thoughtful countenance gives hint of some deeper inner strength—or is it inner turmoil? I have often seen him stand off alone and observe the activity in the camp and I have wondered what he is thinking, what he is feeling at the time. He is said to have a family, wife, and children in Nairobi, yet he is well-known and well respected in this area. In this soft flickering light, his peaceful face is seamed with concern.

"When the water goes down, we must move."

"Where to?"

"I am not sure. But we must move away from here. Away from the airstrip. They know we are here and it will not be safe anymore."

"You don't say!" Robbie says.

"Yes. Now we are safe but soon we will be attacked. They will want the supplies."

"Who, pray, are 'they'?"

"Subclan militia."

"I thought you had everything under control, Yusuf," Robbie says. There is an edge in his voice.

"No man controls the subclans." He stands and walks out into the dark. Very uncharacteristic.

"I do believe he's heard something," David says.

"Wonder how?" I say. "We're pretty isolated."

"Word gets around. Probably during one of the trips to the villages or over the radio."

Robbie says, "Maybe our Somali friend is working both sides. . . ."

The water, however, this night continues to rise.

A discussion after we bedded down, as if we were all awake expecting one of us to speak first:

"I think I heard a lion, David."

"I believe I heard it too, Robbie."

"You know that inimitable grunting sound."

"Quite. Not so far away."

"Rather near, I'd venture."

"Night, Robbie."

"Night, David."

"Night, all."

Frog croaks and cicada ratchets, a soothing pastiche of night sounds, have been upstaged. By laughter. It *is* laughter, not from within the camp and not laughter that any human could create: not a cackle, not a snigger, not a rollicking good belly laugh, but three clear and sharp "Hahaha!" This series is joined by another from somewhere out there and then others, and the ensemble turns idiotically hilarious. Lying on my back in the tent, I can't help but chuckle, and were it not for the fascination, the mystery of the laughter, I surely would be caught up by it for it is irresistibly infectious—*hahahahahahahahahahaha*—like watching someone laugh so hard you can't help but laugh yourself. I try to picture the sort of creature that could create such a good-time noise—its size, its head, the shape of its mouth. I don't want to sleep. I want to keep laughing.

19.
Blood Sport

THE sunrises are brilliant and come on fast: tangerine sky in the east above low, gray night clouds, silver stars against the blue-black in the west, squalls out over where the sea should be. The haze and smoke from the early-morning cooking fires cling to the surface of the water. I wade out in the half-light toward the boats for my daily performance. The flood level is no higher than it was last night, possibly even a little lower.

I don't use the platform today. Squatting in the water like the Somalis seems more hygienic—let the current carry it away. I feel a little nibbling on my butt. A half dozen catfish have been attracted to my efforts; they don't seem interested in the excreta but more in my shiny white cheeks. A splash of the hand sends them scurrying.

The catfish are clever. Our compound not only feels like a garbage dump but is taking on the trappings of one. Scattered over the site and in the water are the empty Humanitarian Daily Rations, bright yellow plastic packs that contained halal food acceptable to Muslims. Each of these HDRs, with an American flag decorating the front, provides about 2,200 calories, enough to sustain a person for a day. Each costs the American taxpayer $3.93; with door-to-door delivery, this is one of the most expensive meals in the world. Inside, the chef's surprise: foil packages of lentil stew, or pasta with tomato sauce, or red beans and rice, and always shortbread, peanut butter and jam, fruit bars, and a book of matches, also decorated with the American flag. It is because this stuff is put together in Texas, I suppose, that there is included a packet of crushed red chili pepper.

Those yellow plastic packages floating throughout our campsite are evidently feasts for the ravening sea life. Catfish shove their noses into the torn-open packs to get at whatever leftover food remains inside—crumbs, sauces, spillage. To watch an empty HDR break the surface and zip through our compound lake like a yellow submarine makes you briefly forget why you came here in the first place.

Out here there is time, finally, to reflect, to breathe, to observe. There is time to ask questions, to wonder, a luxury we never had in Kismayo. It took Kismayo to appreciate the ability to collect. In the mainstream, we have the opportunity but we are usually too busy.

In mid-morning, when the sun warms the last of the dry land to the south, storks and giant white pelicans freewheel in the thermals above, reaching ever higher in great sweeping circles. They are a joy to watch until they spiral so high that they disappear. Somewhere in the bush there is also a bird I have never seen that teases with the mock of a child: *nana-nana nah, nana-nana nah*. I hear it every time I pull out of the campsite; I'll not rest until I've seen it. In the evening a pair of black and white sacred ibis, stilt-legged with curved beaks like a hand scythe, flap over the strip, noisily bickering in raucous and impatient yawps. These are the birds revered by the pharaohs as the embodiment of Thoth, the god of wisdom. The ancient Egyptians described Thoth as having the head of an ibis; there is nothing known about the sound of his voice. At about the same time, hundreds of white cattle egrets skim low in silent graceful flight, undulating just above the surface of the water like a shining white satin ribbon. We have a resident marabou stork, a carrion scavenger with a wingspan of about five feet. With a scabrous naked head, a sack that hangs below his neck like loose skin, and square black shoulders, he is suggestive of an undertaker—certainly one of the most repulsive birds on the planet. He stands on stilt legs midway down the runway, silent, observing, waiting for death. This is the type of bird I first saw in Kismayo Bay tearing apart something meaty and large.

* * *

YUSUF and some elders board the go-fast for an early-morning delivery to Marerey. A swarm of white butterflies sweeps across the flood just above the surface and briefly engulfs us in their gentle white cloud. "Flood will soon be finished," Yusuf says. "They come when the water begins to drop."

The villagers are there waiting. They stand atop the dike looking down at my inadequate contribution in baleful silence, and only when I greet them in Somali do some respond. The youngest children run along the base of the dike as we approach, excitedly splashing into the water toward the boat. With the swirling current it is difficult to maneuver, but the teens keep the younger ones under control.

"John-John!" the children call. One of the children at this village had asked my name on an earlier delivery. "John-John!" The distance from Captain *Diep Maleh* to John-John is about twenty miles and, it seems, a lifetime.

The brash boys, the shy little girls, the smaller naked children, always make me feel welcome. They are a good audience. I make funny faces and they laugh. I even dance a little jig in the boat and they respond with a similar dance on shore. I act the madman, and they squeal with delight. A fifty-something white-blond-haired relief worker stands in a boat belting out at the top of his lungs before a depressed and helpless group of children:

> Peanut butter sitting on a railroad track,
> His heart was all aflutter,
> Along came a train along the track,
> Choo choo pea-nut butter.

I have no idea where I picked that one up.

They don't know what it means, but it is a silly childish melody and it makes them laugh. To experience their genuine pleasure and their open expressions of unquestioned trust is a great personal joy. For a brief period, I ease them out of their mud-stuck drudgery, and it is then that I begin to feel that I *am* helping and personally getting some good out of it. They make me feel like the Pied Piper, a wandering Muppets show. To make people smile, to laugh—those who need to smile, to laugh—I have some idea why Bob Hope entertained the troops year after year. If this personal joy is what relief work is all about, then I could stay on for more.

"John-John! Good morning!" An emaciated little boy of about six or seven wearing only the bare remains of shorts wades through the water and hands me a "baggie" of tobacco. The old man on top of the dike grins and offers a little salute with his walking stick.

I recognize the child. He was the curious one who first asked my name. I taught him "good morning." Through him the other children learn. I answer him and the others chime in, just as eager to participate but too shy to be the first to ask. They teach me: "Much water," I say, sweeping my hand over the flood in front of them. *"Bia bidan,"* the children say, *"bia bidan."*

"Diep maleh—means no problem," I say. "No problem," the children shout back.

The child is reed-thin, ribs like a washboard, evidently very, very hungry. His face is angelic, highlighted by quick, intelligent eyes and a wide, bright smile.

There are about a dozen HDRs still locked in the forepeak of the boat from our preparation for escape from Kismayo. Most people don't eat the main meals unless there is nothing else available, but the fruit bars and peanut-butter-and-jam packets are like candy, a sugar fix. I pull out a foil-packed fig bar and hand it to the boy as a reward for the tobacco.

The cheerful sounds of the surrounding children suddenly stop.

The silence lasts for about as long as it takes the child to realize what comes next. The children only moments before so cheerful and happy scream as one in outrage. As a pack they charge down the slope and attack the boy. Clawing fingers try to pry away his precious reward. The child holds on and gathers it tightly into the pit of his stomach and tries to run. He dodges and twists and splashes through the mud along the embankment, chased by the mob of frenzied children. He tries to run up the bank but is blocked by the older boys who, with their arms crossed, form an impenetrable barrier. He turns, runs back down to the shallow water toward me. The pack again surrounds him and wrestles him into the mud. He manages to wiggle out, crawl on his hands and knees into deeper water, carrying several of the punching and scratching children on his back. It is like a shark feed. He is in water up to his waist and he seems about to break away when the mob re-forms and attacks him again. He disappears under the surface. The children continue jumping, pounding, slapping blindly at him below the surface. Finally, his tiny black head breaks the surface. He gasps for air. Older boys grab the child and drag him back into the mud and continue to beat him while another tries to prise the treat from his little fist. He curls into a ball. An older boy kicks the child in the head, once, twice, three times.

The villagers who are not involved press around the boat for a better view of the battle. I cannot get out of the boat, there are too many children, too many adults who have now come down to the water's edge to watch. The adults do nothing, say nothing. It has become gladiatorial, a blood sport. I yell to the adults to stop the beating. They tamp their open hands downward, orders for me to relax—just kids. The child stumbles away from the attack and falls onto his knees in the shallow water. His eyes are nearly closed from the beating, and he is bleeding. There is no sign he is crying. He still has something in his hand.

Three older youths leap off the land onto the boy's back and punch him in the head. One pulls his legs out from under him, sending him facedown into the water. They are trying to drown him. I can stand it no longer. I jump out of the boat and bull my way through the crowd. A sudden shout and the biggest boy, in his early teens, raises his hand victoriously with the crushed silver packet of a fig bar.

I reach down and pull the child up and out. He is sputtering and gagging and half conscious. The battle is over, and he and I are ignored as some of the villagers begin to disperse and slowly return up the hillside, the entertainment concluded. He opens his eyes and, seeing me, shrieks with fright and passes out.

I stand before a wall of strange people, no faces, only a black curtain of hostility. It is a standoff. The children so violent a moment before stand in silence on the shore, looking at me as if waiting for me to make the next move. The adults above look down with savage condemnation. Is it because I did something so stupid? Because I didn't give every single one of them a little goody? Maybe they think I treated them like animals in a zoo. That I was consciously manipulative, toying with their primal instincts, their most basic needs.

A young woman with eyes flared fights her way through the villagers. Seeing the boy at my feet, she utters a cry and stumbles down the embankment and drops to her knees at the child. Her colorful *kanga* swaddles an infant to her back who, awakened, begins to scream. She grabs the boy's face with two hands and shakes, but the child remains unconscious. She looks up at me and, in a shrill that deafens, screams unintelligible frightening charges of accusation. I retreat slowly, walk backward to the boat; I dare not take my eyes away or she will attack. My own standoff with her is my only defense. Yusuf elbows his way through the back of the crowd.

"You come now! *Now!*" he says, and grabs me by the arm and pulls me to the boat.

The woman's voice slices through the sound of the outboard, even, it seems, when we are out of sight.

"Is he going to be all right?"

Yusuf shrugs. "Bantu."

I suppose that could make me feel better, but I feel like shit.

Back at the base, the Somali with a headset at the HF radio

calls me over. The radio shack has been improved: a new tarp strung over the card table to protect the equipment, a cement block in front of his chair to keep his feet dry, and freshly cut poles to keep the antenna wires out of the water.

"Juliet Bravo back," I squawk into the mike without much enthusiasm.

"Hey, John, Alpha Kilo here!"

"Andrew! Good to hear from you. What's up?"

"I have a rotation coming your way; might be too late today, so probably tomorrow, first thing. Unimix, BP-5, blankets, maize meal. And a French photographer. Word is we have to be good to the photographer. You copy?"

"Roger, Alpha Kilo—another tourist. We'll make sure he gets what he wants."

"And I've got some, uh . . . Mombasa water aboard. The photographer is looking after it—making sure it doesn't go astray. You know those pilots. . . . I assume you'll take care of that too."

"Yeah, sure. Good to hear the flight is bringing in the important things. Thanks. Anything further?"

"No, that's all. How's it going your end?"

"Not real great. I just—" and I decide not to get into it. I still don't understand. "Water on three sides, and if it gets much higher, we may find ourselves washed down to Kismayo. You?"

"Dodgy. Still the dispute about the number of camels—the price of a life! Anyway, I hope to get out there one day. Cheers. Alpha Kilo out."

The Somali radio operator looks up. I shrug.

David and Robbie are relaxing under their shelter, each reading their respective magazines—one the conservative, the other the literary, and both are drinking scotch. Occasionally Robbie breaks the silence by reading a passage he thinks will interest his partner.

"Rotation on the way," I announce quietly. "Probably coming in tomorrow morning."

"Anything interesting?" David asks, looking over his reading glasses.

I don't tell them about the beer, in the event it gets hijacked on the way. "A journalist."

"Oh, swell. Our name in lights, David," Robbie says. "You drink whiskey?"

"Not usually, but today I think I need it. Had a fuckin' crazy day!"

"Do tell."

". . . So he finally gave up his prize," I say, recalling the frightful scene. "Rather, he wouldn't give it up—that was the problem; he would have rather died than let it go—but one of the older kids finally got it from him. When you have twenty hysterical children all going for a small piece of food, whoever won got no more than mush."

"What happened to the boy? Is he dead?" Robbie asks.

"Christ, I hope not! The last I saw of him he was unconscious; he was lying in the mud with—I guess it was his mother screaming bloody murder. I thought she was going to get a piece of me."

"Oh, boy."

"It is not like I did anything to the kid. . . . But I was responsible."

"I wouldn't worry too much about it," Robbie says. "Certainly, it is not the sort of thing they teach you in your basic humanitarian training course. It is something you learn the hard way, although I must say, it is too bad a child has to suffer so that an aid worker can learn a lesson."

Before I respond, David says, "Better stay away from the village for a day or two. I'll take the Marerey runs."

"It is quite a common mistake, actually," Robbie says in a tone more ironical. "Swamp water with your whiskey?

"Most soldiers without experience make the same mistake—must be a carryover from the Second World War, when your GIs rolled through Europe introducing us all to American chewing gum. I remember American soldiers in Mogadishu were also guilty of such well-meaning but destructive generosity and gave candy bars to the street children. I suppose it is human nature: Give something to someone and you hope to win their loyalty, their love in return. I tell you, not the proper way to pacification, sport. We Brits learned long ago in Northern Ireland that handing out sweets to the children does not win any favor. Indeed, the Yanks found that out in Mog: Twice as many children returned the next day—the word was out—and when the sweets ran out, the children became resentful and began to throw rocks. They were joined by the townspeople, and the soldiers ended up firing over their heads. That was the beginning of the end of the Americans in Somalia. So, here's to lessons learned, J-B." He leans over and hands me a glass. It is filled with eighty percent whiskey, five percent mud, and ten percent water.

"Now, David, what have we done today?" Robbie says, reaching for a notebook. "How many sacks of Unimix, boxes of BP-5s, blankets, etcetera?"

I duck into my tent, a little tipsy, less disturbed now because I discussed it. I did not need Robbie's avuncular insight to define my mistake, but I do appreciate having been able to talk about it—not that it absolves my guilt. Or my foolishness.

Closing the mosquito flap quickly behind me, stripping off my clothes, I lie down on my sleeping bag and pull a cotton sheet over me. My balls itch. I scratch and feel a small insect fastened to the base of my scrotum. I can't get it off. In the light of a torch, the tick is no bigger than a gun pellet. I grew up in tick country, have removed many from myself and from my dog. Back home, we used to take a hot poker or a cigarette to swollen ticks embedded in the dog hairs and they would fall off. So no big deal, but these are African ticks. Perhaps it is the whiskey, but I know only one thing: I have got to get it off, get it to withdraw its head voluntarily from under my skin, or I may get the fever.

Robbie doesn't smoke, David doesn't smoke, and I don't smoke. But some of the workers do and it is not too late. Cigarettes to these people are not bought by the carton or by the pack; they are sold individually, and each cigarette is a precious item. Determined—no, desperate—I dress, walk out through the mud to the string of cots under tents of mosquito nets. Cigarette must be a universal word; at least I hope it is.

A circle of men is gathered around a fire. I could take a stick from the fire, but I ask them for a smoke. Several pull individual cigarettes from behind their ears and offer. It is generous and I feel I should pay, but then might I give insult? I have already committed one grievous error today.

They pat the ground beside them and, thinking I am being social, insist I sit with them and share their *ugali*. I need to scratch my balls. No, no, I say, just a cigarette, thanks, but they won't listen and insist even a little louder, and I join them. Those who offered cigarettes hold them in their outstretched hands, not sure I still want one. I am extrasensitive now: If I take one cigarette, will I insult the others who offered? If I take cigarettes from them all, will I be considered greedy? Smooth, gentle Yusuf always seems to be there when he is needed, and this is no exception. His tall dark figure enters the circle of light and he greets me with surprise.

"It is difficult to explain, Yusuf," I say. "All I want is a cigarette." I have got to scratch my balls.

"Ah, but you don't eat?"

"Tell them that I just had an HDR. All I wanted was a cigarette."

"I didn't know you smoked."

"No, just on special occasions, Yusuf. Now is one of them."

He says something in Somali, and the cigarettes come back from behind the ears and are pointed at me.

I take one at random, light it in the coals of the fire, take a long drag, close my eyes to express my extreme pleasure to the donor, and then, rising, thank them all, bow, and withdraw into the darkness.

Back in my tent, the operation is hardly straightforward. With flashlight in my teeth, I lean forward, lift up my balls, and spot the little critter as he digs his way into my spiritual center. Taking another long drag and flicking the ashes out under the net, I place the burning ember against the tick; my hairs singe and curl and the surrounding sensitive skin begins to heat up. The tick holds fast. I take another puff but, not used to smoking, begin to feel a little fuzzy, and this time my aim is none too good. That is going to hurt in the morning. The third time, the tick comes out easily and I flick it outside. I think I would rather live through the fever.

20.
Heaven Is Just a Sin Away

ROBBIE perks up at the sound of the aircraft, tucks his shirt into his skirt, and prepares himself for his well-rehearsed ritual.

"I'll get it," I say. "I'm expecting something on this flight."

"No bother, really. Must show the flag, you know."

We march out to the landing Cessna with marionette-like stiffness, without revealing it is a competition, without making fools of ourselves. Because of his long legs he doesn't have to worry. Well, fuck it, neither should I. Anyway, I can't keep up. Like Good Soldier Schweik he marches powerfully up to the plane and stands at attention, grinning, ready to welcome. The race is lost. The side door opens. Fine, he gets the journalist, I get the beer.

Boxes and bags are unloaded first and then a small backpack is thrown out and lands in a heap in the dirt. A lanky blonde in her late thirties ducks out through the cramped entrance. She pauses at the top of the steps, takes stock of her surroundings. Her face brightens.

"Robbie!"

"Why, it's Gabriele! Welcome to Marerey Base. Didn't expect you here. Or maybe I'm not so surprised."

"And I didn't know you were here. How wonderful," she says cheerfully, kissing him on each cheek.

"How is East Africa's favorite disaster groupie?"

"I love you too. How is Carol?"

"Good. Taking care of the *shamba*."

"Is David with you?" she asks.

"Of course! I wouldn't come out to this primeval swamp without the expert, you know." He picks up her pack and leads her down the runway toward the camp.

She turns to me. "And you're the American. John, *n'est-ce pas*?"

"*À votre service.*"

"Oh, good, you speak French. Robbie, why haven't you ever learned to speak French?"

"Don't have to. I'm marrying a Yank. I am learning to speak American."

The photographer turns to me. "I have something for you from Andrew."

"*Magnifique.*" I feel childish, as if I were trying to impress.

"Well, we have just enough room for you, Gabriele," Robbie says outside his shelter. "I sleep here normally and you can sleep there, next to our well-stocked *bibliothèque*."

She looks over at my living quarters next to my tent, just another tarp on poles but without the dirty dishes, the molding potatoes and onions, the bags of maize and blankets. "I will sleep there, in there." Who could argue?

"Now, perhaps we should go to see some villages, eh? I don't have much time." Robbie looks over to me and grins lewdly.

"How do you know Robbie?" I ask as we walk toward the boat. She hands me one of her bags of camera equipment.

"From Nairobi. East Africa is my territory. I've known him and his fiancée for years. And his partner, David. Robbie is something of a bore, don't you think?"

"Sometimes." Why had I felt there had to be some kind of competition with Robbie? I start to relax. I can do so in a woman's presence. For the moment, I'm on home ground.

"When do you have to leave?"

"Tomorrow midday. I have a lot of ground to cover."

"Well, no shortage of sinking villages." I am about to suggest Gadudey, where I taught the children to high-five, but Yusuf, who joins us in front of the radio shack and introduces himself, suggests Marerey. I shoot him a hard look; it is the last place I want to go, the day after.

No trip is made empty, without bringing supplies, a couple of armed guards, and a passenger or two. It is with understandable nervousness that she sits clutching her camera gear atop the bags between the guns in the overloaded and delicately balanced boat.

We wind our way through the submerged rooftops. Ahead, some boys on a raft of insulation push-pole bags of WFP maize meal through the branches of nearby mango trees. She wants to go closer. It is not easy. There are trees and poles and metal things under the muddy surface, and the current is swift. But closer, closer, she asks. I have to spin the wheel in one direction, then the other, countering the whirlpools that swirl around the broken dike system. As we approach she speed-shoots the children. These bone-thin urchins clad in only scraps of cloth are some of the most impoverished the world could offer. They wave and smile gaily.

"Damn!" Gabriele mutters through her lens. "They see a camera and they want to smile at you in their misery."

I find her compelling, not because she is a woman, but because of some natural vitality and open spirit. She is undeniably attractive, in a sort of masculine way: angular face, high cheekbones, dark green eyes, and a youthful bouncy manner that so many French women have never lost. She asks questions, she wants to know about the deliveries, the health conditions, she asks about the Somalis. She asks about me. I tell her what little I know about the local situation. I dodge questions about myself. This is the one effect I do recognize from Kismayo. I no longer consider myself terribly significant in any respect. Certainly not to anyone else. I may blather from the mouth sometimes, but it is just that, mindless blather requisite to communication.

The adults line the top of the dike; it is as if nothing had happened the day before. The children are there and greet me with "John-John! John-John!" "John-John?" she says. I grimace and nod. There's some admiration in her eyes. She smiles. I turn away. I don't need this. I search the faces of the children. The little Bantu is not here.

"Come with me?" she asks. I dare not leave the boat. She shrugs and, lugging her bags of camera gear, struggles up the muddy embankment and disappears through the mob of villagers.

The children resume their greetings and practice words they learned from earlier deliveries. I am not much in the mood. I still feel like a fool and I still hurt for the little Bantu. Offsetting that, however, is something more reassuring. I sense that I am being renewed, that her presence is injecting me with some kind of positive energy that I have not been able to provide myself. It is a vague feeling, a hope that this nagging disorder, the emotional chaos that has been building within, might not be so permanent after all. I guess I won't know until I'm out of here.

We motor slowly back to the base. We have left one guard in the village and the other rests his chin on his hands over the business end of his gun, staring mindlessly ahead. We are alone.

She leans back against the side, staring into the landscape of destruction. While I pay attention to my driving I study her. She is a lovely creature. I am in a foxhole—how could I know? Her greenish eyes are direct and warm and cheerful. She carries herself with some assurance, yet without the arrogance or overcompensation common to working women who have had no easy road to success.

There is a sensuality about her that quietly challenges me. It frightens me. She need not speak, need not appeal. Maybe others do not recognize it in her. Perhaps sensuality is an individual affair, unique, chemical, animal. Am I sensual to her? I must assume so. Could hers be one-way? I feel it is not. One tantalizes the other until recognized.

We both see the crocodile breaking the surface at the same time—long, lethal, and ugly. We are close to where Robbie, David, and I bathed the other day. The beast, about the size of the boat, swims lazily across our path, and I slow down to avoid it; a crocodile slapping a boat with its tail and overturning it is not unheard of. She snaps away, commenting as she shoots: "Ah, there. Yes, that is a good one. Just a little further, yes, that's right, good!" I watch the croc's big slow blinking eye watch us.

"Absolutely wonderful," she says, turning around. Her eyes are radiant with her pleasure. "Thank you!"

I didn't produce it, I just avoided it. "How long were you in Kismayo?"

"Overnight. A long overnight."

"Violent place."

"I know. There was a shooting at the airport just before I arrived. Something to do with the *miraa* plane. Your friend Andrew—what a lovely boy—said they have plans to evacuate."

"They always have plans to evacuate. But they never will. Not until someone gets shot."

"I think it may be serious now. I don't know the story, but Andrew says Unicef is now refusing to pay the families some blood money. Someone was killed, yes?"

"Yes—a woman." So, things are no different today from when I left last week. There is still a working boat at the port that they could use—unless it has been stolen.

Back at the base, we pass the mysterious woman in the dark chador still sitting cross-legged, watching, waiting. Gabriele considers a photo opportunity. The eyes of the two women meet. The photographer, however, lets the strapped camera fall back against her body, smiles warmly, and we return to the shelter.

Robbie ferries Gabriele to another village upriver and then briefly to the Red Cross distribution site being built on a dike north of that. I have the afternoon off—that is, time to refuel, to repair the damaged propeller.

Yusuf calls me over to the supply tent, where the men are stacking bags of flour, wheat, and maize meal brought in on this morning's rotation.

"Those are for you," he says, pointing to a carton of bottled water, a box of spark plugs, and some oil. The water is most important, and while our resident bush wallahs may not feel the need, it will make me feel a little more secure. Unless we have already picked up some mysterious Somali scourge. "This also arrived." The Japanese writing on the side of a large box placed at the entrance offers no clue to what is within. "I have never seen these before. How do we use them?" Yusuf pulls out a thin, bright pink blanket with an electric cord attached.

"You have got to be kidding!"

Two hundred electric blankets, baby blue and shocking pink, should go a long way toward keeping the villagers warm—when the snow falls and electricity comes to this part of the world. "Tell your boys to cut off the cords and we'll try to hand them out."

* * *

GABRIELE lays out her sleeping bag and I rig a mosquito net above. She is not very well equipped, but she was told that Marerey Base had everything she would need. I cannot imagine who would tell her that, certainly not anyone who has ever been here.

David has prepared a leg of goat in Gabriele's honor. He is an accomplished bull cook—a bush chef. The meat is roasted under strips of sugared mango, and with Yusuf, the five of us feast to the sound of the crackling fire and the din from the shag.

Robbie suddenly breaks into song:

> "I see cannibals munchin'
> A missionary luncheon . . .
> Like the hopes that were dashed
> When the stock market crashed . . ."

And I belt out:

> "And that glorious morn,
> Jack the Ripper was born,
> Those were the good old days . . ."

It is hard to believe that we should be singing a Broadway tune around a campfire in the middle of the Somali bush. I never sing, but I could not resist. I haven't heard or thought about that tune since I was a child, and somehow it just blurted out. Robbie, effeminate, enigmatic, blustery, sits back against the bags of maize meal, looks me uncomfortably in the eye, and grins. "Well done, sport."

Turning to Gabriele, he asks: "Now, do tell us, Gabriele, any new adventures, any yarns to spin around our campfire? What have you been doing—surely not hanging out at the Muthaiga Club?"

"Sudan—Bahr-el-Ghazal, Robbie. Government planes bombed a drop zone the day after I left."

" 'The world's in a terrible state of chassis,' " David says. She looks at him, puzzled. "Sean O'Casey, one of Ireland's finest."

"Yes, I hear the government is beginning to play hardball," Robbie says. "Although I hardly think it likely that they were mistaking some of us for a bunch of rebels. Did you meet Roger, the Frenchman. . . ." They talk among themselves about mutual acquaintances, old times, and Robbie's upcoming wedding. I excuse myself and walk outside and look up at the night sky. I cannot deny that I am attracted to her.

She joins me in the dark and slips her arm into mine. I feel vulnerable and awkward.

"I don't suppose there is a latrine in the camp," she says quietly.

"Out there." I nod into the darkness.

"You come with me?"

We walk through the low smoke from the small cooking fires down the runway that slips into the shag. A voice calls out softly from a row of cots tented by the willowy nets:

"Mzee! Simba mingi sana!"

"Asanti, bwana."

"What did he say?"

"Uh, have a nice walk."

"Oh, how nice!"

I need this trek into the crisp fresh night. I need this walk with her. I wouldn't cut it short because of some warnings in Swahili about plenty of lions out here.

In the dark she takes down her jeans and pees, unashamedly and without reservation, while I awkwardly stand above, keeping watch for animals, gunmen—anything but keeping watch on her.

We walk further into the night. Lightning bulges within some thunderstorm in the distance. "It is special here," she says, looking up at the heavens that bristle with specks of light. "Here I don't feel under the stars, I feel among them."

We turn and look back at Marerey Base. It is a memorable sight. The twinkling cooking fires on either side of the runway outline a descending tunnel into darkness. There is no other light save from the stars.

While I put things away, she undresses in the dark and slips into her sleeping bag under the net. "Stay and talk to me," she says, as I am about to duck into my tent.

I sit next to her on the floor.

"Now tell me about you."

"There's really nothing much to say. I drive boats."

"*Alors*, you do not just drive boats. Andrew told me some things. You are a writer."

"Sometimes. When I'm published, I am a writer. When I'm not, I am unemployed. I would rather admit to being a commercial fisherman, which I was once. A far better 'day job.' "

"But you are a writer."

"I guess we are whatever we call ourselves at the time. I was in the upper Midwest in the States writing a book and working on an oil rig. I was buying supplies when the shop owner asked me what I was doing up there. Instead of saying that I worked for Cactus Drilling on the Shell rig, I said I was a writer. He said, 'Oh, you mean you are unemployed.' So I just say I am whatever it is I am doing at the time."

"But you are a writer. You've been published."

"Yeah. A dime novel, TV soaps, speeches, some stories. Funny thing. I guess I realized at an early age I could be a writer. I was raised at an all-boys boarding school. Like all little boys, I was exploding with horniness. So I wrote my own pornography and—well, it was very effective."

She bursts into laughter.

"I sold it to the other kids for twenty-five cents a page."

"That's marvelous!" she says.

"I say, David," comes a voice from nearby, "sounds like our Gabriele and the American chap are hitting it off."

"Indeed it does, Robbie."

"And now I meet this famous pornographer out in someplace like this. Are you writing? About Somalia?"

"Taking notes. Not sure why—instinctive, perhaps. Maybe one day I will try to write the Somali story. I don't think I am enough of a writer to express the sorrow, the rage, the vulnerability. For it to be honest it would have to be autobiographical, and I wouldn't feel comfortable with that. For it to work, so much depends on how we understand what happens to us. I do not understand a thing. If I can't put this into some personal perspective, then there is probably nothing to say. No, I don't think I can write it. Still, for some reason, I take notes."

Except for the babble from critters outside, it is silent. She incites me. Without her knowing, she is ripping something out of my soul and making me wear it. I need to spill my guts, to gush, to release the accumulation of fear, grief, confusion. Up to this point, I have been walking without a shadow, have become invisible to all but myself, and so I wished to remain—to get through life leaving no trace. She is a stranger, however, and it is easy to confide, to shed this mask of anonymity.

"Before Somalia," I continue, "I had never seen anyone die. Not even my parents; I was simply told it happened. Now I've seen death—and people in the process of dying, which is even worse. . . . When I see someone die, and am involved somehow in that death, I feel something inside of me goes with them. Part of me, part of my spirit seems to just evaporate. Like I am losing something vital. Yet I know how absurd that is; doctors, nurses, firefighters, and cops—they see it every day. Do they get so inured to death that it has no effect on them? I cannot imagine. At what point do these people begin to accept traumatic death as a way of life? I don't know—maybe I haven't yet seen enough death. Hell, Gabriele, you've been there."

"I am a journalist, not an aid worker. I don't get the blood on my hands."

"No, I suppose not. When I was a reporter, I could look at suffering through a protective lens. In Washington, there was a plane crash, a P-3 Orion antisubmarine plane. It was a big plane. It went down in some woods near Andrews Air Force Base close to a highway. I was one of the first on the scene. It was terrible weather—sleet, rain. I walked to the site. They were still putting out the fires. I looked up and spotted a charred helmet wedged among the branches. And something that looked like a face in it still. I just stared at it; it was merely interesting, fascinating. I was a reporter—it was not my job to connect. Only to write the story. Odd, but that day has come back to me a few times since I've been here—as if I had missed an opportunity to feel, to prepare myself. As journalists we managed to shield ourselves. I suppose if I did years of this relief work, that shield would be of sterner stuff. But today, today I can't hide behind journalism, and I don't have the calluses from years of relief work.

"And you know, Gabriele, my real concern is that because of all this, I could become incapable of ever again having any real feelings, that I could lose that vital element that separates me from a rock. Then I guess there would be nothing more to lose, would there?"

My voice is unsteady.

"I think you must write it."

"Yeah. Sure."

Her hand slides out from under the net and reaches for mine.

21.

A Rolling Stone and a Squeaky Wheel

GABRIELE wants some soft-light shots, and we motor slowly through the mist of daybreak.

"Oh, look—under the tree!" She points to a large humpy white bird on stilt legs about three feet tall with a brilliant crimson face. Its yellow beak is nearly as long as its body. We approach it with some delicacy, expecting it to take flight, but it merely cocks its red head and looks inquisitively at us with a large dark eye.

"Yellow-billed stork, David tells me."

"You wonder how it can get itself off the ground."

"They do. Look up there." Hundreds of the ungainly birds float effortlessly a thousand feet above us, riding thermals in slow lazy circles.

"I wish I didn't have to leave." She brushes loose strands of hair away from her face and looks up at me expectantly as if for guidance.

We glide quietly through the pallid morning light, savoring a sort of youthful swoon; it is as if we had been adulterous and are hesitant to walk out of the afterglow. We do not speak. Even the engine seems muted. Our moment of languorous contentment that we are about to acknowledge is brought up short by the sound of an approaching aircraft.

"The damn thing is too early!" She pouts. "We must go back."

When we return from the shoot, the plane is on the runway, waiting. She doesn't even have time for a cup of coffee. While I slept she had packed her gear and stashed it in a corner. She tosses her kit on her back, gathers up her equipment, and in silence we walk toward the plane—a distance far too short to sort out the confused mess of exhilaration, sadness, and guilt.

"Call me when you get to Nairobi?"

"Where can I reach you?"

"I left my number in your tent."

"Good."

She turns, kisses me on each cheek, then with a lingering look: "Call me."

"I will."

She walks toward the plane and calls over her shoulder, "Promise?"

"Yes."

At the steps she yells over the sound of the engine, "Four times promise!"

"Yes. Four times!"

The plane turns, points down the runway, and begins to roll. I wave, not knowing which side she is on.

Yusuf joins me on the airstrip. In a tone respectful of my private thoughts, he asks me if I would mind taking him downriver. I welcome the diversion. I wince when he says he wants to go to some village just upstream from Hum Hum.

"Yusuf, that's pretty close to the Green Line. If we couldn't get there from Kismayo, how can we get there from here?"

"We will stay in our territory. Very safe."

"But across the river is enemy country."

"We don't go so far. We will take extra guard."

The boat is less loaded than usual. We carry just a token of what we eventually will deliver if Yusuf can get this run organized. But we do have aboard three young militiamen and a village official with a very pronounced *singda,* the darker callused spot on his forehead from years of prayer five times daily; the thickness of the *singda,* it is said, usually reflects the depth of devotion. Since he couldn't cross the Green Line from Kismayo, he was flown here to be ferried twenty miles back down the river, a long, circuitous route to his village, only about ten miles up the road from the port city. It is to be a two-hour trip each way, a real outing, so I load up with drinking water, HDRs, a Snickers bar, extra fuel, and a little anxiety. Yusuf and the official strap on life jackets. Unlocking the locker in the forepeak, I pull out the flak jackets and combat helmets and pile them at my feet by the steering wheel: I know about Hum Hum.

Because of the receding flood level, this passage to Marerey where the canal joins the river is more of a challenge. Out in the middle of the flooded field, we pass Robbie and his guards standing waist-deep, struggling to push his boat off some unseen underwater obstacle. While considering offering Robbie a hand, we run aground on a submerged hillock and momentarily hang suspended. The propeller spins uselessly. The current takes control and pushes us off the rise and backward into the fast waters of the canal. Throwing the boat into gear, we shoot forward and continue on our way.

The entrance of the Jubba is marked by a copse of handsome mango trees. It is not hard to imagine how beautiful and peaceful the area must have been before the floods, before the war, the kind of scene that evokes Huck Finn sitting in the shade of a tree with a fishing pole. We bottom out again under the fruit-heavy limbs of a mango tree. The guards jump out and begin to fend off.

"Stop! Wait! *Mia! Mia!*" No, no, I shout.

Standing on my seat, I reach for a low-hanging branch and pluck half a dozen juicy mangoes. I have wanted a mango since I arrived. Keeping one for myself, I give the others to my passengers. "Okay, *sasa sasa*." It is, apparently, a very good year for mangoes.

Our passenger points toward the water as the last guard begins to mount the swim ladder. A mamba, three feet long, iridescent green, narrow head weaving just above the surface, slithers through the bottom rung just as the man lifts his foot. It is one of Africa's most venomous snakes.

There was a time when the rising river poured through these

broken dikes and spilled onto the surrounding countryside. Now the water from the thousands of square miles of flooded plains has begun to return to the river through the narrow slots in the dikes, and with an alarming force. Funneling into the holes in the wall, the water rides up against both sides of the gaps and explodes skyward in a haystack. I choose one such opening for our entrance and slam the throttle forward. "Hold on!" White water lifts us and hurls us through the gap like a pinched watermelon seed. I throttle back and relax, satisfied.

One sunken village after another speeds by, villages that I never knew existed. The sound of the engine precedes us by miles, and above each village, straggly groups of distressed homeless stand on remnants of broken dike, waving flags of rags, beckoning. I wonder why we haven't been serving these villages and why we are going so far downriver to feed another.

It is possible to follow the general course of the Jubba but impossible to determine which is the river itself. Were it not for the flood, the Jubba would not be very wide or for that matter very fast. It is said that during the dry season, it is a peaceful and placid stream and even shrivels to a trickle during the frequent droughts in the area.

If I remember from the air, it is near here that it doubles back like a winding mountain stream, but there are no indications of sharp turns or switchbacks. I take a wrong turn. Rather, not seeing any turn to take, we continue downstream until we start bumping over the ground, kicking up mud. Yusuf confers with one of the gunmen, then points to a line of trees ahead that once delineated the riverbank.

"Look. Careful!" Yusuf's attention is fixed on some disturbed water, an odd crosscurrent that churns up darker bottom mud near an uprooted mango tree about twenty yards off to the left.

We go closer.

"No!" Yusuf puts a restraining hand on my arm.

A low wide wall of water pushed by some large creature rolls ominously toward us. Flared orange nostrils and two heavily lidded eyes pop above the surface; their size belies the mass of the creature hidden beneath. It must be big. We are starting to rock from the wake of the water it displaces.

The hippo lifts its head above the surface and with movement slow and menacing opens its huge mouth as if measuring whether it is wide enough to chop us in half. This cavernous yawn is a warning.

Yusuf answers an unasked question: "We are safe. Because we can see it. But go now!" We turn down the river and leave its territory.

He impatiently motions more speed, and loaded with less than usual, we skim over the surface and rise to a plane. High ground ahead forms a spit out into the river where the Jubba doubles back. Tall acacia and large ancient mango trees drape themselves over the river and cast their darkness onto the other side. It is a gloomy junglelike section, palliate and secret, that hides the unknown, the unexplored, and a hint of evil. It is not much different from the wooded area around Hum Hum where someone used us for aerial target practice. I don't worry much at this speed—combined with the fast current, we are hitting about fifty knots. They would have to be pretty fair shots and use something far more accurate than a Kalashnikov. We each nurse our own private thoughts, fears, nervousness. I feel Yusuf's tension; I am sure he feels mine. Within a few minutes, however, we round the point and come out from under the shadows into the sunshine. We do not say anything about that stretch and it seems foolish to do so, but each of us is well aware that against the current we will have to return this way at a considerably slower clip.

A haphazard collection of tumbledown shacks on a high embankment lies directly ahead. The river disappears in a sharp turn to the north. From here the settlement looks like it is sitting at the end of a blind alley.

Yusuf indicates by a nod that this is our destination. A crowd awaits us at river's edge. He puffs up a little, pulls down his long sleeves, and appears to primp. He seems pleased, possibly relieved that we made it.

"You have been here before?" I ask.

"Oh, many times—but not since the flood."

Each temporary shelter on a dike, settlement, or village possesses its own aura, a special feeling, and through my antics I am usually able to get a sense of its spirit, to gauge its level of hope or despair. However, this place—I do not even know its name—projects an atmosphere tense and saturnine. The people on shore don't welcome us, they just glower. The assault rifles are many and the men wear them slung on their shoulders like they do in Kismayo. It feels like an armed camp. And where are the children, the excited little urchins who run down to the water so happily curious to see the strangers and the strange boat? There are no children here, at least none so young that they cannot carry a gun. The crowd parts as if on some silent order, and a tall older man of some evident authority—long white beard, bright clean white robe, and Moslem cap—greets Yusuf and our passenger, who quickly vanishes beyond the villagers. The elder points to one then another of the sour-faced men with his walking cane, and with grudging compliance, they rest their guns against the stump of a dead tree to help off-load the sacks of supplies.

A murmured discussion, words barely audible, develops between one of our militiamen and one of the villagers waiting below for a fifty-kilo bag of Unimix. Initially, it appears this is a meeting of old friends, but they do not look at each other. The voices grow louder, the tone turns ugly. It is clear there is a personal problem. Our guard lifts a bag onto the edge of the gunnels, and when the villager steps forward to take it, our man pushes it off and drops it on him, sending him reeling backward into the mud. The villager shouts at our guard, turns toward the embankment, and slips and scrabbles on hands and knees up to his rifle. The women scream and scatter. The village men cock their guns and aim them at our own idiot hothead, who stands defiantly next to me as if my presence is going to stop him from taking a bullet. Yusuf waves his arms furiously and barks in short guttural expletives at the gunman in our boat. The old man swings his cane through the air and shouts at the offended villager. Our guard, outgunned or persuaded by Yusuf's demands—I will never know—places his rifle gently against the side of the boat without moving his eyes from the armed men on shore. It is still cocked and ready to explode.

Within minutes the unloading begins anew. Yet the incident is not forgotten. I am beginning to think Yusuf may have miscalculated or misread his maps. I think he is lost.

Yusuf wisely stays close to the boat, holds a brief discussion with the village chief, and on parting shakes hands in the Islamic tradition of respect: an extra little bow and a self-effacing tap to his chest. Then he wades back and climbs onto the boat with our guards. *"Sasa, sasa,"* he says tightly through his teeth, but he is smiling and waving at our host. The villagers respond with a glare that is sullen and challenging. As we ease away, our gunman shouts a parting Somali obscenity. I throw the throttle forward and roar out, kicking a plume of white water.

Yusuf regards our young guard who precipitated the violence not with accusation but with regret. He joins me behind the steering wheel.

"It was my fault," Yusuf says. "We are from the same clan but there are problems—this man here, his father's father was killed by the family of that man."

"These people don't forgive or forget, do they? But for Christ's sakes, Yusuf, didn't you know that before we took him along?"

"It was . . . a miscalculation. I needed him. He knows the area better than anybody."

"Bad call, Yusuf."

"Yes. But my job is to help everyone in this area." He pauses. "I am told they now may be with General Morgan."

"General Morgan! You mean we are on the other side of the Green Line?"

"Perhaps. Today it is here. Yesterday it was not here. We must hurry."

"No shit! Here, better take this." I reach down and hand him a heavy flak jacket, but he shakes his head. He would rather wear his life vest. He takes a helmet that is several sizes too big, and were this not so serious, it would be comical. Yusuf's long thin face is swallowed up by the big blue helmet, his eyes peek out from below the brow.

"Which side of the river is the problem side?" I shout.

He shrugs, points to the line of trees ahead to the right. "Maybe there. Maybe some problem."

We are approaching the densely forested high ground at the river's edge that in our imaginations had been cloaked with threat. We hug the opposite shore of open fields, scrub, and remaining pools of floodwater and mud; it is unlikely anyone could find much cover there. The three guards face the starboard with guns pointing into the wood. The overhanging trees close over our heads like the vault of a tomb.

We are halfway down the line before the shooting starts. It is not how I would think an ambush is made, no sudden withering barrage of bullets as we cross some invisible line but rather an undisciplined scattering of automatic fire as we speed past. Our guards return fire and shoot into the line of trees. We are on the far side of the river but well within range. Deafened by our own shooting, I can't hear the incoming. I don't have to hear the gunfire to be scared, but then, I don't have much time to be. I drop to my knees and drive, peering through the steering wheel, trying to keep as close to the bank as possible without running aground. At the same time I'm hoping to avoid broken trees that lean crookedly out over the bank. Worse, at this speed if we run over a fallen tree that lies below the surface, we've had it. Kneeling on the flak jackets, I slap a helmet onto my head and crouch even lower, seeking protection from the remaining bags of maize meal. We speed out of the shadows and out of range into blazing sunshine. The floodplain extends benignly in all directions.

I feel shaken, exhilarated, thrilled, and rewarded by a vague sensation of heroism, a touch of invincibility. It is childish and arrogant and dangerous. And fraudulent: I did nothing. I should feel something else, but like at the airport on the first day when the lone shooter was firing at us, this also seems too remote and unreal and impersonal. This is what it feels like—immediately.

My reaction is tempered by Yusuf's cool, almost nonchalant reaction. He does not seem to be too affected by the incident, but our guards jabber excitedly among themselves.

It is becoming easier to understand these Somali gunmen. They have grown up with the gun as the Almighty. They know the dangers and accept the risks, and the risks of death have become part of their psychological makeup. It is their way of life. From here on the ground, so far away from the corridors of power and influence, it is presumptuous to think that any foreign power would feel the need to step in to end the fighting and disarm them, to force upon them a form of democracy. (The Norwegians submitted a proposal before the UN Security Council for a nation-building program in Somalia, which would gradually disarm militias and train a national police. The United States opposed the resolution on the ground that it was premature. I would add futile.)

The Somalis have never known democracy. They know democracy only as a fanciful concept represented by such things as a calendar in Harun's home. Democracy is nowhere in their history; the concept of one man, one vote here is a cultural absurdity. Too factionalized to accept Western democracy, they would rather be governed by an iron fist. T. E. Lawrence wrote that Arab populations could only be ruled by autocrats, tribal chiefs, and strongmen; they cannot manage freedom as we define it in the West. Yusuf agrees and wonders aloud whether his people were not better off under the rule of Siad Barre. Then there was a form of law and order (at least for the indigenous Somalis), even with an unrepresentative government. Moreover, there had been electricity, food, water, schools, telephones, and commerce. When the infrastructure that held the country together collapsed, social services in all but a few pockets in the capital ceased to exist. Indeed, today nine out of ten children have no access to basic education. Under the heel of a dictator, there was some stability. Remove a dictator and watch chaos grow.

On the return to the base, we stop in Marerey town to pick up some elders.

The villagers crowd the boat; there is no sign of my little Bantu friend. The children chant, "John-John," and it is reassuring. The next time children are not at waterside, I will just turn around.

While I wait in the boat for Yusuf, one of the older boys yells something in Somali. "John-John," and the rest is gibberish.

A helpful voice from the crowd translates: "He ask about girl. Girl sister?"

It takes a moment to realize they are talking about Gabriele. Could that have been only yesterday?

"*Mia, mia*. No. No sister." With our similar beaky features and blondish hair I suppose it is not inconceivable to be considered siblings.

Another question from somewhere in the crowd. "Wife?"

"*Mia, mia.*"

A small voice from within the crowd yells something. The villagers laugh. I shrug. I don't understand.

Another ragged boy reams his forefinger into a curled fist.

I think I know what he means. I grab onto an imaginary ass in front of me and pump obscenely. I don't know what is happening to me. I would never do such a thing—but I am *alive*. The crowd's laughter at my lewd gyrations is spontaneous and loud. The older villagers, usually reserved, laugh heartily, and the women turn to each other and giggle.

"*Whus, whus,*" some of the children shout.

"*Whus?*" I grab and bump-grind.

"*Ha ha! Ha ha!*" Yes, yes.

So *whus* means fucking. Joking about fucking to a stranger in public doesn't seem to be in bad taste.

"*Mia whus*. No fucking! *Mia whus!*" I shout. Some in the crowd are laughing so hard they are dancing, stamping their feet in the mud.

It is almost too much. One minute scared to death, minutes later loving these violent unpredictable people whom I make laugh. Could a person's emotions go through such a ride without some damage? I feel like a runaway engine with no governor, screaming to its maximum until it breaks. Or explodes. I need this. I need more.

Bouncing over the flooded field back to the base, I wonder if making these people laugh isn't something of a higher calling. The bureaucrats chalk up the tonnage of relief supplies delivered. Fighter aces chalk up the kills on the fuselage of their planes, the militiamen with notches on their guns. I should paint on the hull of my boat a long-tongue Rolling Stones smile for each villager I get to laugh.

"Yusuf," I shout over the outboard. "What about the little boy? The one I gave the biscuit to?"

Yusuf hears me but looks straight ahead, abstracted.

"Yusuf? The kid, I didn't see him today. Or yesterday."

Yusuf turns slowly.

"Yusuf?"

"He is dead."

"What! How the hell could he be dead?"

"I do not know. He is dead. They told me today. It is not important."

* * *

BACK at camp, David lies back against a pile of blankets, his baseball cap over his eyes, a paperback autobiography of Winston Churchill folded open on his lap.

"You awake?" He probably is not but I must talk.

"Yes."

"The boy died."

"Oh. And?"

"And shit! The boy is dead!"

"Yes. What can you do about it? You think it was your fault?"

"Of course it was. If I hadn't given him the fucking fig bar he would still be alive. The villagers didn't show any signs—like it didn't matter. I mean, we could have done something. If it was that serious we could have sent him to the MSF hospital in Kismayo. David, I killed that little boy."

"That is a little extreme. I wouldn't spend too much time on it. They say life is cheap here."

"Yeah, I saw how cheap. Measured in a number of camels. Maybe you have been on this godforsaken continent too long to know the value of life."

He lifts his cap off his eyes and looks up. His stubbled face darkens, creases with insult and threat. I do not want to alienate this good man. "Sorry, David, I am a bit strung out."

"Life in Africa is not measured by you and me. It is measured by them, Africans. We are here to save lives. We do what we can. But if we didn't, life would continue; people live, people die. You are a European—an American—with entirely different values. Maybe I *am* too African, but that is the way it is. In this business you see these things."

"But I caused it."

"Indirectly. But you did not kill him. They killed him. Africans killed him. It will do you no good if you dwell on it. It will tear you up. Someone once said: Keep your sense of humor in the face of the absurd. Wise counsel, I should think."

"Humor is not the word that comes to mind. Sanity is more like it."

The child's startled look as I gave him the fig bar will stick with me forever. It was not of gratitude. It was of horror.

"Are you going to see Gabriele again?"

It is an unusual sort of question, probably a diversion. I have never heard him ask about anyone's private affairs.

"Shit, I don't know. Yes. No. I told her I would."

"Quite a woman."

"I wouldn't know. I never found out anything about her. We never talked about our personal lives. I don't know if she is married or spoken for, and she never asked me"—David begins to interrupt—"but I think it is better that I do not know. No, I probably won't see her again."

I reach into my pocket for Jacqueline's photo, ever close at hand. She has become less of a person to me than something to hold on to. I am re-creating her in my mind, recalling and placing events—the good times—out of proportion. The happiness, the comfort of those times, have become far more solid than they really were. She has become an anchor, and the holding ground is poor, and I use her to keep from smashing into the rocks.

I feel I am being watched. Perhaps it is because of my loud

American voice, the tone of my distress. Across the other side of the campsite, the eyes of the figure in the chador who sits immobile like a block of granite are on me. I might have thought, might have wished for her accusation, her condemnation, but from this distance her eyes are without expression. Yusuf's young assistant brings her a bowl of *ugali*. Without taking her eyes off mine, she accepts it.

The afternoon quiet is broken by the sudden roar of a ground-skimming flyby. The Twin Otter, a high-wing two-engine turboprop, zooms just above the top of our tarp city, gains altitude, banks to the right, and circles back for a landing.

I have no interest in the flight. I just hope there is no VIP who wants us to tell him what we are doing out here. The plane is on the ground for only about five minutes, then roars off into the afternoon sun, leaving us all in relative quiet. David hasn't moved and I begin to doze off.

An awful ear-grating scraping—as piercing as fingernails down a blackboard—and tiny swear words like the angry chirping of a little bird rustle me out of a fitful slumber. I had been thinking or had been dreaming about the little boy. I raise my cap to watch a small figure silhouetted by the late sun—female, apparently—back down the runway, pulling a heavy lock trunk.

She turns and, seeing me observe her, straightens, puts hands on her hips, thrusts out her chin, and demands:

"This is Marerey Base, is it not?"

"Yeah."

"Very good." She stands with passive expectancy on the side of the strip and waits. She is clad in an outfit better suited to the city than the Somali heartland: designer jeans, khaki shirt, new unscratched hiking boots. She has a round, little girl's face with big innocent eyes. By her posture, it is evident she is used to getting her way.

I get slowly to my feet and take one end of her trunk. "What brings you here?"

"I am an aid worker."

"Oh."

"I am here to drive boats. My boat should be here in a day or two."

"Really!" I look at this childlike apparition with some amusement. A boat driver?

"No. Yes, well,. that is what I am—a boat driver. You may call me Amelia." She takes my hand stiffly and pumps.

"I may? If I didn't call you Amelia, what would I call you?"

"No, really, please just call me Amelia." She offers a shy smile, then looks away as if embarrassed.

"Okay, Amelia it is." I do not feel very charitable. Minutes ago I was trying to make sense of the day and now comes this, this little girl with a squeaky voice who, despite her peremptory manner, looks very worried.

"You bring a tent?"

"I wasn't told to."

"Net?"

"Oh, yes! I brought that—I'll just get it." She starts to fuss with the locks on her trunk. "It's in here someplace."

"You don't need it right now, Amelia. I'm trying to get you set up for the night. You can sleep here with me."

"Oh, no! I couldn't do that."

I just stare. This is not happening. I want the luxury to revel in kinder thoughts. "Not with me, of course—I just don't know you well enough, do I?"

She looks at me blankly. "Amelia, you sleep *alone* under your net under the tarp there." She frowns. "A photographer—a woman—slept there last night. It's perfectly safe." She is still frowning. "Well, where else would you like to sleep? In my tent?"

"Silly!"

"Well, there are no hotels, I'm afraid. As it is, your shelter is three-star. David! Wake up. We have been sent a boat driver."

"So I see," he says. With his forefinger he lifts his cap just off his wrinkled eyes and gazes critically at the new arrival. "Invite her over for a cup of tea when she gets settled."

She stands above me in silence, her hand on her hip, watching as I help make a spot for her under the tarp.

* * *

DAVID concocts a vegetable curry for the occasion. Robbie, who had spent the afternoon in Gadudey, drinks whiskey with David, Amelia drinks tea, and I have a beer. Amelia admits to Robbie's prodding that she is from one of the wealthier families in Nairobi, a third-generation Kenyan.

"Then why are you out here?" Robbie asks suddenly. "Not for the money, certainly."

"Why, the same reason as we are all here. I just want to help people."

"David! I do believe we have a true altruist at our humble base. I never thought we'd find a real one. You?"

Amelia reddens, embarrassed that her motives are questioned or, worse—in our eyes, she suspects—wrong. However, no one laughs or teases; it's her business, but none of us believes it is as simple as that.

"I know of your family," David says quietly. "From Karen?"

"Oh, yes! You know my parents?"

"Never met them."

I seem to be more surprised than Robbie and David that Amelia has joined us, that she has become a relief worker, that she will be handling these difficult deliveries. A member of a well-known family of white Kenyans, she lives in a wealthy Nairobi suburb (named after Karen Blixen, author of *Out of Africa*), and when asked teasingly by Robbie about her handicap, tells us of golf with her older brothers on Sundays at the country club after brunch, a family tradition of generations. It will be interesting, if not amusing, to see if she will be any more able to survive in the bush than someone ripped out of the Upper East Side of Manhattan. Something in her nature, however, tells me that she is going to turn out to be a very tough little girl.

Yusuf joins us from out of the shadows and casts a curious look in my direction. He brings his own *cha*, asks Robbie for some sugar.

"You know," Amelia addresses the quiet Somali, "I was taught that too much sugar in one's tea will rot your teeth out. They will actually fall out. Did you know that?"

I am amazed. So are the others.

Yusuf keeps his eyes on his cup and smiles diplomatically. "Well, you see that is not such a big problem in Somalia. We don't have much sugar here." Looking up at us, he adds, "The water goes quickly."

He addresses our greatest concern. It won't be long before we will find ourselves high and dry, unable to get our boats away from the strip, much less deliver aid to any of the villages. We should shift camp to a spot closer to the river, perhaps above the irrigation canal.

"Yes, that would be a good idea. The helicopter can land on the dike," he says, but it is evident this is not his main concern. "But the dike is also a road, and when the water goes down then I think there will be some trouble."

"Do tell," Robbie says.

"As I say before, I am hearing the militia will attack and steal the supplies. When there is no more flood, they will come across the land. I do not have enough men with guns to protect you."

"Perhaps this nostrum of international goodwill will be declared over by that time."

"I just got here!" Amelia blurts.

I walk out into the night, down the runway toward unidentifiable animal noises. I won't go beyond the loom of camp lights but I am tempted. I need some clarification. The sound of this girl's voice remains in my ears.

This night is like last night but different; nevertheless, the pleasant memory fills me with some comfort, a positive reinforcement. Gabriele has given me a sense of hope, some reassurance that apparently still holds, tenably, despite the events of the day. I detect a noiseless movement behind me and I turn with a start. It is our new boat driver.

"Did I scare you?"

"No, I was just listening to the lions. I thought maybe you were one of them." I think this will frighten her and she will scurry back to the shelter.

"Oh, yes, I've heard them. Not too close."

"You know about lions, Amelia?"

"Yes, my family and I go on safari every year. But it's not like this. This is quite different."

"What is the difference?"

"Oh, you know, we bring the servants, of course. And we have big tents, and chairs and tables and wines—my brothers, they like champagne, so my parents bring champagne for them, but I drink juice only—I don't like alcoholic beverages—and we have a wonderful good time, really. Now, my oldest—"

"Do you do the cooking when you go on safari?" I need to put an end to this febrile chatter.

"Cooking? I can't imagine, really. That's not for us to do."

Later as we prepare to bed down, I ask Amelia how she got the UN job. She says she had friends who helped. Qualifications? "Well, I do drive our ski boat during the holidays." Then she confides from under her mosquito net: "This is my first real job."

"In your life?"

"Yes. You won't tell anyone, will you?"

"How old are you, Amelia?"

"Thirty-one. You will help me out there, won't you, John?"

In excited whispered tones she begins to relate endless rambling tales about her brothers, her father, her favorite servants. One cannot be critical; she has held steady at sixteen, has never been permitted to mature. She is a woman and I wonder, with her protected background, whether she has any experience. "Well, of course, I do know what it is all about, Robbie," she snapped back earlier when he began to pry into her love life. "I have gone out with boys, you know."

I find it difficult to work up any interest in her tales of her personal life. I am no family member, no father confessor, no handholder, no babysitter. I do not want to adopt a little girl. She is talking to the wrong guy. It is a pity that I am all there is.

The falling water level has taken away those riotous good-humored noises, the magic night sounds. It is a sad thought. That mysterious idiotic laughter was nothing less than a lullaby.

So now I have Amelia. As I am drifting off to sleep, a small voice breaks the silence: "John, tell me, what is it like out there—out on the river, in the villages?"

22.
One of the Boys

"JOHN! Where are you going?"

Soap in hand, I had begun walking through the compound to the communal toilet. Amelia, dressed only in a bathrobe and felt slippers, had come running out after me, flip-flopping through the mud, breathless, desperate.

"Amelia, for God's sakes. I am going to take a dump."

"You needn't be vulgar. I just want to know how it is done, that's all."

"How it's done?"

"Where to go!"

A few dusky figures squatted ankle-deep in the water. She watched the performances with startled eyes.

"Well, how do you do it on safari?"

"Why, we have a portable loo that our servants take care of."

"Well, kiddo, it is *au naturel*. Out here, there is no loo."

She was horrified.

"Most of the men are up at dawn and drop their pants shortly thereafter. The area is usually pretty empty by this time."

"But everyone can see!" She stood like a small pillar, her fists clenched tightly at her sides, her worried eyes fixed on the men hunkered in the water.

"Why don't you do what David does: walk the other way—down the runway and into the grass?"

"Oh, yes! Thank you!" She hurried back to the camp.

Some Somalis sitting on their haunches around a cooking fire had watched Amelia march off down the runway. "Mister John!" one of them called, "You many wives. Many wives."

"Mia whus, mia whus!"

The men laughed and took up the chant: *"Mia whus, mia whus."*

Amelia apparently was successful and she returned cheerful. When she smiles that eager little-girl smile, there is something attractive there.

"What does *mia whus* mean?"

"Where did you hear that?"

"Oh, one of the men said it to me when I passed. Is that like—good morning?"

* * *

DURING the past days, the atmosphere at the base has become more relaxed, less urgent. Yusuf is not as eager to use us as he had been, possibly because the crisis has eased or because he is under pressure. It is not as if there is nothing to distribute. We still get deliveries to the base—bundles, sacks, and crates of supplies stacked ever higher on reclaimed land. We had discussed it among ourselves last night.

"He certainly uses the little polystyrene rafts," Robbie said. "We have boats that will go everywhere."

"Not mine, Robbie. With my V-hull, I am spending more time pushing us off than under way. I got stuck three times in a half hour. With the falling levels, our usefulness may be drawing to an end, at least in this area."

"Rubbish. I, at least, can go anywhere they can. I mean he *pays* those little naked boys with their rafts and poles to make *our* deliveries."

"Good social economics, Robbie," David says.

"Quite. But if he can't use us, then he should lose us. It beggars the question, what in God's name are we doing here?"

Therefore, I am surprised when Yusuf asks me to go on a delivery run. First, an unusual request:

"Do you have a mosquito net?"

"Of course."

"You don't need it?"

"No, I have the tent."

"Would you let her use it?" he says, pointing to the woman in the chador sitting across the compound.

"No problem. What's her story? Why is she here? She just sits."

"She has children in Nairobi and has Kenyan identity card but she is Somali. Her home and I think most of her family were lost in the flood. She now has no papers, has nothing. She waits for plane to Kenya."

"Oh."

"There is nothing we can do," he continues. "My NGO is trying to help, but without papers, she has to stay."

I dig out the net from under the tins of vegetables and instant noodle meals in my lock trunk and walk over to the austere and solemn figure. I have never been quite this close to her before. She is not dressed in black but in robes of dark deep purple and a black veil with a two-inch opening for her eyes. I am captivated by what little I can see of the woman. There are no other distracting body parts, and her silent eyes offer all there is: Nestled behind long curled lashes, they are beautiful, direct, and somewhat challenging, and it embarrasses me. Does she smile under that veil? Or does she sneer at this fascinated infidel?

"Here. For you." She withdraws her hands from the folds of her robe and accepts the bundled net. By the appearance of her lithe and delicate fingers there is little indication she has ever had to do much manual work. One might get the impression she is from a family of some wealth, accustomed to slaves.

"What is your name?"

She lowers her eyes. "My name is Asha," she whispers. Her English is precise.

"My name is John," I volunteer.

"John," she repeats, and says nothing more.

"I will try to help." Her eyes meet mine. As I turn to leave, she whispers something in what sounds like Arabic. She lifts her palm to her face and appears to blow across it. It is a strange, incomprehensible act.

Amelia is wandering around alone in the camp like a lost puppy. "Let's hit the road, kiddo," I call over.

"Oh, good! Where are we going?"

"Upriver. Downriver. Who the hell knows? Wherever Yusuf points us. Thought you might like to see how it's done before your boat gets here."

"Oh, what fun! Thank you!"

We are running out of gasoline for the outboards, but mixing it with Jet A1, a kerosene-based aviation fuel, seems to work. After I siphon the fuel from the forty-four-gallon drum, Amelia offers to take one of the twenty-liter jerry cans; I am not sure she knows how much twenty liters weighs but, pausing every five yards, she gamely manages to lug it to the boat.

No matter how many times it is explained or demonstrated, the boat is being loaded haphazardly, blankets on the bottom, where they will get wet, and the watertight bags of meal on top of them. I tell the workers to unload and do it properly, and without complaint they do it right.

Yusuf, Amelia, an elder and his croupy three-year-old daughter, and two armed guards board the boat. We are precariously overloaded; water slops in from over the sides. It will be a very slow trip. Another guard wades toward us through the knee-deep water, gun in one hand and a sprig of *miraa* in the other. Without a word he tries to scramble aboard.

"Hey, you—*Bes, bes!* Stop, stop! *MIA, MIA.*"

The young gunman has one leg over the side, and as he tries to hoist himself aboard, the boat nearly turns turtle. "Hey, dickhead! Get out!" I shove him with both hands and he falls back into the water. Out of the corner of my eye I see the little girl begin to roll off the supplies and I lunge for her, but too late. She falls overboard. Her shrill screams rend the air and join the frantic shouts of her father and the sputtering anger of the sodden gunman. The guard gets to his feet, stumbles through the water, and jams his rifle hard into my stomach. I have not heard him cock the gun and I think this registers. On the other hand, maybe it doesn't. Without thinking, I push the barrel away and jump into the water and grab the terrified child by the back of her thin T-shirt. The water is not deep, and if she had not panicked she could have stood up. The elder is shouting, the gunman is shouting, the little girl is screaming. I lift the frightened kicking child up by her armpits and turn toward the guard, who has his gun leveled at me, finger on the trigger. I realize with horror that I am inadvertently using this hysterical little girl as a shield. The gunman snarls something ugly in Somali. He is not insane; it is not in his eyes. He is just angry. It is not like that kid at the roadblock.

Turning my back to him, I pass the girl up to her father. Yusuf is bawling at the guard, who reluctantly lowers his gun, turns, and skulks back toward the camp.

"Yusuf." I try to mask the fear in my voice. "I don't bring this boat back to camp until that man is gone, off the base."

"It is nothing. It is over."

"Yusuf, I've heard that Somalis have long memories."

"All right, I will see to it."

"No, my friend. You see to it now. I will wait." His black eyes spark. "Sorry, Yusuf, that is the way it has to be." He nods and carefully climbs down from the boat into the water.

We finally motor through the fields toward Hargeisa. I am consumed by the incident. Scared. This is the sort of event that is the most frightening. An incident that turns personal; it is one thing to be caught between two angry guns, but to find oneself the target of some hothead's personal enmity is downright dangerous. I wonder if I will not have to start watching my ass, sit with my back against a wall.

"You have to watch the fucking currents, Amelia. Excuse my French. You also have to watch the hotheads. You never know what gets you a bullet in the back." I force a smile and manage a more cheerful tone: "Here the currents run in one direction, then—you see there? A few yards away, in the other."

"That's all right. I speak some French." Is she a step ahead of me, with me, or way behind? The boat slews in a sudden crosscurrent. "Yes, I see what you mean." Her eyes widen with fascination and thrill. "How ever do you find your way?"

"With difficulty. Took me days before I stopped asking directions. Now that the water is falling, it's even more difficult—every morning we have to find new routes, deeper channels. Loaded like this, you can't afford to have an accident."

Amelia cocks her head and regards me as if I was speaking a foreign language. "Didn't you understand?" I ask her.

"Quite. Why do you always do that?"

"Do what?"

"Why do you keep wiping your face with your hand? It's like you have something on your face, like you walked through some spiderwebs or something."

"I don't do that, do I?"

"Lots."

"I am getting neurotic," I mutter. I catch myself before doing it again. How could I not be conscious of it? What sort of strange neurosis have I developed? I do it again and she laughs.

I do not feel like being a clown in the village today, getting people to laugh, getting them to forget about their problems. I could have plenty of tongues stenciled to my boat. So what? It was probably the newness of it all that got me to act like such a fool. The villagers standing in the stinking mud are not looking very friendly either. Subdued, more somber than usual. The village boys unload the relief supplies in silence while Yusuf meets with the elders.

"John, Amelia—please come," Yusuf calls down. "The boat is safe."

We climb up the slippery hillside and into what is left of the village of mud-and-stick homes. There is a soft, mournful sound, a reserved and plangent keening from a small crowd gathered under the last mango tree.

"We must help," Yusuf says quietly.

Corpses of three children and four adults have been placed in a row under the shade of the huge tree. The bodies are frozen in the rictus of death, vacant jellied eyes, mouths locked open in the futile struggle for their last precious breaths. Every orifice visible appears stained and caked with blood, dried nearly black. Flies wander over the lifeless, bloating flesh, walk on the eyes, and dart in and out of the gaping mouths. The bodies have begun their initial stages of putrescence, and the cloying stench is gagging. I think I recognize one of the children but it is impossible to tell. Amelia is no longer with us; I suppose she is off somewhere vomiting.

"We must help," Yusuf repeats hoarsely.

"Jesus, how?" Staring at the dead, I have a strange sense of emotional remove. Is this the beginning of the disconnect? The surrounding villagers look at me with pitiable expressions, plaintive, appealing, as if John-John could bring these people back to life or rid them of this disease.

I expect Yusuf to ask me to move these corpses, to take them away in the boat, to touch them. "You call Nairobi on the radio from base and you tell them what you see. Maybe they help."

"I think this is something for the Red Cross. Don't they have a camp somewhere near here?"

"Ah, yes, that is a good idea."

"Do we just leave them here?"

"They will be taken care of. But they cannot be buried because of the flood. They will do what they have done before. They will cover them with mud and wait for the rains to stop."

On the way back, I ask Yusuf about Asha's strange gesture. "It looked as if she was blowing me a kiss."

Yusuf's smile is tolerant, almost reproachful. "It is from the Koran. It was to make you invisible to all who surround you. You are now protected."

The Russian-built Mi-8 sweeps over the camp ahead, turns toward us and hovers above, then flies back to base. It is waiting for us on the strip as we jump off the boat into the waist-deep water.

Andrew, hands on hips, blue baseball cap cocked on his head, stands grinning under the blades of the helicopter. We offer each other a quick awkward hug. The crew is no longer the rugger boys from South Africa but three beefy gold-toothed Ukrainians, smoking cigarettes nearby.

"I thought that was you down there," he says, pushing back his cap. "We were on our way to Sakow when I saw some *musungu* in a blue ski boat coming back to base. Not many people look as ugly as you do from an altitude of five hundred feet."

"I get prettier when you are on the ground. What brings you out here?"

"Inspection trip of the delivery sites—see what can land where."

He brings news: The Buffalo, the cargo plane that makes at least one stop a day at Marerey Base, crashed on landing at Jilib yesterday, a write-off. It is surprising that we don't lose more aircraft. They seem to spend most of the time in the air with quick turnarounds, brief stops to unload and fuel, then back to Garissa or Nairobi for another pickup. There is not much time for anything but a little midnight maintenance by an overworked Kenyan crew. The loss of the Buffalo cuts our access to supplies by almost half. It may not make much difference; Andrew reports that Unicef is soon going to declare the Somali Flood Emergency over. Just as well. The El Niño rains are moving south and flooding parts of Kenya, destroying camps on the Tana River that house a hundred thousand Somali and Bantu refugees. With the quickly falling water levels here, boat deliveries are becoming more restricted and less efficient. As well as more dangerous. David ran aground yesterday. Not unusual, but as his guards climbed back onto the boat, a ten-foot crocodile sped past with what David claims was a covetous gleam in his eye.

According to Alpha Kilo, the sixty thousand tons of food promised by the European Community may never be sent. The donors have heard too many horror stories: Subclans and factions within subclans have ended their suspension of internecine warfare and have renewed fighting in what is/was the disaster area; the clans are planning raids on distribution bases like ours; relief workers have been kidnapped in the north. I presume news that my cargo plane was shot at also has gotten out (I suppose it had to be reported to some aviation authorities somewhere).

"So how is life in the bush?"

"In a word—weird." I need to tell him about the gunman I pushed into the water—that is still very much on my mind. I need to tell him about the little Bantu boy in Marerey. I need to share; maybe it will sort out my confusion. However, what occurs out here is probably not much different from what other aid workers go through elsewhere. "Yeah, weird. Kismayo? Same-o, same-o?"

He was mugged in the control tower. He was talking-in the C-130 when a couple of *miraa*-crazed gunmen raced up the stairs, fired some shots through the tower windows, took his radios. Then they fired at the Hercules as it was landing. "Bloody glad to be away from that lunacy for a few days—this is like a holiday."

"And Jeri? Still that tightly packed little package that nobody can unwrap?"

"Still. You had something going with her that I didn't know about?"

"No, why? She say something?" I feel that awkward brush of a kiss on the cheek even now. "She is a hell of a woman. I wonder how she can put up with what she does day after day. Oh, thanks for the beer, by the way."

"Right. The French photographer, *he* didn't drink it all?"

"You could have prepared me."

"What would you have done? Scrub up?"

"Something like that. You don't have any bottled water on board, do you?"

"Beer?"

"Real water."

"I'm taking a case to Sakow. Could give you a couple bottles. You don't have water here?"

"A thousand square miles of it, give or take."

"I mean to drink."

"That's what I mean. We shit in it, piss in it, bathe in it, brush our teeth in it, and drink it." He looks shocked. "Oh, we have had the occasional bottled water, but for the most part, this is our water source. We have asked Nairobi for water, but it seems that out here we are pretty well forgotten. Actually, it was all right when the flood was high and fast-moving, but now it's mostly mud and hardly moving at all. We end up drinking a gritty slurry—picking rocks out of our teeth."

"I'll give you guys the case and tell them at Sakow I forgot."

"Terrific. That will keep cholera at bay for another few days. Oh, yeah, would you pass the word to Nairobi and Garissa that there is some kind of strange hemorrhagic fever going on here? People bleeding from the nose and mouth and dying real fast. Seems they get it one day, then they're dead a couple of days later."

"They already know. From that old man you sent us the other day. Who died, by the way. The fever is big news. In fact, I got a chopper-load of World Health Organization doctors, scientists—people like that going to Bardera. It's worse up there."

"I hope it's not contagious."

"You and me both."

"Last thing before I forget it—can you take a passenger to Garissa?"

"A live one or a dead one?"

"Very alive. Over there." Asha is watching us. I think she knows I am asking for her.

"Of course. Does she have Kenya papers?"

"Yes. Or she did. Yusuf says they were lost in the flood."

He frowns and shakes his head. "Then we can't. They all say that, and it worked in the beginning. But we aren't responsible for the refugees. They go to the camps and then UNHCR handles them. If it were up to me I'd take her, but it's the pilot's choice. Without papers, Kenyan immigration won't let her off the chopper." He shrugs. "Not much we can do. Sorry. Oh, the chopper will be returning later today with a delivery."

While I see the helicopter off, Robbie is concluding a conversation with Saskia on the HF radio:

"So there is no earthly reason to stay here, at least David and me. The American chap has a boat that can go almost wherever we can, and the girl's boat should arrive any time. It is quite ridiculous to keep all of us here. After all, our delivery count is quite dismal, as you probably know. The NGO is using us less and the water level is dropping precipitously. You should have trucks in here within a few days.

". . . Yes, yes, of course. There are places we can go—upriver, of course. Or we could follow the rains south. Haven't you got an operation in Kenya?

". . . Well, I would have thought that it is more expensive to keep us here idle than to fly us to where we are needed.

". . . Well, there is that too. It *is* a wretched disease, whatever it is.

". . . Good. Then we will leave it you. Cheers. Romeo Tango out."

* * *

THE Mi-8 returns, makes a sweep over the camp, then settles down on the strip. The Ukrainians lead us aft to the open tail ramp. Amelia's red river boat, an eighteen-foot Sea Canoe, gleams inside like a long-promised Christmas present. She runs to the lowered gate.

"Oh, John, it's here!" She dances. I haven't imagined her expressing much enthusiasm about anything; it is good to see her this way.

"Well, let's get it out and rigged up, kiddo."

"Oh, yes, let's do."

The porters drag the boat to water's edge, considerably further away than when I first arrived.

After preparation and loading, she mounts her red stallion like Jeanne d'Arc. The outboard engine is nearly as big as she is, and the moment of truth is nigh. She tries to tilt it forward to lift the prop out of the water, but she is just too small. Robbie and David, who have been helping outfit the boat, give her a few hints but she is near tears in frustration. She chews her lower lip with short, quick bites. "Leave it in," David says. "If you hit something, it will bounce out." He offers to accompany her on her first delivery and I will follow.

Amelia has to steer by tiller, by moving the outboard directly; there is no wheel as there is on mine. I would give her my boat, but it is just too powerful and too unstable for her. Moreover, that is her boat. This is what she signed up for. Hers is more of a regulation deliver-the-goods-and-turn-around motorboat.

Because of the lack of business, we take the opportunity to recce a location for a new camp south of Hargeisa. Marerey Base will return to a full-length airstrip in a few days, inaccessible to boats. The narrow dike above the irrigation canal, wide enough for a helicopter-landing site, would be ideal. However, it is in the heart of crocodile country; nearly every day one of us either sees a croc or the slithering tracks of one that scar the muddy slope.

The trip is not one for beginners. David, with his experienced eyes, seems to be able to spot a course by instinct and navigates for Amelia. The water runs more swiftly through the gullies and ditches and fields now that there is less of it. Amelia seems to be doing all right and she looks behind to me, smiles happily, and waves, something she must have done a thousand times on her family's ski boat.

"Amelia!" The current grabs her boat and slams it broadside into a thorn tree. Throttling back to avoid running into her, we watch helplessly as inch-long needles rip her clothes, her bare arms, and her face. David had ducked to avoid the razor-sharp spikes. The boat has run up onto a hummock, its bow firmly embedded in the mud under the tree.

Amelia sits on a bag of maize meal with her head in her hands, and I imagine she is finally crying. Blood runs through her fingers from facial cuts. She looks up at David and forces a grim little-girl face of determination. She jerks the starter cord angrily and snaps at him to help her shove off the island with an oar. On the trip back, she stands facing forward, as solid as Nelson at Trafalgar, the tiller clasped tightly in her hand.

At the campsite, she has regained her composure and, resolute, carries herself with newfound defiance. In the period of a few hours, she has seen death and she has been injured. She is a sliced and punctured mess, and for a time she does not remove the smears and rivulets of dried blood, whether for our benefit or for the Somalis who had yet to take her seriously. We notice but say nothing.

Back at our tarped-over meeting place, Robbie has begun dismantling his squirrel's nest. Carefully folding sheets, stacking his magazines—"I've read these, you want?"—removing canned food from makeshift shelves of the moment, and stashing them into his lockbox.

"What's this? Deserting a sinking ship?"

He laughs. "Marching orders. We are being sent to Bardera. Then, if the gods smile, back to Kenya, where we will continue our mission of mercy closer to home."

"When?"

"First light tomorrow. Saskia called on the HF while you three were doing battle with the local flora. David and I will take the boats upriver. An absolutely ghastly trip, I'm sure."

"What about us. Amelia and me?"

"Haven't heard. Carry on regardless, I imagine."

Watching him pack his gear is a bit sad. I feel lost, deceived. We were coming to know each other, had worked well as a unit, but more personally, I was beginning to feel comfortable, was beginning to let these guys in. It had been an investment in a relationship, and while the relationship was not particularly close, it had the cohesion of a family in which each of its members knows the needs, the preferences, and the oddities of the other, in which one knows best how to deal with the other. We had established some sort of routine, a big step in the maintenance of sanity. You go through hell together, help each other, discover the other, get to know the other in the most trying and intimate of circumstances, then, without warning, some faceless administrator declares the unit in which we have invested so much merely a memory. That is the nature of relief work, I suppose: You go where they send you, where you are needed. We did not come out here to make lifelong friends, and no one was running a summer camp. It is no big loss, of course, but the suddenness, the finality of the end takes some adjustment.

* * *

OVER the fire, Robbie breaks an awkward silence. "I say, David, have you told your menials we'll need extra jerry cans for our perilous upriver adventure?"

"Yes, Robbie."

"You know it is one of the perks of being a menial—not to have to plan for things. Just doing. Do you ever think we are on the wrong side, David?"

"Not often, Robbie."

Robbie turns to Amelia: "Sing us a song, Amelia!"

"A what?"

"A song, dear girl. A ribald sea chantey to make our American sailor blush."

"Robbie, I am waiting for my tea."

"David, you fix our nightingale a cup of tea, there's a good chap. Now, Amelia, there is no excuse, is there?"

Amelia whitens, trapped. She looks to David, then to me. "Robbieeee."

It is David who bellows out—off-key:

> "My father was the keeper of the Eddystone light,
> And he slept with a mermaid one fine night.
> From this union there came three,
> A porpoise, a porgy and the other was me.
> Yo ho ho, the wind blows free,
> Oh, for the life on the rolling sea."

"Oh, that is wonderful!" Amelia squeals.

"A bit lame, I'd say, David," says Robbie. "But entertainment for our last evening, nevertheless. Come on, Amelia, give it a go, then, shall we?"

"I don't know anything like that."

"Well, just something!"

"Oh, well, then:

> Wynken, Blynken, and Nod one night,
> Sailed off in a wooden shoe,
> Sailed on a river of crystal light,
> Into a sea of dew."

She raises her shy eyes for approval. "It was something I learned as a little girl."

"Well, Amelia. You have succeeded in surprising us. However, I thought you knew one to make us fairly shrivel with embarrassment."

"I'm sorry, Robbie."

"I say, we should all tell stories tonight. John, won't you tell us a sea story?"

"What? You some kind of camp counselor?"

"A what? Is that another Americanism?"

"Social director, Robbie. You know, someone who organizes shuffleboard on cruise ships."

"You have a point, my good fellow," he laughs. "I do seem to have that tendency, don't I? Must be going troppo."

It is hard to get upset with the man. I just don't think he really knows who he is. "But I do have a few sea stories."

"I imagine you have."

"Bores the hell out of land people, though."

"Yes, well, I am sure they might. By the way, why have you spent so many years at sea? Must be frightfully monotonous."

"Not often."

"But why the sea?"

"It is a refuge."

"Ah, yes, understood. Well, another time, then. So. A toast to our lovely and winsome little heroine of the Jubba. You earned your stripes today, dear girl."

Amelia blushes. "Oh! Well, I'd like tea instead," but she takes a glass of whiskey mixed with swamp water.

"To the Queen of the Jubba," I say.

"Well, if you really wanted to earn your stripes, you'd be three feet tall, with a flat head and toothless."

"Why, Robbie?"

We laugh. Surely she has heard that one. If she hasn't we won't give insult with an explanation.

"You know," she says. She pauses; her tone is serious—she wants to be heard. "I like working with you—you men." It sounds as if she is trying to imitate George C. Scott doing Patton. It is difficult to take her seriously. Yet the respect she has earned is unspoken.

23.
Death of an Angel

THE nearby sound of automatic gunfire nearly throws me out of my skin. Eyes pop open. Instantly awake. It is dangerously close. It is safer to stay put inside my tent—in this instance only inches above the ground—than go out to investigate who is shooting whom.

Minutes later I peer outside, expecting to see the militia storm the base. It is just dawn. One of the workers outlined by the rising sun returns through the mist down the runway, rifle in hand, proudly carrying a lifeless guinea fowl by its tail feathers. I am surprised there is anything remaining but a feather or two, filled as it probably is with a clipful of bullets.

Robbie and David putter away from the camp. I don't see them off. Their departure has increased the doubts about our value here. I suppose we can expect a call from Nairobi within the next few days, moving us to another location with a new mission, new people. It is the nature of relief work to zip in and out of people's lives, for them to flit through mine. It would not surprise me that I will never again see Robbie, David, Amelia, or Andrew. I could see Gabriele again, but will I? The ones we work with, those with whom we have shared so much—one doesn't get to know them intimately. It is not as if we had trained together as soldiers in preparation for combat and together were tossed out onto the front with a common purpose. It is not as if we expected to be lifelong friends.

We are now two boats, and one of them is driven with a learner's tag on the hull. Where Amelia goes, I suppose I should follow. I had always assumed responsibility for her but had known there were others here who could help. Now there is no one else and it is forced on me.

She approaches and, by her body language, I know there is a problem.

"You are coming?" she asks hopefully.

"No, Amelia."

"I'll get lost, I just know I will."

"Yusuf will show you how to get there. He'll help. Just keep your eyes on the road and you will do fine."

"Please come!"

"Got things to do. You need this solo flight, Amelia."

She frowns, pouts, and turns toward her boat. My heart aches for her. She acts the little girl who has been unfairly scolded, and I cannot help but feel a little accountable.

A Twin Otter lands at the strip, and now that I have no one to race, I wonder if I should go out there at all. I do. I have nothing else to occupy me except for some old magazines, and I don't want to attempt another effort at Dante's *Inferno*.

There is something amiss on the way to the plane, something different. That sentinel figure in the chador is gone. Perhaps she got a lift with Robbie and David—in any case, it is no longer my concern. The Twin Otter pulls up, shuts off one engine and keeps one spinning in idle. The side door opens, and a uniformed crewman in white shirt and black pants walks forward with some boxes to be delivered to the Red Cross camp.

There is a commotion by the nose of the plane; the copilot shouts angrily. A purple blur of color dashes toward the open door. More frantic shouts. We all start screaming. Motherfuck! *STOP!* It is too late. The blades of the right engine slice through fabric and skin and bones in an explosion of human debris. Asha's body lies in the dust. I stand in shock, unwilling to move, unable to help.

Day after day, it just goes on and on, one miserable event after another. As David said, God favors no one, not those who perish, not those who serve. The misery of the world will continue with or without our gallant efforts. Let others replace me; let others try to save the damn world.

Epilogue

THE Somalia Flood Emergency continued for another month. When the crisis ended, twenty-five hundred people had been killed by drowning, snakebite, crocodile attacks, malnutrition, and disease; nearly a half million people displaced; more than one hundred fifty thousand acres of crops and farmland destroyed, and thirty-five thousand livestock lost. Yet it never was much of a news item.

Like other multinational relief efforts, the humanitarian mission just petered out—no self-congratulatory plaudits, no hearty well-done, no acknowledgment by anybody, really, that tens of thousands of people were fed, thousands of lives saved. The rivers returned to their banks, the fields dried out, the dead were buried, the livestock that had survived were fed, bred, and marketed, the UN and the nongovernmental agencies packed their tents and went elsewhere to other humanitarian crises.

Warlords resumed their reign of terror over those who only wanted to live in peace, who yearned for some security and stability, education for their children, a job, and a life without persecution or crossfire. Peace conferences—punctuated by fistfights and the occasional murders of delegates—were held in Kenya, agreements were negotiated and signed and broken. An interim president was "elected" and he took office in some rooms in a hotel in downtown Mogadishu. If he was king of all he surveyed, then he was ruler of a couple of hotly contested city blocks. The Marehan clan did retake Kismayo, and General Morgan was driven out in a lengthy seesaw conflict. During that local war, I am told, Harun, my driver—a popular gunman of Morgan's subclan militia—was killed in one of the many battles for control of the port. Today Somalia is still not a real country. It may never be.

Those with whom I worked were assigned to other complex emergencies, and today they are in Darfur, Afghanistan, Angola, in any of the eighty-two countries where WFP is feeding the starving and the malnourished. Few of the players ever see each other unless posted to a humanitarian crisis near their homes. Those Kenyans who work out of Nairobi occasionally bump into each other in Sudan, but relief workers are an individual lot and they go their own way, meeting and working with new colleagues and then, in the instant of an HF radio transmission, ripped out of the fabric of a relationship and sent someplace else. A Band of Brothers we are not.

Some of my colleagues were more fortunate than Harun; another was not.

Andrew remained with the WFP and was sent to Sudan full-time, where he concluded it was more profitable (and perhaps even safer) to be a relief worker in the rebel-held areas of the south than try to start a party business in Nairobi.

Matt Wolff, an impatient man who had trouble controlling his reaction to the Mickey Mouse of bureaucracy, got the sack soon after the end of the Somali Flood Emergency for his tantrum with the finance officer. Matt's demise, I discovered later, occurred trying to get material to us on the rivers. I recall my own frustrations trying to outfit the boats without tools, engine oil, anchors, rope, or GPS. I had been angry that he sent us out there without proper gear. Russ Ulrey, the regional logistics officer, put things straight:

"Matt tried hard to get things for the river operations. He knew what you needed, but he ended up in a shoving contest and he got fired for it. He was no schmoozer; in that job you had to be very creative, very patient, and know all the rules backward and forward.

But he had a short fuse. The finance officer was a haughty, arrogant bureaucrat, and so this was a perfect match for a hothead.

"Matt even went out and bought things for the field out of his own pocket. He was on your side."

Shortly after Robbie left Marerey, he was laid out with malaria, which turned cerebral. He was lucky and he survived. David and he worked the Tana River, distributing emergency supplies to the locals in their own backyard. Robbie married his American girlfriend, and their safari camp, rebuilt after the floods, caters to adventurous tourists today.

Amelia went back to her home near the country club in suburban Nairobi, wiser, older—very much a woman of the world.

Chet Sloane retired to his villa on the Kenya coast overlooking the Indian Ocean.

Russ Ulrey, an expert at logistics, became the WFP's liaison with the Pentagon's Central Command (CENTCOM) during the invasion of Afghanistan in 2001 and again with CENTCOM in 2003 during the invasion of Iraq. As a result of his experience in Sudan and Somalia, he thought he knew how to assure the delivery of humanitarian supplies in Iraq: He urged the Coalition to first disarm the local population, if not for the future stability of Iraq, then in the short term for the security of relief workers and the work they were doing. His advice went unheeded. "And you can see what happened there," he said. The looting and destruction immediately following the end of the official war was said to have caused more damage to the Iraqi infrastructure than the war itself and set back nation-building efforts by two years. Soon after George W. Bush stood under the banner that declared "Mission Accomplished," Russ left Iraq in frustration and returned to the U.S., where he was in the process of remodeling his house on a lake in the Boston suburbs. He is on call.

Saskia von Meijenfeldt, our logistics officer, was murdered nineteen months after the flood crisis. Saskia was one of eight UN officials sent to the Muzye refugee camp in southern Burundi to determine the food and medicine needs of civilians forced from their villages by Hutu rebels. It had been an urgent, hastily arranged trip, apparently also without much concern or assessment of the dangers of the mission. When armed uniformed men stepped out of a nearby house, Saskia realized the gunmen were impostors and that rebels controlled the camp. The eight foreign nationals were lined against a wall and, one by one, robbed. One rebel stole Saskia's glasses, clowned around, and then returned them. The gunmen began to walk away when, according to survivors, one rebel, a child soldier, demanded aloud: "Why should they be allowed to live?" At point-blank range he shot Luis Manuel Zuniga, a fifty-three-year-old Chilean who ran Unicef's operations in Burundi. He then swung his gun toward Saskia and shot her. The six remaining relief workers survived by fleeing into the jungle.

Russ Ulrey had hired Saskia, taken her under his wing, given her a position of responsibility. "Aid workers are no longer sacred; used to be the locals would invite you into their homes, were thankful for your help. Today they think we are just rich aid workers making a bunch of money. They think that if they got money in their pockets, let's rob them. If they are helping others, then let's shoot the bastards. I cried when she was killed." So did we all.

There is no known specific reason for the murders. It was possible her killers were furious she was aiding the Hutus, or they thought the relief workers were spies, or they were murdered because of what they represented. Possibly the attacks were an attempt to make some form of political statement, or the rebels resented them simply because they had clean clothes.

Saskia's husband, Elias Habte Selassie, demanded to know why the Burundi mission had been arranged only the day before without an adequate security assessment. Why had there been so little consultation and planning? And why, in a subsequent investigation, did the UN not even visit the site?

Such killings have become more frequent in the thousands of dirty little regional, intrastate, and local conflicts; combatants drive people from their lands, force homeless into refugee camps, take advantage of natural disasters, and use food as a weapon of war. Saskia's murder brought the WFP 1999 death toll to a dozen and came less than a month after a doctor for Unicef was murdered in Somalia and a day after a UN relief worker was killed in Kosovo. The year I worked in Somalia, the WFP lost nine staffers. Such a high death count is incontrovertible evidence that security was not an issue that was taken very seriously in 1998.

Other than that brief beer bust at the casino in Nairobi at which we were warned about snakes and hippos, we had no idea what we were to face and had no idea what to do when we faced it, at least not in Kismayo. There had been little official guidance or policy from those at the top, and there was no training in security on a local level for those of us sent out into the field. The safety of many UN personnel had been handled on an ad hoc basis—survive as you go.

I came to realize how ill-prepared we really were in Somalia during a trip to Iraq in the summer of 2003. I had gone to Iraq specifically to find out what measures were being taken to protect humanitarian workers in a declared war zone. While relief workers daily go unarmed into combat areas—whether or not there are soldiers to protect them—I did learn that today they are at least somewhat better prepared and more security-conscious than we had been.

Before visiting the villages of southern Iraq with WFP food monitors, it was strongly recommended that in Basra I take a security briefing that finally had become standard for all UN relief workers stationed in hostile areas.

Basra, a desert town not unlike Kismayo, triggered an emotive recollection; I found myself back on the streets of Kismayo, surrounded by the sensation that combined taste, smell, gut feeling, raw fear. I felt I had been in this dusty desert town before. My senses were sharpened and I felt the tension, the building anger, the future that seemed without promise. Basra, like Kismayo—parched and windswept—seemed to be a town holding its breath; any moment a single hot temper could trigger an explosion. I saw it on a street corner one day where a large man lay sprawled out, still living, blood spreading on his white robes. He was mostly ignored by passersby and my driver shrugged, said it was only a *tasifya,* a vengeance killing that, since the occupation, occurred daily.

So Basra was an appropriate place to get what is called Just-in-Time training, a short but thorough high-tech presentation that bears no resemblance to the indifferent watch-out-for-the-hippos warnings over a few beers. Indeed, this multimedia show on CD, abbreviated for my purposes, fascinated and angered me. It took years of bloodshed, unnecessary deaths of humanitarian workers, to give staff security the attention it deserved.

My instructor was an attractive ex-narcotics cop with a ponytail from South Africa whose most recent assignment had been in the jungles of Southeast Asia with Interpol. "Relief workers work for peace, but we still are soft targets," Nicoline Landman said. A woman with hard blue eyes, Nicoline was pure police officer.

I had told her some of my experiences in Kismayo and those later in Marerey, and she simply said, "Well, at least you will be prepared for Iraq." As if reading my mind, she added, "This training is for both permanents and those on contract."

One of the most dangerous moments for us, the course emphasized, was the approach to a checkpoint, a roadblock. Today's policy requires every vehicle to radio the compound when arriving at a barrier and then again when passing through. "These are very easily bad situations. If you are ordered out, get out, do not argue, swear, or raise your voice. Remember, those guarding the checkpoint probably have been standing in the sun all day and any sign of resistance is inviting trouble." In Kismayo, we had no idea.

I wanted to know what advice they offered about child soldiers. Because so many relief workers are confronted by them, I expected that the WFP security briefing would include some warnings, some preparation to enable aid workers to survive meeting a kid with a gun. There wasn't a mention. Possibly it was just too complex, too variable, too demanding to consider.

"Every confrontation with a child soldier is different," Nicoline explained. "You have to treat it on an individual basis."

"But wouldn't you think they would discuss it here? That there would be at least some reference that child soldiers are out there and that the confrontation can get a relief worker killed?"

With an inscrutable dismissive smile, she went on to talk about kidnapping.

Relief workers are kidnapped or held hostage with increasing frequency each year. A relief worker kidnapped often means ransom money to buy more guns and bullets. When a hostage-taking goes wrong, the aid worker is injured, killed, or simply disappears.

"It is important to accept that a kidnapping is going to be brutal. You must realize that your captors are under a lot of stress," Nicoline said. "Most victims have never been handled roughly; many have never even been yelled at. They see violence only on television. How you react to any dangerous situation in the first fifteen to forty-five minutes determines whether or not you survive.

"When you are captured"—she said it so convincingly that it was an assumption that soon you would be—"take a deep breath, control your fears, be cooperative, emphasize that as a UN employee you are not involved in politics. Do not try to be a hero, do not resist, don't study your captors' features, dress, and mannerisms, don't beg, don't plead, and don't cry. Oh, and try to maintain your sense of humor.

"Very important," Nicoline continued, "is preparing for your reaction to a violent or potentially violent event. Occupational stress is an issue which can no longer be ignored. Often we are asked to confront situations without the appropriate skills to cope with them. Disaster-relief and humanitarian-aid workers are in the same occupational groups as firefighters, emergency medical personnel, police officers, and search-and-rescue personnel. These are the people who are exposed to psychologically traumatic events.

"But stress is also just being in a strange place, without friends, with terrible food, lack of sleep, lack of routine, and living some things that they have only seen on television."

Before my brief discussion with Mike Dunne on the pier, stress management was not an issue I had ever considered before. I had always thought of stress as an affliction of high-powered businesspeople with consequent rashes, ulcers, and strokes. The discussion about stress illustrated that unless we are made of stone, we are all affected by it one way or the other, even when physically removed from the event. (It was a surprise to me to read that as a result of the terrorist attacks on the U.S. in 2001, ninety percent of the American public was reported to have felt symptoms of stress and forty percent were severely impaired, suffering from clinical anxiety, depression, or other mental illnesses.)

While much of the advice in the briefing was common sense, it was necessary to be reminded. I had recently spent time with seafarers who were victims of modern-day high-seas pirates. While many had been taken hostage by pirates and hijackers and had survived, some were not so lucky. Their bodies were found washed up on some lonely beaches. As a former merchant seaman, I know that some would have lived had they the benefit of the UN briefing—presuming ship owners bothered with that sort of thing.

* * *

A security briefing covering such contingencies as child soldiers, roadblocks, kidnapping, and stress before going to Somalia might not have given me much more confidence than my own God-given sense of survival. However, it would have provided some added strength, a knowledge that someone outside the small cadre of internationals and a cautious security officer in Kismayo did give a damn for our safety.

I confronted Russ Ulrey, the man who created the WFP Somali operation, about the cursory bonk-the-crocs security briefing at the casino and about the lack of security for the river operations generally.

"That [casino briefing] was certainly less than was needed," he said. "The fact that you did not receive a security briefing is news to me as we speak. There was a security officer who was supposed to give you guys a briefing. It was probably a case that he was to give it to Wolff and Wolff was to give it to you. It was only about crocs and hippos, you say? Well, Kismayo was a total Unicef operation. Matt got the [security] information from Unicef. They would have said everything was fine in Kismayo. Matt didn't come and ask me.

"We could have done better by you when you went into Somalia. And I apologize for that. But at the same time, no matter how much we did, it would not have been enough. It could be a four-year university course and it would not have been enough. You could go to the field and something would come up that you would not be prepared for. There is no way that you can have enough training to go to the field and be an aid worker."

The lessons in today's WFP security training are those that, God forbid, a relief worker should not learn firsthand. They are lessons that no doubt were learned the hard way—I could add a few that were not covered. Once learned, however, you pass them on to someone else. Or write the manual and hope that such experiences will save the lives of others. The idea of this Just-in-Time training occurred long after the Somalia operation had closed down. To some back at UN headquarters in New York at that time, security evidently was not so important.

* * *

IMMEDIATELY upon my release from Somalia, I disappeared into Mike Dunne's vacant flat in Nairobi for three weeks, and stocked with food and drink, I locked the doors, drew the blinds, and remained inside. I had been in a fragile, confused state, and I knew I had to put the two previous months into some perspective for my own sanity and for the health of my relationship with Jacqueline. Sometimes we are our own best therapists. I reverted to what I knew best and found my salvation behind the armor of journalism. I felt that if I could put into some sort of order the notebooks, the scraps of conversations, the documents I had collected, I could remove myself from the events. I thought I had succeeded. It was an absurd assumption, of course. Had I looked at the events as they were occurring as a journalist, I might have been spared the personal effects of the experiences. In the beginning, I had no intention of writing about Somalia, reporting the shooting of a woman and schoolboy or relating any of my own experiences, and I certainly did not set out to investigate or criticize the UN's policies on security for its staff.

While writing this did serve as therapeutic balm that partially healed the wounds of Somalia, it could not affect the change in attitude and outlook that resulted from such experiences. There are a few short-term, a few long-term effects, both salutary and deleterious. In any case, I cannot recall the person I was before Somalia. It is for damn sure that I sometimes do not recognize the person I have become.

Afterword

The Broken Gate

RELIEF operations in Somalia in 1997–1998 took priority over the security of those hired to carry out those operations. To my surprise, I discovered that this policy had not changed five years later. The bombing of the UN compound and loss of life in Baghdad on August 19, 2003, was the direct result of this negligent attitude.

Field workers today are briefed and trained to protect themselves and survive the unexpected. This is an improvement. However, it means little if at the top the policy on security of staff is guided by geopolitical pressures, outside interests, and a woeful lack of proper assessment of the conditions on the ground. In the summer of 2003, there were few in the United Nations and in the Coalition of the Willing who did not know that the UN compound and its staff were targets. Indeed, despite warnings of suicide attacks, security at the compound was considered by those who worked there to be a joke and, in one case, an invitation to catastrophe.

Backed by U.S.-led Coalition forces and secure with the shield of neutrality of the United Nations, one could be forgiven for feeling that Iraq was not much more dangerous than any other assignment. However, in spite of the presence of the military, these relief workers were as unprotected, as alone, and as isolated as we were in Somalia. After the Just-in-Time training in Basra, I had felt safer, not because of what I learned but because I was told that it was now official UN policy that the safety of its personnel was paramount, and in some cases even more important than the operation itself. However, that policy became subverted to Coalition interests; despite the repeated warnings, threats, and intelligence that an attack was likely, the UN, under pressure from its main donor, continued to place its staff unnecessarily at risk.

Baghdad was a war zone, yet the city was classified as Phase Four, which enabled the UN security boss in New York to permit international staff "directly concerned with emergency or humanitarian operations or security matters" to remain. A pretty wide brush, since most of the internationals serving in Iraq were directly concerned with humanitarian operations. The next category, Phase Five, on the other hand, required all internationals to leave and had to be approved by the secretary-general.

(Somalia was also, curiously, classified as Phase Four. Had it been Phase Five, they would not have created the flood-relief program. Kismayo was incontrovertibly Phase Five, and it was finally evacuated two months later during the buildup of militia forces prior to the final battle for the city.)

Had the UN secretary-general declared Baghdad as Phase Five, the international staff would have been evacuated out of country and operations would have been maintained by local employees of the UN. However, to evacuate would have been an admission that Iraq was more dangerous after the liberation by Coalition forces than before—a further embarrassment in light of the failure of Washington and London to find weapons of mass destruction or bona fide al Qaeda connections to the Saddam regime. Such lumpen acquiescence was so set in stone that UN Secretary-General Kofi Annan refused to close down UN operations even after the bombing and the death of many of his staff. It was not until after a second bombing and further loss of life that he decided finally that it was too dangerous for internationals to remain in Iraq, no matter what the Coalition claimed in the daily Pentagon briefings.

* * *

IT was not difficult to imagine history repeating itself: Baghdad reminded many of the conditions in Mogadishu in 1993 when the bodies of American soldiers were dragged through the streets by young militia and frenzied locals. (Indeed, in March 2004, four civilian American contractors were killed in Fallujah near Baghdad, their charred and mutilated bodies dragged through the streets and strung up on a bridge.) So concerned was Mick Lorentzen, chief of security at WFP headquarters in Rome, that immediately upon his return from Iraq, he fired off an e-mail to UN security officers worldwide that warned Iraq "is deteriorating and has all the hallmarks of another Somalia." The urgency of the warning was prescient. The same explosive ingredients found in Somalia were creating a cocktail for anarchy in Iraq. Pockets of lawlessness were spreading across the country; foreigners filtered across the Iranian and Syrian borders intent on bagging an American or British soldier; unchecked looting was widespread, and trucks delivering humanitarian supplies were routinely looted and hijacked. Jobs were scarce; electricity, water, and sewage disposal were less available than during the war itself.

Many Iraqis who earlier had welcomed the Coalition forces were beginning to admit—at first reluctantly, then louder in demonstration—that they were better off under the repressive regime of Saddam Hussein than they were in the hands of the bungling and ineffective Coalition Provisional Authority, the interim administration created by Washington. One young father in Basra had told me it was better to fear the knock on the door in the middle of the night from a Baathist henchman than a future of no electricity, no water, no jobs, and, above all, no security from gangs of looters that swept through the darkened neighborhoods. This reminded me of Yusuf's claim that a dictator was better than anarchy. Iraq, once a modern secular country, looked like it would join Somalia back in the Stone Age.

* * *

THE WFP headquarters in Baghdad were located in the UN compound, the former Canal Hotel; during Saddam's reign, this sprawling complex had housed UN weapons inspectors and the WFP offices that administered the Oil-for-Food Program. As invading American forces gathered on the outskirts of the city, looters gutted the place. After remodeling and repainting the building in UN colors, the WFP, WHO, Unicef, mine-clearance teams, and other agencies returned.

When I first arrived, the UN compound was not a Kismayo fortress, but it would not be long before it was to become one—at least to all outside appearances. The entire property was ringed with a wall of shipping containers, which we were told was protection of a sort against car bombs. Following increasing guerrilla attacks against the Coalition forces, a cement-block wall, topped by rolled concertina wire, was hastily erected on the highway side.

The relief workers slept in large air-conditioned refugee tents laid out in rows in the hotel parking lot, a tent city created by the Swedish Rescue Service Agency with Ikea efficiency and precision. You checked in with the Swedes like at any hotel and were handed a plan of the area. Showers, portable toilets, and a tent with weights and a cycling machine had been set up in the back near a barbecue grill. A makeshift men's room, with urinal crafted from an inverted water jug (a target large enough for several beery long shots), opened out onto the field that led to Sadr City, a center of anti-Coalition opposition. Between a hostile Iraq and us was a thin chain-link fence. One morning at daybreak, I went to relieve myself, and rubbing sleep out of my eyes, I looked up at an Iraqi youth with a Kalashnikov passing by. He was as startled as I was and we stood facing each other, a weapon in his hand, a weapon in mine. He looked down, grinned, then walked on. It was not lost on us that despite the impressive fortifications at the front, anyone with a mind to take down a few UN staffers, or to check out the size of non-Arab penises, could casually walk across the field and pop us off one by one through the wire fence. Or slip an RPG through the fence and lay waste to our tent city. (Indeed, so lax was security that an NGO staffer entered the UN compound by merely showing the guards her New York driver's license.)

Under the stars of a gritty Baghdad night, humanitarian workers gathered around the barbecue grill and a cooler of beer at the far end of the tents. Most never left the compound; no staff was allowed outside the gates on foot. A few beers and some hamburgers on the grill after their ten-hour day was all the recreation they could expect in this war.

It had been a depressing twenty-four hours. I had just returned from a briefing of security officers—all ex-combat veterans—assigned to various UN agencies and NGOs. Each reported information they had about the security situation nationwide and in Baghdad. It was a gruesome picture, which as the days passed only got worse: There were an average of ten attacks a day against Coalition forces in the city; a convoy of six vehicles of a British news crew was attacked that morning by a gang driving pickup trucks and a silver Mercedes; a Red Cross helicopter was fired at near Hella. More macabre was the latest intel that the Fedayeen were capturing cats and dogs, disemboweling them, and stuffing them with explosive devices. The animals, placed along the street as roadkill, were detonated remotely when convoys passed. There was some talk that resistance forces soon would increase their attacks on the softest targets: humanitarian agencies and their staffs. It was one thing to be well-armed soldiers on an ill-defined mission, cleaning up the chaos that they themselves had created by invasion and occupation. It was quite another to be an unarmed relief worker caught in the crossfire.

The previous night, over the whir of air conditioners, the tent city had been rocked by the sound of an explosion. An American convoy was being ambushed at the underpass down the road; one soldier was killed and three wounded. We could sleep around the shooting, the helicopter gunships chasing the attackers back into Sadr City, but it didn't improve our disposition to awaken to a blue-black sky that morning; sandstorms had been predicted, but there was something else in the air. A mysterious black pall covered us like a shroud; there was a taste of sulfur in the air. During the night, two hundred fifty kilometers to the northwest, saboteurs had blown up the crude-oil pipeline from northern Iraq to Baghdad's Doura Refinery.

I found myself wondering once again, as I had done so often in Kismayo, what it would take to shut down the UN humanitarian operations. How dangerous does it have to get before relief workers are told that it is too dangerous and they should prepare to withdraw? The decision to terminate any humanitarian mission before its time, while refugees are being relocated, the starving fed, the injured and sick healed, is not one that is reached without careful consideration. In many remote and lonely outposts—Somalia, Burundi, Afghanistan—wherever aid workers are stationed, the decision to evacuate must be made at a moment's notice, on the spot, when and where the bullets fly, not eventually through the chain of command that lands at a desk thousands of miles away. In 1998, a year of unprecedented killing of World Food Program field staff, someone somewhere finally realized that there was not much guidance in the manuals about when and how to evacuate. Security for the WFP had come a long way. There was, after all, the Just-in-Time training.

At our tent-city barbecue, a laptop connected to external speakers fed us sounds of ancient Madonna, and a French couple danced nearby. None at the beer cooler was a stranger to combat areas. Most had served in places like Kosovo, Afghanistan, Liberia, Angola, and Sudan. From nations as unconnected as Ecuador, Greece, Ghana, Croatia, Mozambique, the Netherlands, the U.S., and the UK, the lingua franca was English, but inevitably the French spoke mostly to the French, the Swedes to the Swedes and the Americans, the British and the Australians to anybody with a beer in his hand. Elizabeth once worked for a New York literary agency, Jane from Melbourne had been a schoolteacher, Pierre, a Belgian, was a Unicef security officer recently returned from Afghanistan, Anders, from the Swedish Coast Guard, had just come in from Sierra Leone, Jim, a former U.S. Navy SEAL, had been in charge of security for Unicef in Sudan.

This evening the laughter came a little too easily and we made jokes about things that were not so funny. It reminded me of that night in Nairobi. Then we laughed from fear, from the unknown. In Baghdad, it could be said, we laughed more just to be heard over the rattle of the gunfire. But there was a baleful desperation to that laughter as well.

The talk was of shutting down the UN operations in Baghdad and getting the hell out before the Saddam Fedayeen, foreign terrorists, or simply an angry mob of locals laid siege to the compound or blocked the roads leading out of the city. Barring a catastrophic event, however, abandoning the fort would come only in stages. Noncritical and clerical staff would be the first to leave, then those involved in organizing distribution of relief supplies, and then, finally, those needed to close down and lock up.

The lamps under a large umbrella and table provided the only light. At the beer cooler and over the grill, we were little more than shadows.

There was a short burst of gunfire.

"That keeps the juices flowing," I said, watching a lone figure, towel around his waist, drift past us toward the showers.

"The adrenaline never stops in this place." The speaker was Jane, a pert thirty-something Australian. Her job was in programming, but that was a misnomer, for she, together with the security officers, was the first in and last out of a country, setting up the operations in complex emergencies. She had been to all of them. "I do the paperwork, I sit behind a desk, most of the time," she said modestly. Her last assignment was in North Korea.

"Do you get out to the field?"

"Quite a bit, actually. But this posting is a cushy city job. Oh. That's closer," she said to the sound of new gunfire.

"Would you rather be back in Melbourne?"

She threw her head back. "Are you kidding? There is no rush in Melbourne."

"Rush? You're here for the adrenaline rush?"

"That has something to do with it. Why are you here?"

"You could be a housewife," came a deep voice from behind.

She turned and playfully kicked the voice in the leg.

Charles Forbes, chief of WFP security for Iraq, an ex–Royal Marine, emerged from the shadows. "Not much different from anywhere else. You were in Somalia?"

"During the floods in '97 and '98."

"I heard that was where people were being eaten by crocodiles and bitten by poisonous snakes," Jane said.

"Interesting times. In Kismayo, we spent much of the time trying to figure out how best to evacuate."

"We call it relocating these days," Charles said. "Going to another place in-country. 'Evacuation' means leaving the country. Things have moved on in the last few years."

"Change in policy?"

"Probably not. Maybe just definition. No, check that. Security is taken very seriously today. We know we are all easy targets and you don't mess around with staff safety. The head of the office can now make the decision, or the security officer can if there is one. Doesn't take that much. Rioting, demonstrations that might get out of hand, attacks on the office—you don't need the permission of the country director anymore or someone in New York. At least this is how it is on the books. They are already relocating the office in al Amara where One Para was attacked today—being sent to Basra."

I thought about Kismayo: Had not the shooting of a woman and a child, the shooting of cargo planes, and the ambush of relief boats warranted evacuation—or at least relocation?

"What about Baghdad? There still is a war going on outside."

"But your President announced that the war was over," Jane said.

"That was for domestic consumption only."

"Evacuation won't happen here," Charles said, a veteran of humanitarian postings in Afghanistan and Kosovo. "Evacuation is a political statement."

Jim, security officer with Unicef, a tall square-shouldered ex-SEAL from South Carolina, rubbed down a thick mustache and merely snorted: "Politics."

There was a muttered agreement. Politics and the aid trade go hand in hand. The major donors make the policy, not the Security Council. This is the way it has always been. In Iraq, the United States contributed $395 million to the controversial Oil-for-Food Program, more than the total of all other donor nations. This helped feed twenty-seven million people, just about the entire population of Iraq. Thus it was never questioned that the U.S. would have solid control of the agency that distributed its generosity. While the subject of evacuation was one that we could discuss, it was never going to be an issue as long as the Coalition forces were in town.

"What will it take?" I asked. "Soldiers are getting killed every day. One of us gets killed? That do it?"

"I don't think so. It will take a lot more than that," Charles had said with prophetic clarity. "Too much at stake here."

Evacuation is generally based on risk. This night, Baghdad was not dangerous enough to consider evacuating. Nevertheless, we all knew that was rubbish. There was no question in our minds that with the war still being fought just outside the compound walls, we could soon be a target.

As Charles spoke, a sudden storm of gunfire, heavier than the usual Kalashnikovs, indicated that the Americans had brought in more firepower. That meant we could soon expect to be blessed with silence.

"What about the front gate, Charles?" asked a voice out of the dark.

"I might as well do it now," Charles said.

The heavy steel door that opened onto the street had finally fallen off its hinges and the entrance to the compound had become an open thoroughfare. This was the security of the day at the compound.

"Maybe we should just keep it open. If we have to escape," Jane said, "we won't have to wrestle with it. Much faster that way."

"Or someone with a car bomb could drive right in," another said.

Charles returned a few minutes later with fresh beers and announced that he had parked a UN vehicle across the entrance.

* * *

FIVE weeks after this evening, a suicide bomber drove a truck laden with a ton of explosives alongside the outer north wall of the UN compound and blew up the headquarters. Twenty-two humanitarian workers were killed, more than a hundred others injured. Among the dead was career diplomat Sergio Vieira de Mello, the UN special representative in Iraq. His last words to a rescuer uttered from under the wreckage of the building were:

"Don't let them pull the mission out."

The dead were listed as:

Rick Hooper, 40, U.S.
Jean-Selim Kanaan, 33, Egypt
Chris Klein-Beekman, 32, Canada
Fiona Watson, 35, Britain
Naval Captain Manuel Martin Oar, Spain
Arthur Helton, 54, U.S.
Gillian Clark, 47, Canada
Alya Sousa, Iraq
Renam Al-Farra, Jordan
Saad Hermiz Abona, Iraq
Martha Teas, United States
Leen Asaad Al-Qadhi, Iraq
Ranillo Buenaventura, Philippines
Alyawi Bassem, Iraq
Reza Hosseini, Iran
Ihsan Taha Husein, Iraq
Sergio Vieira de Mello, 55, Brazil
Raid Shaker Al-Mahdawi, Iraq
Emaad Ahmed Salman, Iraq
Omar Kahtan Al-Orfali, Iraq
Khidir Saleem Sahir, Iraq
Nadia Younes, Egypt

They died serving humanity.

Author's note:

Two investigations into the Baghdad bombing sought to determine how the United Nations compound could be so vulnerable, especially in light of the warnings. An outside commission reported that humanitarian and political pressures caused staff security to be "compromised without an appropriate assessment as to the possible consequences." Further, it added that despite the war that raged outside the compound, there was a quixotic belief that "the UN was protected by its neutrality and its humanitarian mandate and that the staff and its installations would not be directly targeted."

An in-house panel was far more critical, and its conclusions showed that not a hell of a lot had changed since Somalia 1998. The panel, headed by Martti Ahtisaari, former Finnish president, concluded that the UN security system was "dysfunctional" and "sloppy," and that the UN flouted security guidelines, ignored warnings, and provided "little guarantee of security to UN staff" in high-risk areas.

It surprised none who served in the field that the investigation also found that UN management had not adequately prepared its employees—"who felt 'extremely vulnerable'—for deployment in combat areas."

J. S. Burnett

Notes

Chapter 1

P. 17 **One witness told of an old man . . .** Yusuf Hersi, NGO coordinator, Marerey Base.

P. 19 **"Unusually heavy . . . rains . . ."** *FEWS Watch,* November 3, 1997. Famine Early Warning System Network is a USAID-funded activity that collaborates with international, national, and regional organizations and governments to provide early warning and vulnerability information on emerging or evolving food-security issues.

P. 20 **Then suddenly there . . .** The official definition of a complex emergency, the term that defines the amount of security required, is "a humanitarian crisis in a country, region or society where there is total or considerable breakdown of authority resulting from internal or external conflict and which requires an international response that goes beyond the mandate or capacity of any single agency and/or the ongoing United Nations country program." Such complex emergencies are typically characterized by "extensive violence and loss of life; massive displacements of people; widespread damage to societies and economies; the need for large-scale, multi-faceted humanitarian assistance; . . . hindrance or prevention of humanitarian assistance by political and military constraints; significant security risks for humanitarian relief workers." *Orientation Handbook on Complex Emergencies,* Office for the Coordination of Humanitarian Affairs, United Nations.

P. 25 **Problem: How was he . . .** *Shifta* is a name for wandering tribesmen without property. *The Tree Where Man Was Born,* Peter Matthiessen, Dutton, New York, 1972.

P. 28 **Security measures were . . .** The UN's security phases describe those security measures to be implemented based on the current conditions in a country or part of the country:

- Phase One, <u>Precautionary</u>, is designed to warn staff members that the security situation in the country or a portion of the country is such that caution should be exercised.
- Phase Two, <u>Restricted Movement</u>, imposes restrictions on the movement of all staff members, and staff members have to remain in the quarters.
- Phase Three, <u>Relocation</u>, indicates a substantial deterioration in the security situation. In this phase, internationally recruited staff may have to be sent elsewhere either within the country or to another.
- Phase Four, <u>Program Suspension</u>, enables the designated official, the resident coordinator appointed by the secretary-general with the responsibility for the security and protection of all staff members at the duty station, to relocate outside the country all remaining international staff except those "directly concerned with emergency or humanitarian operations or security matters."
- Phase Five, <u>Evacuation</u>, can only be declared following approval by the secretary-general. All remaining internationals are required to leave.

Chapter 3

P. 48 **The contract . . .** The contract with the WFP is a standard Special Service Agreement with the UN Development Program.

P. 48 **The U.S. had not paid . . .** The more than one billion dollars that Washington owed the United Nations in back dues had become hostage to anti-abortion forces in the House of Representatives, which had attached an amendment to a bill containing funding for both the UN and the International Monetary Fund.

Chapter 4

P. 57 **The mobile gun . . .** These guns on wheels, used during the wars in Afghanistan and Iraq, got their name during the UNOSOM days in Somalia when relief workers had to call on clan leaders for protection from other clans. These armed gunmobiles of the militia were often provided as security for the relief workers and payment to them was filed under "technical assistance."

P. 58 **According to a UN report,** ***miraa*** **. . .** *Report of Panel of Experts,* UN Security Council, March 25, 2003, Stefan Tafrov, Chairman. Doc. S/2003.223.

P. 60 **It is apparent . . .** The *qat* leaf, looking a little like basil, is a natural stimulant from a flowering evergreen plant grown in East Africa and southern Arabia. On our way down from Europe, the harbormaster in Aden offered Jackie and me a chew; we found it bitter and only mildly stimulating. In Yemen and elsewhere, it has been used for religious and social purposes, even preferred to coffee. Some reports indicate that eighty percent of the population in Yemen chews *qat*. From what I saw, nearly all males in Kismayo chewed it. Because it contains cathinone and cathine, the U.S. government put it in the same category as LSD and Ecstasy and classified it as a controlled substance in 1988. *Qat* is legal in most places in Europe including the UK, which in 2000 imported about ten tons per month. *Qat* has long been a replacement for alcohol; during Ramadan, it is used to alleviate hunger. *Report of Drug Enforcement Agency Intelligence Division,* April 1, 2002, Washington, D.C.; *Psychological Medicine V19*, Christos Pantelis, Charles G. Hindler, John C. Taylor, Cambridge University Press, 1989.

Chapter 5

P. 73 **"Blood money . . ."** In many parts of Somalia, women are considered no better than slaves. There are even some who believe that women have no souls. It is not unusual for a Somali girl to be beaten upon marriage by her new husband to ensure "proper respect" in the future. Infibulation (sewing of the vulva—an extreme form of female circumcision) is still practiced.

Chapter 6

P. 87 ***"Subah wanaqsan . . ."*** I have spelled Somali words phonetically as they are spoken. *Subah wanaqsan,* good morning, is actually spelled *subax wanaaqsan*. Somalis have had a written language only since 1972.

Chapter 7

P. 103 **The BBC Somali Service . . .** *Focus on Africa,* BBC World Service, by Somali journalist Ali Musa Yusuf, 1998.

P. 110 **Mohamed Sahnoun . . .** *Somalia: The Missed Opportunities*, Mohamed Sahnoun, United States Institute of Peace Press, Washington, D.C., 1994.

Chapter 8

P. 120 **It is written . . .** In Africa, 3,000 people, mostly children, die from malaria every day, and each year between 300 and 500 million get the disease and a million die. The infant mortality rate in Somalia is one of the highest in the world. An average of 120 out of 1,000 children die before they reach their fifth year. *Report on Malaria,* World Health Organization and UN Children's Fund.

P. 125 **The air-fleet . . .** *Humanitarian Update,* UN Coordination Unit, December 12, 1997.

P. 127 **Last thing. There is no . . .** Author's message, hand-delivered and repeated by telex, written December 1, 1997.

Chapter 9

P. 139 **There are three hundred thousand . . .** Human Rights Watch.

P. 140 **"My boys, they are afraid . . ."** *Innocence Lost: The Child Soldiers of Sierra Leone Tell Their Story,* Radio Netherlands, January 21, 2000, producer and writer Eric Beauchemin.

P. 140 **There is not much . . .** *Daily Telegraph,* London, March 29, 2002.

P. 141 **The United States, which has . . .** In other cases, notably the Mine Ban Treaty, the international Covenant of Civil and Political Rights, and other human-rights treaties, the U.S. has either refused to ratify or has entered reservations to exempt the U.S. from any requirements that exceed U.S. law.

The UK was one of the last countries in Europe to sign the protocol, and it did so with strong reservations, using language strikingly similar to that of the United States:

> "The United Kingdom of Great Britain and Northern Ireland will take all feasible measures to ensure that members of its armed forces who have not attained the age of 18 years do not take a direct part in hostilities. The United Kingdom understands that article 1 of the Optional Protocol would not exclude the deployment of members of its armed forces under the age of 18 to take a direct part in hostilities where:
> a) there is a genuine military need to deploy their unit or ship to an area in which hostilities are taking place; and

b) by reason of the nature and urgency of the situation:

i) it is not practicable to withdraw such persons before deployment; or

ii) to do so would undermine the operational effectiveness of their ship or unit, and thereby put at risk the successful completion of the military mission and/or the safety of other personnel." *World Report 2000,* Human Rights Watch.

Chapter 10

P. 145 **A coastal tanker . . .** Ships are often hijacked by modern-day pirates for the cargo they carry. After the cargo has been off-loaded and sold, the vessel is turned into what is known in the maritime industry as a Phantom Ship, with a new name, new country of registration, new flag, new crew, and new paint job. The ship is then used in cargo scams, running drugs, arms, or illegal immigrants. In 2003, an average of two ships a month were hijacked somewhere on the world's oceans; often their million-dollar cargoes and their crews simply vanished. Hijacking, piracy, and maritime fraud cost world commerce $35 billion a year. *Dangerous Waters, Modern Piracy and Terror on the High Seas,* J. Burnett, Dutton, New York, 2002.

P. 147 **The second dhow . . .** Shortly after the Somali flood-relief mission, terrorists blew up the U.S. embassies in Nairobi and Dar es Salaam, Tanzania. The material used in the bombing was transported to Mombasa, Kenya, aboard a container ship and aboard a dhow, which had made landfall in Kilifi, Kenya, just up the coast. Some intelligence sources also are convinced that much of the material used in the attacks was off-loaded from ships in Mogadishu and Kismayo and was carried overland through the porous, poorly defined Somalia–Kenya border. *Op. cit.*

On November 28, 2002, terrorists bombed the Paradise Hotel in Mombasa, killing fifteen. That same day, terrorists fired surface-to-air missiles at an Israeli airliner taking off from Mombasa airport. A UN report released on November 4, 2003, provided evidence that an al Qaeda cell, responsible for the bombing and the missile attack, used Somalia as a base for training, supplies, and cover. Weapons smugglers, the report said, were able to violate the arms embargo using Arab dhows to ply the ancient trade route across the Gulf of Aden from Yemen with hundreds of tons of weaponry in "microshipments." *Financial Times,* London, November 4, 2003.

P. 150 **"Maybe you should see . . ."** The WFP did finally initiate Re-Entry

Syndrome training for their personnel. By the end of 2000, 5,522 staff members received trauma debriefing within seventy-two hours of an incident. When I worked for the WFP, no such debriefing was available.

Victims of RES are the sufferers as well as their families. Not only humanitarian workers are affected, but also soldiers returning to civilian life and prisoners released from jail. Sixty percent of returning British aid workers were reported to suffer from some form of RES.

Symptoms of RES:

- Initial euphoria, followed by a feeling of loss and isolation;
- Frustration that you just can't communicate the magnitude of the experience you have undergone—or the sense of loss you now have;
- Strong bonds are developed between people working in stressful environments, and upon arriving at home, guilt for leaving your colleagues in the field;
- Being home without purpose conflicts with the overseas aid work, which was totally engaging and urgent and the adrenaline rush addictive.

One soldier returning from Iraq said he had become less tolerant of stupid people, and another who returned discovered he couldn't stand crowds. A staff sergeant from Georgia said she found she had no patience with anybody.

One way to cope with RES is to find a form of words to describe the experience to help work it out emotionally. Not knowing this, I nevertheless felt compelled to put these experiences on paper; I locked myself in Mike Dunne's Nairobi flat for a month, exiting for air and supplies only twice, and compiled these notes, converting them into the first effort of a narrative.

Chapter 11

P. 154 **"Haven't a clue."** A Russian Anotov cargo jet chartered by the World Food Program was discovered to have carried money and arms to troops of one of the warring factions north of Mogadishu. Mohamed Sahnoun, UN special representative to Somalia at the time, later wrote: "The Russian plane's delivery rekindled the old perception of many Somalis that the UN and some countries were biased." A second Russian flight, also carrying suspicious cargo, crashed north of Mogadishu a few weeks later. "Although the UN's name and reputation were at stake, no serious investigation was undertaken," said Sahnoun. *Somalia: The Missed Opportunities,* Mohamed Sahnoun, United States Institute of Peace Press, Washington, D.C., 1994.

P. 163 **"Wife in Kismayo . . ."** Somalis believe that much of northeast Kenya is part of Somalia. Wajir, near the border, is a desert oasis where nomadic

Somali camel herders water their animals. It was here, it is said, that the Queen of Sheba spent the night and watered her stock.

Chapter 12

P. 168 **"I wouldn't know . . ."** Countries with the highest number of aid workers killed (1997–2003):

1. Angola: 58 (mostly as a result of antiaircraft attacks on two UN planes by UNITA in 1998 and 1999 and by land mines)
2. Afghanistan: 36
3. Iraq: 32
4. Sudan: 29
5. Democratic Republic of the Congo: 18
6. Rwanda: 17
7. Somalia: 16
8. Burundi: 11
9. Palestinian Authority: 7
10. Uganda: 7
11. Serbia and Montenegro (Kosovo): 5
12. Liberia: 5

http://www.wordiq.com/definition/Attacks_on_humanitarian_workers

"Almost half of the nonaccidental deaths of humanitarian aid workers (47 percent) were the result of ambushes on vehicles or convoys. These incidents occurred on the road in attacks by bandits or rebel groups.

"Among the nonaccidental, intentional violence incidents, 74 percent of the fatalities were local staff and 26 percent were expatriates. Also, 59 percent of these victims worked for or on behalf of nongovernmental organizations, while 41 percent were employed or under contract to UN agencies. The number of local and/or NGO fatalities is probably higher, since these incidents are less likely to be reported in public sources than the deaths of UN and/or expatriate personnel." *UN Office for Coordination of Humanitarian Affairs,* Dennis King, consultant.

Chapter 13

P. 184 **Hunkered against . . .** *Canto XVI, The Divine Comedy, Hell,* Dante, Penguin Books, London, 1949.

Chapter 16

P. 222 **Both David and Robbie . . .** *The Guardian,* London, by Jeevan Vasagar, February 3, 2004.

Chapter 17

P. 234 **My boat has been . . .** *Food and Nutrition Handbook,* World Food Program, Rome.

P. 237 **Ten Christian . . .** *Christianity Today,* July 2004.

P. 238 **While thousands of . . .** *Trafficking in Persons Report,* U.S. DOS, June 5, 2002.

Chapter 18

P. 248 **David and I . . .** *A Study on Minorities in Somalia,* UN Office for the Coordination of Humanitarian Affairs, August 1, 2002.

P. 249 **The global community . . .** *International Herald Tribune,* by Thomas Crampton, October 13, 2003.

P. 250 **". . . just as surely . . ."** November 26, 2001, speech, cited by Nicolas de Torrente. *Harvard Human Rights Law Journal,* 2003.

P. 251 **Andrew S. Natsios . . .** Speech to InterAction Forum, May 2003.

P. 251 **Such occurred in June . . .** Taliban spokesman Abdul Latif Hakimi. The five MSF workers—a Norwegian, a Belgian, and a Dutch, all three doctors, along with two Afghani staff members—had been attacked in their vehicle in the province of Badghis, about 500 kilometers west of the capital, Kabul.

The victims were: Helene de Beir, Belgian coordinator of MSF projects in Badghis, Willem Kwint, Dutch logistics expert, Egil Tynaes, Norwegian medical coordinator, Fasil Ahmad, Afghan translator, and Besmillah, the driver. *Missionary Service News Agency,* July 28, 2004.

Chapter 21

P. 286 **The Somalis have never . . .** *Background, Somalia,* Unicef, SACB, 1997.

Epilogue

P. 317 **Russ Ulrey, an expert . . .** *News Now, Voice of America,* February 25, 2003.

P. 318 **Saskia's husband . . .** *Financial Times,* October 7, 2000, by Mark Turner.

P. 321 **Before my brief . . .** Dr. Mark A. Schuster, Rand Corp.

Afterword

P. 332 **"Probably not. Maybe . . ."** Six British troops were killed and eight others wounded in an ambush in the southern town of Majar al-Kabir, near Amara. The killings, Iraqis said, were triggered by the anger over weapons searches in private homes. *Beirut Daily Star,* June 26, 2003.

Acknowledgments

Mike Dunne, the tough, black-bearded Scot to whom I owe so much, including my sanity—may you be safe wherever you are. And Russ Ulrey, a humanitarian.

George Corse, of Kilifi, Kenya, whose intellectual influence and fondness for Kipling was almost preparation enough, Arabella Stein and Andy McKillop in London and Nita Taublib in New York who recognized an interesting story, agent Jane Dystel, always there, and Miriam Goderich for her keen eye throughout.

John Flicker, an old soldier and fine editor, Kenny Gluck of Médecins sans Frontières, James Morris, Trevor Rowe, Francis Mwanza, Mick Lorentzen, Said Jannoun, Charles Forbes, Daniela Owen, Jane Pearce—all of WFP, Shawn Owen of Unicef, Ahmad Fawzi, Joe Suits, Jessica Taublib-Kiriat, Matthew Martin.

Steve and Penny York for their tireless hospitality, Marcel and Dounia Zandstra as always, and Sam Coleman.

Richard Roth of CNN, whose concern for the safety of humanitarian workers is well appreciated, and David Shipley and Toby Harshaw of the *New York Times* Op-Ed page, who likewise felt it was an issue that should be addressed and encouraged me to do so.

And to Jacqueline, without whose patient support this book could have never been written.

Bibliography

Eritrea and Ethiopia—From Conflict to Cooperation, Amare Tekle, Red Sea Press, 1994

Report of Panel of Experts, UN Security Council, 25 March, 2003, Stefan Tafrov, Chairman. Doc. S/2003.223

Africa, Dispatches from a Fragile Continent, Blaine Harden, Harper Collins, London, 1993

Scramble for Africa, Thomas Pakenham, Abacus, London, 1996

The Tree Where Man Was Born, Peter Matthiessen, Penguin Books, New York, 1995

The Flame Trees of Thika, Elspeth Huxley, Penguin Books, London, 1959

West with the Night, Beryl Markham, Virago Press, London, 1988

Black Hawk Down, A Story of Modern War, Mark Bowden, Penguin Books, New York, 2000

I Dreamed of Africa, Kuki Gallmann, Penguin Books, London, 1991

The Somali Bantu: Their History and Culture, Dan Van Lehman & Omar Eno, Center for Applied Linguistics, Cultural Orientation Resource Center, 2002

We Wish to Inform You That Tomorrow We Will Be Killed with Our Families, Philip Gourevitch, Picador, New York, 1999

Dangerous Waters, Modern Piracy and Terror on the High Seas, J. Burnett, Dutton, New York, 2002; Plume, New York, 2003

Somalia, The Missed Opportunities, Mohamed Sahnoun, United States Institute of Peace Press, Washington, D.C., 1994

For a shocking and thorough account of events resulting in the deaths of relief workers, I suggest:

Paying the Ultimate Price: Analysis of the Deaths of Humanitarian Aid Workers (1997–2001), Dennis King, consultant, UN Office for Coordination of Humanitarian Affairs. *Chronology of Humanitarian Relief Workers Killed,* www.reliefweb.int/symposium/payingultimateprice97-01.html